IN THE WAKE OF
MERCEDES
GLEITZE

IN THE WAKE OF
MERCEDES GLEITZE

OPEN WATER SWIMMING PIONEER

DOLORANDA PEMBER

Royalties from sales of this book will go into

Mercedes' Trust Fund,

The Mercedes Gleitze Relief in Need Charity,

which is being administered by **Family Action**.

Charity number: **264713-44**

Front cover: Profile of Mercedes Gleitze. (Gleitze archive)
Back cover: Mercedes' second attempt at the North Channel. (*Northern Whig & Belfast Post*/British Library/Gleitze archives)

First published 2019

The History Press
The Mill, Brimscombe Port
Stroud, Gloucestershire, GL5 2QG
www.thehistorypress.co.uk

British Library Cataloguing in Publication Data.
A catalogue record for this book is available from the British Library.

ISBN 978 0 7509 8977 0

Typesetting and origination by The History Press
Printed in Turkey by Imak

Mercedes Gleitze (1900–81)
Pioneer swimmer: long-distance open water and endurance events
Philanthropist: a love of mankind, especially as shown in services to welfare

I passionately love the sea; nothing else moves me as it does.
I love and understand its every mood; and I sometimes fancy that
the sea knows and understands me, too.

'Mercedes Gleitze: A Personal Interview'
(article by H. O'B. of Dublin, 1929).

For my brother, Fergus,

with whom I share enduring memories

of our mother, Mercedes Gleitze.

CONTENTS

ACKNOWLEDGEMENTS

Mercedes left a comprehensive collection of memorabilia covering her swimming career, the contents of which made it possible for me to follow her footsteps throughout her swimming years. As a consequence, her sea career is recorded as fully and accurately as possible.

I am indebted to the news journalists of the day for their vivid descriptions of conditions during my mother's open-water swims and their detailed accounts of the public's interest in them. Many of these journalists accompanied Mercedes on her swims and subjected themselves to the rigours of cold and perilous seas in order to cover her trials. Their on-the-spot accounts, which include verbatim messages carried by pigeon post, provide colour and substance to her story.

One of the most difficult tasks I faced was matching up dates, venues and the names of members of her support groups on the swims, many of the hundreds of press cuttings in the archives having been cropped, but, with the help of local and national newspaper archives in the UK, Eire, Australia, New Zealand and South Africa, I eventually managed to identify most of the cuttings and images, and was able to reference them correctly. I thank all those agencies for their help with this task.

I am also indebted to the local history societies I have been in contact with, for example, the Committee of the Glens of Antrim Historical Society who let me reproduce the 'Barnacle Bill' article; and in particular two local historians – Angus Martin, editor of *The Kintyre Antiquarian*

& Natural History Society Magazine, and Alan J. Taylor, Chairman of the Folkestone & District Local History Society. Both of these historians proactively tracked down and provided photographs and/or memories from local families – descendants of people who knew and supported my mother, such as Alex Russell from Kintyre, whose family owned Sanda Island in the Mull of Kintyre and hosted her during the winter of 1929, and Stanley Sharp from Folkestone, two of whose predecessors piloted my mother in her English Channel attempts.

Other contributors I wish to thank for providing me with images from their personal collections are Jean McH. Roberts MBE, of Donaghadee, whose grandfather loaned his motor launch MV *Kathleen* to my mother and accompanied her on one of her North Channel attempts; Dr Ian Gordon (Chief Medical Officer to the GB Swimming Team at the 2012 Olympics), who responded immediately to my request for relevant photographs from his collection of swimming memorabilia; and two Portstewart residents – Dr Michael Thompson, whose mother, Maudie, as an 8-year-old, witnessed the Foyle swims in 1929, and Maurice McAleese (artist, author and former newspaper editor) for his charming sketch of the Berne, where Mercedes started and finished her double crossing. These images, so generously given, help to bring my mother's story to life.

Heartfelt thanks to Clare Delargy, Director of Delargy Productions, Belfast, who, on her own initiative, researched, secured funding for and produced the documentary *Mercedes: The Spirit of a New Age*. Clare possesses a real understanding of how difficult it was in those early days of female emancipation for a woman to break away from her culturally imposed domestic situation and realise her personal dreams. During the making of the documentary Clare took me to some of my mother's swim sites along the Antrim coast, and on the Isle of Inishmaan in Galway Bay, at a time when I was drafting the biography, and I was able to more clearly visualise my mother being in those beautiful places. My brother and I are truly grateful to all those who participated in the making of this documentary, and to have this visual record that contains interviews with a range of swimming and historical commentators, including Duncan Goodhew, Britain's Olympic swimming gold medallist; Dr Helen Pankhurst, great-granddaughter of Emmeline Pankhurst; historians Lucy Moore and Dr Marilyn Morgan; Dr Ciara Chambers from the University of Ulster; Fiona Southwell, open-water swimmer/coach; and Brian Meharg MBE, an experienced escort pilot across the North Channel.

I would further like to record my grateful thanks to fourteen more women who contributed towards Mercedes' story:

The late Montserrat Tresserras Dou, herself an Honour Marathon Swimmer and Channel Swimming Association board member, who recognised Mercedes' pioneering swimming achievements and helped to secure her enshrinement as an Honour Pioneer Marathon Swimmer in both the International Marathon Swimming Hall of Fame and the International Swimming Hall of Fame.

Actor and playwrite Lynda Radley, who, in 2006, wrote the script for and performed in a one-woman show, entitled *The Art of Swimming*, about Mercedes' life as a swimmer. Fifty performances in various fringe theatres were made during the years 2006–09. Watching one of these performances at the Dublin Fringe Festival in Temple Bar in 2007 made me realise that my mother's story could not only embolden would-be open-water swimmers, but could inspire anyone to make their dream, whatever it may be, a reality.

Fiona Southwell, herself a prolific open-water swimmer, coach and Channel Swimming Association board member, whose recognition of Mercedes' achievements motivated her to record the names of all Brighton-based swimmers who successfully complete a solo crossing of the English Channel. The names – at present totalling ten – are inscribed on a shield donated by Mercedes' family, and arrangements are in hand to display the shield in Brighton's museum. Mercedes spent happy years in Brighton, her birthplace. It is where she learnt to swim, and she would have felt very honoured to know that, thanks to Fiona's efforts, her name is currently being used to encourage her fellow citizens to follow in her wake.

Glenda Exley, the granddaughter of George Allan (Mercedes' trainer throughout the 1927 season). In June 2015 Glenda made a special journey from her home in Staffordshire to spend the day with me. She brought with her photographs and written memorabilia inherited from George's time as my mother's coach, which I have been able to include in this memoir. Glenda told me her Grandpop adored Mercedes.

Author Caitlin Davies, who researched and recorded the names of the all-but-forgotten women and girls who performed many swims of note in the Thames during the late nineteenth and early twentieth centuries.

We were able to share information for our respective projects, and it was so gratifying to see my mother's name included amongst the pioneering female swimmers in Caitlin's book, *Downstream: A History and Celebration of Swimming the River Thames*.

Heather Clatworthy, who as a child growing up on the shores of Portstewart used to gaze out at the land in the distance, wanting to swim across, but not believing it was possible until she read about Mercedes' 1929 feat in a book by Maurice McAleese; in July 2016 Heather became the second woman (and first Irish woman) to swim across Lough Foyle. She reinforced my belief that by publishing Mercedes' story, it could inspire others to realise their own personal dreams. Heather's success has given rise to a permanent plaque being erected by the Causeway Coast & Glens Borough Council on the coastal path in Portstewart on 25 July 2017, to commemorate the swims of both women.

And, as a first-time author anxious for feedback, I wish to extend grateful thanks to local authors, Lucienne Boyce and Debbie Young, and to Dr Jenny Yiallouros, for finding time in their busy lives to read and give welcome advice on my first offerings; to Dr Jean Williams (De Montfort University) and Professor June Hannam (University of the West of England) for their academic reviews; to Faye Cheeseman for advice on its structure, and last, but most definitely not least, to Kay Wright and Dianne Rees who shared the task of copy-editing a very lengthy early manuscript.

My immediate family has been especially supportive of this project, despite the stop-start nature of its compilation. My son and daughter-in-law, Andrew and Vicky Pember, have both been on hand throughout and have responded immediately to requests for advice or technical assistance, and my daughter Claire Langlois and family, and brother Fergus Carey (who gave me access to his share of the archives) and family, have quietly and patiently encouraged me from afar. I thank them all sincerely for this. Mercedes' legacy was to help promote the art of swimming, and my contribution has been to ensure that her five grandchildren and their children can now read her story and appreciate the part she played in the gradual emancipation of women in the world of sport during the early part of the twentieth century.

It is also my desire that Mercedes' story will resonate with the descendants of all the men and women who gathered around to help organise and bear witness to her swims. The names of each and every supporter identified in covering reports, as well as witness statements and additional complementary descriptions of swims, can be accessed on the following website created for this purpose: **www.mercedesgleitze.uk**

Finally, greetings and thanks to all the people I have had the pleasure of meeting at various swimming conferences and dinners – officials and open-water swimmers alike – who responded with encouragement when I told them I was documenting the story of my mother's sea career. Mercedes was one of you, and she would have been delighted to know that she is held in such high regard by her peers.

PROLOGUE

Summer 1922

Mercedes Gleitze, a 21-year-old girl from Brighton, England, stands on the shingled beach at Dover preparing herself for an attempt on the English Channel. Her accompanying pilot boat waits just offshore for her to enter the water and start the swim. This lasts just 3 hours and 15 minutes before her shoulder muscles give out and she abandons the swim.

Mercedes makes her way back to London where she lives and works, disappointed, yes, but buoyed by the knowledge that she had actually dared, publicly, to carry out an attempt to become the first woman to swim the English Channel. It would not be her last attempt by far, because she was determined to conquer that iconic stretch of treacherous water.

INTRODUCTION

A DAUGHTER'S REMINISCENCES

Mercedes Gleitze had three children, and I am the second child. My brother, sister and I grew up aware that our mother had achieved fame through her swimming career during her early life primarily because of her status as the first British woman to swim across the English Channel. However, apart from a dozen or so trophies displayed in a cabinet in our front room, we were not given the opportunity to appreciate fully the extent of her achievements or her fame.

Our mother's natural reserve and increasingly reclusive nature contributed to this. She seldom spoke in any detail about her life as a professional swimmer, although very occasionally, when we were older, she did mention to one or the other of us brief reminiscences about her past. What stood out for me was her memory of how kind and appreciative both the public and media had been to her. It was only after she died and we shared out the photographs, letters and newspaper cuttings – which, despite her peripatetic lifestyle, she had managed to safeguard and store in the attic – that we realised what a major sporting icon she had been in her youth.

After being for the most part uninformed about the details of Mercedes' early life (there were no photographs of her as a child or teenager in the house), and only becoming fully aware later in my own life of the full extent of her self-imposed goals, I was finally able to visualise my mother as a healthy young woman, able to walk unaided, and possessing the freedom and independence to make her own decisions about how she conducted herself. It was such a comfort to know that her life hadn't always been such a struggle.

During our years together it was clear that my mother's overriding desire was to live her days only in the present, never in the past, so I have no childhood memories of her relating stories to me, at bedtime, about her own early life and her adventures in the world of swimming. I think it must have been an intuitive decision on all our parts to allow her that anonymity and not to intrude. I understand now that the memories she was able to evoke in quiet moments, when she was by herself, must have sustained her during her years of ill health. She would have been able to relive a time in her life when she was young, strong and healthy, and able to respond to what she refers to in her writings as those 'calling' waves.

My mother's time as a sportswoman and celebrity in the 1920s and early 1930s was a far cry from the life I shared with her in a small, three-bedroomed terraced house in suburban north-west London; and so, before embarking upon the task of documenting her early life and charting her swims, I journeyed back in my own memory to try to link the woman I had known to the person I was reading about in the archives.

The earliest consciousness I have of her withdrawal from public life is a brief remark she made to me during the early years of the Second World War. I had been sent to buy some groceries from a licensed shop run by a neighbour in her front room, a few houses along from ours. When I returned with the shopping, my mother confided that when she first came to live in the street, the lady who ran the shop recognised her and asked if she was the famous Channel swimmer. My mother told me that she had replied, 'No, that is not me.' As a child, her statement confused me, but I have since listened to interviews with families of high achievers from other walks of life who had also been kept in the dark about a close relative's past accomplishments until after their death, and now realise that this type of reaction is not so unusual after all.

A few years earlier my mother had, figuratively speaking, stepped out of one world and into another – leaving behind a prolific and fulfilling life as a female sports celebrity, and settling down into a then conventional existence as a mother and housewife. Many years later when, at the age of 77, she was asked by a German newspaper to write a summary of her life, she described her domestic years as 'quiet and uneventful due to ill health'.

Mercedes was a very maternal, loving mother, and naturally proud of us, her children. Although confined to the house, she knew the names of all our friends, and I used to catch glimpses of her watching us play in the street from behind the curtain of an upstairs bedroom window. Happily, she lived long enough to get to know her five grandchildren. Sadly, ill health incapacitated her, the main cause being an inherited debilitating blood circulation disorder that manifested itself in her middle years, and chronic arthritis in her knees. The latter condition was exacerbated by swimming in cold seas and by the repetitive sideways thrust of the breaststroke leg action with which she propelled herself through the water. She became completely housebound in the latter part of the 1940s and, later in her life, developed type 2 diabetes with all its enervating side effects. Sadly, towards the end of her life she also presented with early symptoms of dementia and gynaecological cancer.

Although my mother took an interest in and shared all the minutiae of our daily lives, she became more and more inaccessible and only very rarely agreed to see anyone outside of the immediate family. However, she managed to fill her days. She was an avid reader – the walls of her bedroom were lined with books on life sciences. She was a devotee of Sir Patrick Moore, and although she had no formal scientific education, she spent her time reading about and writing theories on how life started on earth.

Mercedes was born into a candlelit, horse-drawn world, but her lifespan enabled her to witness a man walk on the moon. Her interest in the 1960s space programme was passionate. She was hungry for any information she could acquire in order to follow the progress of the astronauts of that era. Because of her own strong desire to conquer new horizons, she was in tune with them, and understood why they took the risks they did.

She was a lover of classical music, especially Beethoven, Mozart and Mendelssohn. She particularly loved Felix Mendelssohn's overture *The Hebrides (Fingal's Cave)* – the music of which I now realise must have reawakened memories of her time spent in the caves on the Scottish island of Sanda where she took refuge during the winter of 1929. However, her appreciation of all genres of music meant that she also found pleasure in joining in with my generation and becoming a fan of the Beatles and other pop artists of the time.

She followed the progress of participants in all sporting disciplines. As a 14-year-old schoolgirl I listened with her to radio coverage of the 1948

Olympic Games, and in particular I remember her applauding the success of Francina (Fanny) Blankers-Koen, the Dutch multi-gold Olympic medallist, who helped to break through the prejudices against women taking part in sport (Fanny received 'hate mail' telling her she should be at home looking after her children instead of running on a track in a foreign country, and also that she was too old to take part in sport). My mother was a great admirer of Sir Roger Bannister, the first sub-4-minute miler, and also of the boxers Sir Henry Cooper and Muhammad Ali. She was an unwavering supporter of the Oxford University boat crew, through good times and bad. She especially loved Wimbledon fortnight. Although her mobility was very poor, one day I found her sitting in a chair on the landing, too nervous to stay in her room to watch Christine Truman nearly win a semi-final against Maria Bueno.

With the installation of a TV in her room she was able to view not only sporting, but political and other events. She called it her 'window to the world', through which she was able to see what was happening both nationally and globally.

She was, of course, naturally interested in welfare issues, and was thankful to have witnessed the institution of the National Health Service in Britain. She also closely followed women's issues – for example, the advent of family allowance, which she explained to me gave working-class housewives with children access to a small amount of money for the first time in their own right.

My mother was essentially a shy and modest person. She once told me of her shock when she boarded a bus and sat opposite a poster of herself advertising a product. However, her aspirations for a swimming career, and the associated need to raise funds to help destitute people, forced her to overcome her natural reticence and appreciate the publicity her status as a sporting celebrity brought her – at least until her charity was up and running, at which point she suddenly and completely withdrew from public life and retreated from practically all human contact.

The fact that during the Second World War her own mother was killed in Frankfurt by British bombs and her charitable homes in Leicester destroyed by German bombs must have been a double body blow, but it was really a combination of issues that caused her withdrawal, and her own natural solitary disposition eased the transition from celebrity to recluse. The debilitating ill health that afflicted her from her middle years facilitated this desire to cut herself off from everyone except her own immediate family.

For someone who took such chances with her own life she was almost paranoid about the safety of her own children and was happy for us to lead conventional lives. However, the parts of her character that I can link to the person she was in her youth – such as her ability to bear disabling pain without complaint, and not to succumb to the blows that life sometimes delivers – shone through. She was in herself a very positive person, and if she ever felt depressed, she seldom showed it.

During my own childhood and adult years, I often had to suppress feelings of both sadness and anger that she was so debilitated and reclusive, and unable to benefit in her later life from her sporting achievements. However, writing this memoir of her career has revealed to me that although throughout her maternal years she had a constant struggle with her health, as a young woman in control of her own destiny she lived ten hugely fulfilling years, during which time she realised most of her youthful dreams and aspirations.

The Task in Hand

Moving forward in time, after my mother's death in 1981 I transferred my share of the archives straight from her attic into a cupboard in my own home and a good many years passed before I felt able to read in depth about her youth and her achievements. When I did, I decided that her story should be accurately and fully recorded – not just for her descendants to read, but hopefully for the publication of what has been described recently as 'hidden sporting history'.[1]

Much has already been written about the group of spirited young women – mainly from Britain, Europe and the United States – who, in the 1920s, all aspired to become the first woman to swim across the English Channel. This memoir, however, is focussed on the personal trials of just one of them. From her extensive archival material I have pieced together my mother's early life and her ten years as a pioneering long-distance swimmer in the first part of the twentieth century. Her letters, and the edifying media coverage, throw light on the way she initiated and subsequently managed a unique career, and also on the way she responded to the occasional obstacles thrown in her path.

The project entailed making working copies of and reading and digesting over 2,000 faint and fragile documents, some four or five pages long, which Mercedes managed to safeguard, despite her peripatetic lifestyle. It is a sign of the times that when, during the Second World War, she organised the records of her career, she had to sew many of them into exercise books bought from Woolworths – glue being a scarce commodity because of shortages during the war.

The archives include photographs, press cuttings from national and local newspapers, notes of interviews, descriptions of swims, letters to and from family, friends, fans, sea pilots, coaches, voluntary helpers, corporation officials and witnesses, and correspondence with companies whose products she advertised. They also include legal documents covering the institution of her charity and the use it was put to in the city of Leicester.

It was an emotional journey, and there were many long periods when I put the project aside, always managing to find other 'more urgent' things to do. It is not easy to step backwards in time into the shoes of another person and try to imagine why they said this or why they did that. Although I was writing about my own mother, with whom I had almost daily contact until she died, her natural reticence had created huge gaps in my knowledge of her childhood and her achievements as a young woman. But after finally studying all the witness reports of her swims, reading about the thousands of people who turned out to watch her, and visiting some of the locations where she swam, I found myself able to visualise clearly a time in my mother's life of which we, her children, had been given only a misty glimpse.

1

THE EARLY YEARS AND FAMILY TIES

Brighton 1900

Mercedes was born in Brighton on 18 November 1900, the youngest of three sisters. Her father, Heinrich Gleitze, was an economic migrant worker from Bavaria in south-eastern Germany, who had travelled to England some time during the last decade of the nineteenth century. On Mercedes' birth certificate her father's occupation is noted as 'Journeyman Baker', and he found permanent work at the newly opened Metropole Hotel on the Brighton seafront.

There was a growing German immigrant community in Brighton at that time and this helped to ease his transition into a new country. Mercedes' mother, Anna Kerr, a governess and language teacher from Hertzogenaurach (Middle Franconia, Bavaria), came to Brighton at about the same time to look for work, and it is here that she met and married Heinrich. They rented 124 Freshfield Road, a house close to the seafront, and it became their family home. It was in Brighton that Mercedes learnt to swim, and she always spoke fondly of her years in that iconic seaside town.

Displacement

Twice in her young life Mercedes was removed from the country of her birth. The first time was as an infant of 18 months, when she was taken by her grandparents to live in Germany for nearly nine years. The second time was when, after being brought back to re-join her parents and siblings in Brighton, at the age of 13 she and her two sisters were taken back to Germany by their mother at the outbreak of the First World War. Both Anna and Heinrich Gleitze had been resident in Brighton for over two decades but had never applied to become naturalised, and consequently Heinrich was interned on the Isle of Man as a German alien. Although the authorities told Anna that she was free to remain in England because her three children were British by birth, she decided, understandably, to be repatriated back to Germany to be with her own relatives, and she took her three teenage daughters with her.

However, it is apparent that from a very young age Mercedes had a strong sense of who she was and, geographically, where she was meant to live her life. This was remarkable considering the era into which she was born. Although many young women from a working-class background had, through necessity, left their family homes to take live-in jobs as domestic servants or governesses, or as industrial or farm workers, most were conditioned to live in the parental home until they married. Mercedes dared to break this mindset, and at the tender age of 17 she was prepared to leave the shelter of her parents' home in Germany, where they had resettled, and make a life for herself in England.

This patriotic feeling for her birthplace was so deep-seated that she couldn't contemplate living anywhere else. Towards the end of the First World War she broached the idea to her parents, but they refused to listen. Her mother also refused to allow her to work because she knew this would give her some financial independence. As she was under the age of consent (in those days, 21 years) she felt that she had no option but to run away. After an abortive flight to England with just 10 Reichsmark in her pocket, sleeping in cornfields and living on bread and butter, she negotiated a return back home to Germany with her mother (who had caught up with her on the island of Wangeroag – a Frisian island off the coast of the Netherlands) on the condition that she would be allowed to find employment. While marking time in Germany she also furthered her education by attending a school for languages in Frankfurt. Amongst her collection of letters is one from Charles Jacobs, the son of the college principal, who recollected she was there from 1920 to 1921 with the Quakers Society.

It is difficult to assess the feelings of rejection a child might have when the realisation comes that they have been removed from their natural family environment and sent to another country to live, albeit with grandparents. Given the fortitude and endurance Mercedes exhibited in the face of adversity during her pioneering swims, as well as during years of ill health, it seems likely that she would have faced those years of childhood separation from her parents and siblings with stoicism. But that act of separation also instilled in her a resolute determination to return to England, and it is clear from her writings that she considered it her birthright to make her home there.

The following passages are extracts reproduced from notes written by Mercedes in 1928, combined with those taken from a short summary she wrote in 1977 for the *Nürnberg Press*. In these two sets of notes she describes her childhood and teenage years, and the deep and persistent longing she felt to return to the country of her birth. They reveal how single-minded and courageous she was, even at such a young age.

A Memoir – in Mercedes' Own Words

My native town was Brighton. I was about 18 months old when my grandmother came to England all the way from Hertzogenaurach because my mother, who at the time had three small children to look after, found it difficult to manage. When my mother recovered from her illness my grandmother asked her 'Could I take your youngest child home with me to Hertzogenaurach?' My mother replied 'Yes'.

Thus it came about that eight and a half years of my life were spent in my grandparents' house in Hertzogenaurach, where I had a happy time raising geese for my grandparents, whilst spending each Saturday delivering the weekend bread to customers far and wide and collecting for my aunt and uncle (Backerei Geschaeft Wagner) the bread monies due for the week.

When I reached the age of ten my mother arrived to take me back with her to England where she lived with my father and my two sisters. Here, in Brighton, I went to school until I was twelve.

At this stage of my life I was sent back to Germany with my sisters to enter the Maria Stern Convent School in Nördlingen. During the holiday we travelled from Nördlingen to Hertzogenaurach to stay for a few weeks with our grandparents, when I had a serious illness and was treated by a Dr Biermann. My mother came from England and the doctor told her that I needed my native sea air to bring me back to full health. So back to England I travelled.

When war broke out in 1914 my father, as a German national, was sent to join the other prisoners of war on the Isle of Man. My mother was told that since her three children were born in England they were of British nationality and, therefore, should stay in England. However she was anxious to return to Germany and so she left England taking her three children back to Hertzogenaurach with her.

...

On the 25th April 1918, on account of a terrible feeling of home-sickness for England which I could not overcome, I decided to escape from Germany and attempt to get back to my native country.

I decided to make my escape on the morning of the 1st May and spent the five days I had left secretly making preparations and studying the map of Germany so as to enable me to find my way easily through the various towns. It was necessary for me to make the journey on foot as no-one was allowed to use the trains that year for the purpose of travelling without a permit, and, not being of age, I could not of course apply for a permit.

The first town I decided to reach was Bamberg; from Bamberg I made my way to Schweinfurt; from Schweinfurt I turned north to Bad Kissingen; from Bad Kissingen to Hersfeld and Fulda.

Eventually I reached the Dutch Border which I had made up my mind to penetrate. However, it being Armistice time, the boundary was strictly guarded in every direction and I realised I would have a very difficult task. One night I decided to make the attempt to get across. About 8 o'clock in the evening I lay in wait behind some bushes in a forest facing a Dutch forest until darkness came on. After waiting for about an hour it began to rain very heavily. Through the bushes I saw guards walking and cycling about. Eventually darkness came on and I emerged from the forest, crossed the road, and then

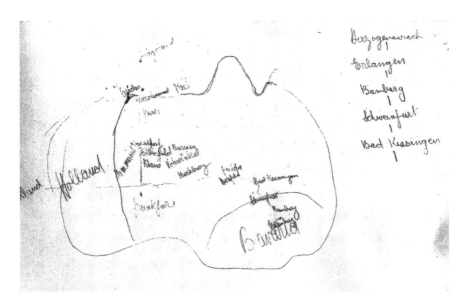

Mercedes' sketch of her planned 'escape route'.

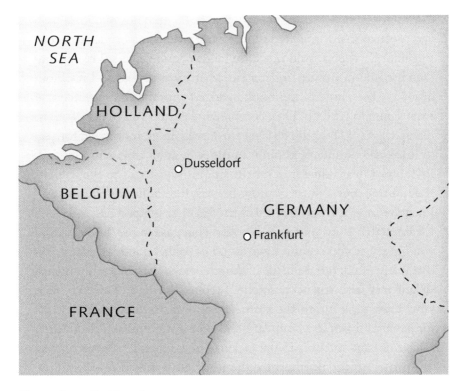

The way home for Mercedes.

into the Dutch forest which I hoped would lead me to a Dutch town. I groped my way through the darkness.

At last the forest terminated and I found myself in a big country road – it was still dark and raining very hard. When dawn appeared the first thing I cast my eyes on was a notice on which was written 'Verbodene Kiostraat' which I took to mean 'Forbidden Pathway'. I was not discouraged and continued my walk until presently I saw a sentry box in front of which two armed soldiers were marching up and down. I hid myself a minute or two and waited until their backs were turned and succeeded in evading detection by these guards.

A little later in the morning I actually reached the first Dutch town, but when I reached the first road leading into this town I noticed, to my horror, that the street was filled with armed soldiers. It was too late for me to turn back, so I decided I could do nothing but walk straight on until I was stopped. It was not long before I was approached by two soldiers. 'Where are you going?' they said to me, to which I replied 'I am going to Church.' (I could not of course have said to them that I intended to make my way to the border to get to England, for they would not have believed me.) The soldiers being Dutch could not quite understand what I was saying, so I took out of my pocket a little prayer book I carried with me and repeated that I was going to Church. They comprehended, and said to me 'With so many beautiful churches in Germany, surely there is no need for you to break the boundary at night in order to attend Mass in Holland.' Presently I heard the church bells ringing and I said to the soldiers 'Excuse me, but I must go now because the bells are ringing and I may be late for Mass.' As I turned to go, they grasped my wrist, and I realised that I was under their arrest. They said to me 'Look around you girl, can't you see the town is full of soldiers, and we assure you that if any of the other guards in the street take you they will not deal so leniently with you as we intend.' I replied 'All right, I will stay with you.' They took me to their officer and induced him to let me off for having broken the boundary, and they got permission from their officer to hand me over to the German guard.

I turned to the north, since the northward direction offered me an alternate water-line where I might perhaps be able to plead for a passage to England. However it was not to be, so I decided to swim out from Carolinensiel in the direction of the Heligoland lighthouse beam, intending to swim through the gap between the off-shore [Frisian] islands of Wangeroag and Langeog.

It was in the early hours of the morning and although I could see the island, it was two or three miles distant. I had never attempted a task like this before but I was confident that I would reach my ultimate goal. I shut my eyes and plunged into the water, fully dressed with the exception of my shoes and stockings. How long I was swimming I do not know, but I kept on battling against the currents which I had never before experienced, and eventually the reigning tidal forces threw me onto the shores of Wangeroag. It was not until later that I was to know my extreme peril. As a matter of fact, it was only providence that saved me from death. It must have been 10 or 11 a.m. My blood was frozen; my lips were blue and I was shivering. I saw a ship lying anchored on the beach. I climbed into it to see if there was a fire where I could warm myself. I found the ship empty, so I left it. Then, in the distance I noticed a group of workmen. I felt too shy to walk up to them on account of wearing no shoes or stockings. Glancing to the left I noticed two ladies walking about bare-footed and I thought to myself evidently this must be the fashion on this island, so I walked up to the group of working men. I said to them: 'I have just swum across the Wattenmeer.' The workmen seemed very surprised and said: 'That can't be true because no one has ever swum across because the currents are too dangerous.' The skipper of a ship offered me shelter in his cabin and gave me food. In the cabin I wrote my third letter to my mother. The skipper, on his way to post this for me, mentioned my plight to the proprietor of a hotel and brought two ladies back with him, and I went to the hotel in order that I might spend the night in comfort.

Here on this island I had my first experience of the extra special kindness shown towards a long distance swimmer. The family of Hermann Rosing took me into their home where I enjoyed the friendship of their daughter, Elfriede, who was about the same age as myself. The family owned a number of guest bungalows and they let me use one of these during my stay on the island. Elfriede and I became close friends and I still remember her pleading voice saying to me 'Mercedes, please don't swim out towards Heligoland'.

'Stay with us.' However, how can one suddenly 'still' a drive to some-how or other look for an opportunity to reach one's native land.

Whilst enjoying this new-found friendship with Elfriede and her parents, events were taking their course. I had given a servant of the Rosing family a postcard to my mother, but before sending it she showed it to the Rosing family, who forthwith wrote to my mother telling her of my whereabouts. Little wonder that a few days later there stood in front of me, not by wishful thinking, but factually, my mother. She was so overjoyed at finding me safe and well that no rebuke was spoken. She told me that she was going to take me back home next morning.

So great was my anxiety to reach England again that I decided during the night to escape. Knowing my mother would peep into my room before she retired, I placed a doll in my bed, leaving the hair showing. Then I ran from the hotel, climbed over the sand dunes and waded into the sea fully dressed. I did not know, but here I was attempting a more difficult feat than swimming the English Channel, for my goal – Heligoland – was 22 miles away. I had not been swim-ming long when I reached a sand bank. It was pitch dark when I started and before I reached the sand bank a storm broke and there was thunder and lightning which made my experience more weird. It was only about 40 yards of sand jutting from the water and when I reached it I realised the peril I was in. I knelt down and prayed and then, on the impulse of the moment, dived into the sea again in the direction of Heligoland thinking that I might reach it. The fury of the seas however increased to such an extent that I was compelled, with a feeling of intense bitterness and disappointment, to turn round and attempt to reach the sand bank again, but my direction was wrong and I had to continue swimming in seas which threatened to overwhelm me at any moment. At last, utterly exhausted, I found myself back on the island and returned to the hotel.

'I will go south with you' I said [to my mother], 'but only if you will let me go to work.' She acquiesced, although she knew that after giving her a share of my future wages, I would inevitably put most of the rest into a Post Office account pending the time when it would suffice to purchase the ticket needed for the return journey to my native England.

… Back now in the country of my birth I set out to get myself a job in London, which I soon managed to do. Thus economically settled, I should have been happy and content. I was, however, becoming more and more aware of the homeless and food-deprived peoples of this world and made up my mind to try to help these less fortunate people.

During the years I spent in London as a typist, I used to practice long-distance swimming in the River Thames. On one of these hours-long swims [Westminster to Folkestone] I nearly drowned because I was pulled under by a very strong downward current. As I went under I *saw* the large crowd that had stood on Westminster Bridge to watch the start of my swim, and I thought to myself 'tonight they will read in the newspapers that I am dead', because the river current seemed to me to be too strong to negotiate. However, contrary to expectations, I suddenly saw the sky again and found myself about a yard away from a boat-full of river policemen who had been searching the waters for me. They said to me: 'You are the only one we know who, having been grabbed by the strong current at this particular spot, has come up again alive. Usually it is only dead bodies that come up.'

My swimming career started with these Thames practice swims. When it was holiday time I travelled to Folkestone where I hired a boat for sea swimming. I made several attempts at swimming across the Channel before I finally succeeded. When I did, I gave up office work to concentrate on long-distance swimming, which I loved to do because it came easy to me, and it was financially rewarding enough to save up sufficient money to buy a 'Home for the Poor'. This wish of mine eventually became a reality in the City of Leicester.

Family Bonds

Although from the age of 21 Mercedes had branched away from her birth family and lived independently of them, she never lost touch. Her eldest sister, Doloranda, remained in Germany with their parents, but before her tragically early death in 1928 from a heart defect, Doloranda visited Mercedes in England and supported her in her 1926 Channel attempt.

The middle of the three sisters, Estella (Stella), had also resettled in England, and although they lived separate lives, Stella also encouraged Mercedes in her swimming ambitions.

In those days it was more customary for children to help support parents in their retirement, and before her marriage in November 1927, Stella sent sums of money to help them. However, after Stella married, Mercedes took over the responsibility. At first, she sent a small but regular weekly money order, and later a more convenient monthly standing order to Anna and Heinrich, who were struggling financially in Frankfurt. She also supplemented these regular payments with occasional larger, one-off sums whenever she could.

Mercedes and her mother corresponded regularly. Anna's letters are written half in English and half in German, sometimes with a language change in the middle of a sentence. It is clear from the letters exchanged between them that a loving bond had developed since Mercedes returned to England at the age of 10, and became an inclusive member of the family.

On 4 June 1928, she wrote to her mother at the time of Doloranda's early death:

It is a pity that she has been taken from us so soon. Stella and I were so keen on having her in London and would have done our best to make her happy. But perhaps God was wise in relieving her from physical pain, as evidently the state of her heart caused her much suffering. Stella and I are so pleased we visited Randa and we shall always treasure the memory of our last meeting with her. You must take things easy now and not worry too much as, after all, we cannot alter God's plans.

Anna wrote to Mercedes, on notepaper edged in black:

Since your last letter with the money order I have seen nothing in the papers about you. Where are you my Darling? Please let me have a line or two to consolate my suffering heart. It is such a joy to find a letter from you in my letter box. I am not well at the moment and I feel so lonely, so sad. Papa is like he was always, not loving to me although I bemother him in every way. I wish you could live with me again my Darling …

My Darling, time is nearing again for your great undertaking [a North Channel attempt]. I feel so sorry for you that you have laid such a difficult, heavy burden on your shoulders. I will pray for you that the Holy Powers of Goodness, Wisdom, Love and Power may protect and lead and help you along to success this time.

Mercedes replied:

My dear Mamma, I am glad Randa has a nice grave in that beautiful cemetery and that she is so near you. It is good of Papa to visit her grave so often …

This morning I sent off your weekly pound.

My Irish and Scotch friends have already made all preparations for me. They have placed a nice comfortable boat with a saloon and nice stove at my disposal. The temperature is being taken for me every day in the Irish Channel and it has already gone up 10 degrees to what it was when I swam two weeks ago. It will constitute a fine historic record if I achieve the swim. Will tell you more news when I write again next Saturday. In the meantime I remain with love to you both.

In a follow-up, Anna informs her:

The postman has just brought me the money order from you. It does help me so. My health is so troublesome, therefore this little money of yours is such a God-send to me. I do hope that you may never be hindered by anything from sending it to me regularly.

I am so glad that people are kind to you. I am glad you have got your dog back and that Stella is able to keep him.

In a later letter, Anna advises Mercedes, '… my dear, never marry into a poor condition or to a man lower than yourself in education and spirit.'

The year 1928 was a tragic one for Anna and Heinrich, losing their first born at such a young age, and Anna's letters convey how desolate she was and how eager for contact with her surviving daughters far away in another country. Mercedes regularly kept her mother informed of her swimming plans as they were unfolding and one of the letters that she wrote in June 1929 reads:

My Dear Mamma,

Today has been a very happy and successful one for me. My swim across the Wash is now an accomplished fact, having landed at Heacham on the Norfolk coast at 6.30 this evening. I had some hot drinks every half hour all the way across and when I felt like having something solid to eat I was given some roast duck. During the whole of the thirteen and a half hours it took me to reach my destination I had musical entertainment – songs and gramophone – and three seals followed me three parts of the way. I expect they were wondering what kind of a fish I was.

About three hundred people witnessed my landing. I was given flowers, chocolates and a gold bangle, and all my expenses were paid.

Enclosed I am sending you a photograph of which I am very proud. It shows a whole shop window at Boston devoted exclusively to photographs of myself. I am also sending you a cutting describing my Wash swim.

The next achievement on my list is Donaghadee to Portpatrick [Irish Channel]. I am going there next week and do not intend to leave Irish soil until this swim is also an accomplished fact.

Trusting that you are both well and happy,

I remain your loving daughter, Mercedes.

From October 1928 onwards Mercedes did not have a permanent home, and she asked her mother to address any letters care of a friend and mentor, Mr William Hope-Jones, a tutor of mathematics at Eton College, who would then forward them on to her as and when she notified him of her current whereabouts.

Separated by War

In 1939, at the outbreak of the Second World War, all contact between Mercedes and her parents was lost. Sadly, this contact was not restored when the war ended. In 1949, after a local search was instigated by Dr Mathias Gleitze (a kinsman), the Chief Constable of Frankfurt confirmed to him that Anna Gleitze had been killed during the war. No actual death certificate was available, but Rechneigrabenstrasse in Frankfurt, where Anna lived – in fact, the whole borough – had been completely obliterated in a bombing raid. All files with the local council had been lost as well. A new register for surviving residents had been established locally in October 1945, but Anna was not listed. As she is referred to in Dr Gleitze's report as 'Widow Gleitze', it must be assumed that Heinrich had predeceased her at some time during the war years.

2

LONDON 1921

Back Home at Last

When Mercedes returned home to England at the age of 21, the First World War had radically changed the way many young women perceived themselves. Throughout 1914–18 women had, of necessity, been asked to step into the shoes of the male workforce that had been drafted into the armed forces. They toiled in munitions factories and as land girls providing food for the country, they drove ambulances, they worked as Voluntary Aid Detachments[2] at home and in war zones, and generally helped to keep the nation's industries running. But at the end of hostilities, those directly employed in war work found their jobs disappearing, and other female employees working, for example, in tram and railway companies or for local authorities, were dispensed with in order to accommodate the returning demobbed troops.[3]

However, for many thousands of women who had contributed in numerous ways to the war effort, their self-perception had changed forever. They had become aware of their own capabilities and were not prepared to return to low paid, menial work in domestic service or textile mills.

Alongside the greater social freedoms these 'new women' were enjoying (chaperones were unheard of after the war[4]), the Suffrage movement, led by the resolute Pankhurst women, was slowly gaining ground in its battle to secure the enfranchisement of all women – not just certain categories – into Britain's political system.

It was into this environment that Mercedes returned as a young woman in 1921, and she gladly embraced this new social order. Although there was a post-war slump in Britain, the changing economy had produced a substantial growth in the number of white-collar positions opening up to women,[5] and she quickly found employment with Messrs T.J. Eaton & Company, a shipping company in Westminster. (In practically every one of the hundreds of press reports covering her career, Mercedes was referred to somewhere in the text as 'The London Typist'.)

It was a well-paid job for a woman at that time. Mercedes spoke both English and German fluently, had a readable knowledge of French and Spanish, and had also taught herself the universal language of Esperanto. Her proficiency with languages, together with her shorthand and typing skills, was reflected in her salary. This enabled her to rent a small flat in Pimlico, buy some furniture on an instalment plan from Drages,[6] and settle down to a life of her own choosing. In so doing, she became one of an emerging class of independent, self-supporting young women.

Dreams and Aspirations

However, despite having a secure job and her own little flat, Mercedes felt that her life was not fulfilling. Although at an age when most young women of that era were contemplating marriage and bearing children, she harboured two very different ambitions that together became her driving force.

Firstly, she always felt she could swim great distances. Indeed, as part of her escape route out of Germany she had planned to complete the final stage by swimming across the sea from Holland to England. And she wanted to use this inherent ability to pursue an aquatic career as a professional long-distance swimmer.

Secondly, living as she did in the heart of London during the years leading up to the Great Depression, she witnessed all around her the homeless, jobless and hungry people. On her walks to and from the office, she became aware of the 'casuals' sleeping on the Embankment or in Trafalgar Square, selling shoelaces and matches to eke out a living – people she believed 'could be reclaimed'.[7] She thought that if she could succeed in becoming a professional long-distance swimmer, she could perhaps earn enough in prize money to fund a refuge home for at least a few of these impoverished people.

The Pioneering Spirit

During the 1920s boundaries were wide open for pioneering individuals such as aviators, mountaineers or polar explorers to challenge, and on the aquatic scene the crossing of the English Channel by a woman would be groundbreaking. And so Mercedes decided that this would be the waterway to launch her career. She possessed a self-belief and winning mentality, and these attributes would help her face up to any obstacles she might encounter on the way. When questioned later by *The Australasian* about her choice of career, she explained:

> I love swimming. I could not give it up. I fight the currents, the roughness of the sea and the cold, and just cover the distance with no attempt at lowering speed records. If it is a rough sea, and you are a good swimmer, you can adapt yourself to it, and be just as comfortable as if you are swimming in a calm sea. The cold is the greatest drawback as it causes such intense pain, and there is nothing you can do to lessen it.[8]

Mercedes is a notable example of a sporting pioneer who had to achieve her goals entirely by her own efforts, compared to some of her contemporaries who came from wealthy families, and those from overseas who were fully sponsored – or, indeed, the athletes of today who enjoy the support of clubs and have access to a wealth of information on coaching techniques, specific diets, specialised clothing, sports psychologists, funding, managers and so on. During the years leading up to her successful crossing, Mercedes at times took on two jobs in order to pay for boat hire, pilots' fees, trainers, travel and accommodation.

Mercedes and the American swimmer Amelia (Mille) Gade-Corson (the second woman to swim the English Channel) were friends as well as fellow competitors. On 26 August 1926, immediately after Mille's own successful English Channel crossing, she quickly made her way to Folkestone to lend support to Mercedes, who was about to make her next attempt.

Mille Corson openly criticised the authorities in the UK for not supporting English girls so that they could have an equal chance of succeeding. To cover her own preparations for the Channel crossing, Mille and her husband had been financed to the tune of $3,000 by American businessman L. Walter Lissberger. Mille put it to journalists at a press conference, 'Why does not England finance an English girl so that she can have a fair chance? I feel almost sorry that I have swum the Channel. I feel it ought to have been an English girl this time.'[9]

The Way Forward

Although the 'road map' leading to her new career was unclear, common sense told Mercedes that to succeed she must be in good physical condition. With fitness training for the English Channel swim in mind, she focussed on how this could be fitted into her weekly routine. Land training didn't present a problem as this consisted of long walks together with Swedish exercises using dumb-bells, both of which could be done anywhere. But because of her long working hours, it was only possible for her to train in the sea at Folkestone or Dover during infrequent summer holiday periods.

Even though she was able to use local indoor swimming pools in London, the warm, fresh, calm water in the pool was no substitute for the conditions she would meet in the cold, salty, unruly sea. She needed to do regular sessions in tidal waters in order to build up her strength and stamina for the task ahead, so her initial step was to organise training swims in the open air, closer to home.

The River Thames, with its waters varying from freshwater to seawater, was her nearest open waterway. She walked along its embankment daily on her way to and from work and realised that this tidal river could simulate some of the conditions she would have to face in the open sea, and so she organised training sessions in 'Old Father Thames'.

In an interview given to the *Rand Daily Mail* later in her career, Mercedes recalled:

When I first took up swimming in real earnest I was a rather delicate girl. Those who watch me swim nowadays may find this difficult to imagine. But think of it – I was a struggling London typist subject to fainting fits and troubled by repeated attacks of bronchitis, when I made up my mind to go in for swimming seriously.

As a schoolgirl of 10 years I had learned to swim, but it was not until 1922 that the idea became rooted in my mind that I must continue my swimming practices at all costs. Usually I worked so hard at business that by evening I was too tired even to go to the local swimming baths. But it occurred to me that it would be a splendid thing to swim in the Thames every Sunday, and I applied to the Port of London authorities for permission to do so. I was granted a special permit and began my training at week-ends.

I had a natural desire to be in the open, and found the joy of swimming in the fresh air intense. A stretch of two or three hours in the water was, I found, long enough for me in those early days. Next morning I was often in such pain – every muscle in my body aching – that it was sheer agony for me to move. But I had made up my mind to go in for endurance swimming, and I persevered.

I weighed only eight stones when I began my week-end Thames swims, but my health so improved as a result of the exercise that when I swam the English Channel in 1927 my weight had increased to ten stones, and I was in perfect physical form. Lung, heart and nose specialists in various parts of the globe have asked to be allowed to examine me, and in every case they have informed me that my health is absolutely sound.[10]

Although her main focus was still very much on the English Channel crossing, an opportunity presented itself in 1923 for Mercedes to set her standard in another waterway – the River Thames.

3

THE RIVER THAMES

1923 – British Ladies' Record for Thames Swimming

On 29 July 1923 Mercedes made an attempt to break the ladies' record for swimming the Thames, which was then held by Eileen Lee, who had achieved 20 miles in 10 hours 17½ minutes. Mercedes started out at Putney Bridge and covered 15 miles on the ebb tide. At the turn of the tide, a swift seaward breeze made swimming back with the flood tide too difficult and she abandoned the attempt after covering about 19 miles in 7 hours 7 minutes.

A week later, on 5 August 1923, she tried again, and this time succeeded in establishing a new Thames record by swimming 27¼ miles in 10 hours 45 minutes. The next day, the *Daily Sketch* reported that Mercedes started from Putney Bridge at 10.19 a.m. and reached Tower Bridge (8 miles) at 12.49 p.m. Rough water was experienced, but at 2.35 p.m. she arrived at Greenwich (12 miles). On the journey upriver, she was cheered by crowds at Tower Bridge at 4.30 p.m. and made steady progress despite a drop in water temperature, reaching the 24-mile mark at Putney some 9 hours 7 minutes and 30 seconds into the swim. The last leg took her past Hammersmith and on to Barnes, where she landed at 9.02 p.m.

This was Mercedes' first officially recognised swimming record, and it demonstrated that she was physically and mentally gaining in strength and endurance from the part-time training in the Thames that she was able to engage in outside of her office hours.

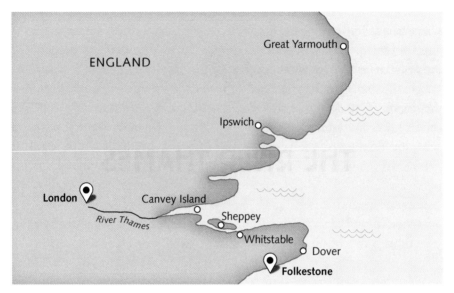

Along Old Father Thames – an innovative marathon swim in set stages.

1927 – London to Folkestone, in Stages

During the previous four or five summer seasons Mercedes had made several unsuccessful attempts to swim the English Channel, but she was still in training for another try. However, in order to widen the scope and variety of her swims, and to gain publicity for a potential new career, she fitted a different trial into her schedule. This was to swim from Westminster Bridge in central London, down the Thames and around the headland to Folkestone – 120 miles in an estimated ten stages, swimming for 6 hours each day depending on tides.

Near-Death Experience

The swim was not without mishap. Mercedes narrowly escaped death when treacherous currents drew her under some barges in the Thames at Wapping. She had set out on her first stage from Westminster Bridge at 5.30 on the morning of 18 July 1927 and was swimming strongly through the dangerous Pool of London when horrified spectators saw her disappear under a row of barges moored on the Rotherhithe side of the Thames.

For what, according to one of the watchers, seemed hours but was actually about a minute or two, there was no sign of her. At last the current propelled her to the surface and she reappeared feet first and obviously distressed. Despite the fact that she had been on the verge of losing her senses, and powerless to resist the undertow, she refused to abandon the swim. The spot is known as Church Hole and is notorious for its currents. It has been the scene of numerous fatalities, and a bargeman commented afterwards, 'It takes a strong and cool-headed swimmer to get out of a trap like that. In nine cases out of ten anyone getting under the barges in this sort of water would not get out alive.'[11]

In a later interview in Cape Town with *The Outspan*, Mercedes gave her own perspective of the incident:

> When I undertook the swim from London to Folkestone I remember that there was a crowd of newspapermen and cameramen on the Westminster Bridge to see me start, and though I paid little attention to them – my mind being on the swim – the sight of them came back to me in a curious way.
>
> I had covered a few miles down the river when I approached three stationary barges moored amid-stream, and I tried to swim away from them. But a strong current drew me towards the nearest barge, and, try as I could, I was forced nearer and nearer until I expected to be flung against the steel hull of the barge. Just as I seemed about to strike it the current sucked me down below water and I held my breath and went with it without struggling. This seemed the only thing to do and, as it happened, was the safest course. But as I sank below the surface there came to me an astonishingly clear vision of those newspapermen standing on Westminster Bridge and I could even 'see' the cameras levelled at me as I went under. I must have lost consciousness under water. The current carried me right under the three barges and I was told later that when I came to the surface I bobbed up suddenly as if propelled by the current and commenced to swim automatically. I came up quite close to the river police patrol boat which was accompanying me, and if I had not started swimming they would have pulled me out. My head cleared, however, and I refused to leave the water.[12]

An Extended Police Escort

Mercedes hurriedly moved away from the accompanying police boat when they offered to pull her out of the water, swam the tide out and finished the first leg at Erith (18 miles) at 11.30 a.m. In the accompanying motor launch were Mr Garman (skipper), Jack Weidman (trainer) and Miss Hayden (a friend). Following the near-death episode, she was escorted down the river by relays of Thames River Police.

During the first two days of the swim she took only liquid food when in the water, but from the third day solid food was added to her diet – sandwiches, omelettes and so on – to keep up her strength. She went on to successfully complete the whole course on Friday, 29 July 1927, twelve days after leaving Westminster. She had planned to arrive at Folkestone on Wednesday, 27 July, but was delayed for two days by rough weather.

At the finish of the last lap (Dover to Folkestone), when Mercedes waded out on Folkestone beach at approximately 8.30 on Friday evening, she was accorded a great reception. For some time after her arrival she was besieged in a hut by the crowd. She told a Press Association representative that she felt 'as fit as a fiddle' after the swim, despite her right arm being pitted with red spots. She said:

> Those are from cuttle fish between Canvey Island and Whitstable. The sting from them resembles the sting of nettles, and is very painful at times … It was a case of adverse winds nearly all the way. I swam mostly with the tide, but the cross-tides were difficult, and at times the sea was rough.[13]

This second Thames record swim moved her closer to her aim of becoming a professional swimmer, and she must have taken much heart from its completion.

4

THE ENGLISH CHANNEL
(1922–27)

The Channel swimming season is limited. It takes place during high summer to early autumn in order to take advantage of the higher sea temperatures. If a swimmer doesn't succeed in one season they have to wait until the following year before making another attempt. Nowadays it is possible for would-be contenders to train in warmer climates during the weeks leading up to the most favourable Channel swimming period, but this wasn't an option for Mercedes and most of her contemporaries.

The date on which Mercedes actually boarded a train in London and made her first journey to the coast is not recorded, but it would have been sometime during the early summer of 1922, when she was 21 years old. As she packed her suitcase she would have felt both excited and apprehensive about the task ahead. Even today it would be quite daunting for a young woman to plan and organise an undertaking of this scale on her own, but in 1922 it was remarkable because of the restricted life most women led. However, Mercedes had declared – at least to herself – that she was going to swim across the English Channel, and so, when time permitted, she would have made one or two preliminary visits to Dover and Folkestone to find out how to go about organising a swim of this nature. She would have needed to gather information on suitable tidal conditions, starting and finishing points, how to employ a trainer, how to hire a pilot and boat, the sustenance needed during the crossing, whether travel documents would be required when landing in or leaving France, and, of course, the cost of such a venture.

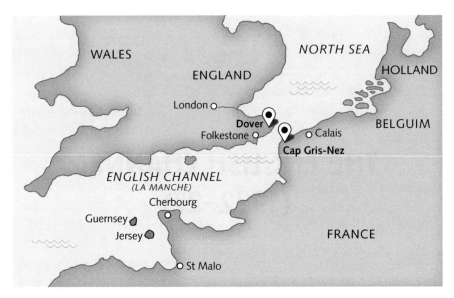

Across the English Channel – still today, the benchmark crossing for aspiring open-water swimmers.

During these short visits, she would also have tested her own strength in the sea. She would have learnt that there is nothing constant about the Channel tides. They are liable to develop all sorts of mysterious offsets and currents at the most unexpected times. Even today, despite the advanced technology available for predicting sea movements, long-distance swimmers can still get their timings or their courses wrong.

These early trials would have given Mercedes some idea of her body's ability to withstand the buffeting of the waves, the extreme cold and the overwhelming desire to sleep that long-distance swimmers have to fight against. She would also have learnt about the benefits of covering her skin with grease to stop it wrinkling and the need to wear a veil on her face for protection from salt spray as well as – in the absence of modern sunblocks – to shield her from the sun's rays.

During the swimming seasons Mercedes met other would-be Channel swimmers and occasionally, in order to minimise expenses, shared swimming coaches and training sessions, but generally she kept herself apart from the crowd. Many of the swimmers congregated at Dover, but Mercedes established her training headquarters further along the coast at Folkestone.

Trainers and Pilots

Trainers

In August 1922 a Mr Taylor accompanied her on her very first attempt.[14] It is unknown who her trainers were (if any) in the years 1923–25, but in 1926 Mercedes employed two trainers – Horace Carey for her 24 July attempt and Sydney T. Hirst (Honorary Secretary of the London-based Amateur Swimming Club) for her 18 September attempt. However, throughout the 1927 season George Henry Allan was her trainer, and he was with her on her successful crossing as well as on her subsequent vindication swim.

George had an engineering background, and during the First World War and beyond he worked as a civil servant, monitoring armament production. After the war he returned to London and lived in Kensington with his wife, Helena, before eventually moving to Watford. It was during his time in Watford that he became involved in coaching, and in 1927 he became Mercedes' personal trainer.

Pilots

On her first attempt in August 1922, a Mr Driscoll (who had accompanied Montague Holbein on his pre-war attempts) piloted Mercedes. But during 1926 and 1927 Henry Gare Sharp and his son, Henry (Harry) James Sharp, were employed by Mercedes, with Harry piloting her on her successful crossing and her vindication swim. Both Sharps were men of the sea – fishermen from Folkestone – but apart from fishing, they also used their navigating skills to guide would-be swimmers across the English Channel during those pioneering years. The crew at times included other members of the Sharp family – Harry's brother, Arthur, and Arthur's wife.

English Channel Swims

1922

On 3 August, Mercedes turned up in Dover 'unknown and unheralded, announcing that she was going to swim the Channel. When asked about her training and preparation she confessed that she was without either.'[15] During the summer of 1922, Mercedes' visits to the coast and the opportunity to do any meaningful training would have been very limited because she worked a five-and-a-half-day week in London. Consequently, this lack of training took its toll, and after being in the water for 3¼ hours, and covering 6 miles, her shoulder muscles gave out and she abandoned the attempt. The *New York Times* – one of many newspapers to cover the event – reported on 4 August:

> She dived at 7.30 this morning from Shakespeare Cliff, Dover, using a powerful breast stroke. A strong easterly tide swept her along, but soon diverted her towards Deal. Abreast Saracen's Head, near Goodwin Sands, Mercedes complained of a pain in her shoulder, but continued swimming until the suffering caused her trainer, Taylor, to lift her from the water.

In the press, details on her were minimal, but with this first swim she had begun to establish herself in the media as a serious contender in the race to be the first woman across.

1923
Two swims were recorded in the press this summer lasting 3 hours 30 minutes and 10 hours respectively, but they appear to have been discounted as formal attempts – just test swims. No details are available about the sea conditions or the distances swum.

1924
There are no records of any attempts this year – Mercedes had a short spell in hospital that may account for this.

1925
Note: The records state that Mercedes succeeded on her 8th attempt. Her initial competition swim in 1922 and the two trial swims in 1923 described above have been discounted as formal attempts, and the count starts as from 1925.

According to newspaper reports, two formal attempts were made from Folkestone on 25 and 30 August. They both ended in failure due to cramp, after 3½ hours (7½ miles) and 5 hours (10 miles) respectively. Criticism was levelled at her in the *Dover Express & East Kent News* (4 September 1925) for starting the swims from Folkestone Pier. They said it was a well-established fact that the crossing would be impossible from such a westerly point. This is unlikely to have been a decision made by Mercedes, though – she would have taken advice from those responsible for charting the course.

1926

First Attempt

Her initial attempt this year was on 24 July from Folkestone beach, from where she was cheered on by a crowd of 2,000. Her pilot was Henry Gare Sharp, and Horace Carey (himself a Channel aspirant) acted as her trainer on this one occasion. During the early stages of the swim Horace's swimming and training partner, Mona McLellan (aka Dr Dorothy Cochrane Logan), kept Mercedes company in the water for a period of four hours.

However, heavy seas and bad weather hampered Mercedes' progress. The buffeting was severe, often hiding her from the sight of those in the attending boat, which was repeatedly swamped. It was reported that the wind was 'blowing half a gale', and after strong pressure from both her trainer and pilot, she was taken out of the water 9 miles from the French coast. After five hours in the water, 19 miles had been swum. During the swim, pigeons were released from the boat to let the people waiting in Folkestone know of her progress.

Second Attempt

Again from Folkestone, Mercedes' second Channel attempt of 1926 took place on Thursday, 26 August. The next day the *Daily Mirror* reported that the attempt was abandoned 10½ miles out from the English coast, after covering a distance of 27 miles in 7 hours. This zigzag course was due to the abnormal strength of the tides which kept carrying Mercedes back towards England.

Another great, and unusual, inconvenience during this attempt were the swarms of thousands of flies. Harry Sharp told the *Gloucester Citizen* (27 August 1926) that he had never before seen anything to equal their numbers – his boat was black with them and understandably they sorely tried the swimmer.

Third Attempt

On 18 September, the third attempt, the decision was taken to try the reverse direction, from France to England. Sadly, this attempt also ended in failure after nearly 11 hours in the water.

The *Folkestone, Hythe, Sandgate and Cheriton Herald* (25 September 1926) reported that prior to the commencement of the swim a consultation was held between Mercedes' acting coach, Sydney Hirst, Harry Sharp and fellow Channel aspirants, Jabez Wolfe and Ishak Helmy, as to the best course to follow. It was recommended that Mercedes should swim the course recently identified by William Burgess – a successful Channel swimmer in 1911, since turned coach.

The attempt started at 5.07 p.m. on Saturday, 18 September, her departure being witnessed by Calais' Mayor Leon Vincent, Ishak Helmy, J. Costa and a large crowd. In the pilot boat *Ocean King*, together with skipper Harry Sharp were Sydney Hirst and his three club colleagues (C.B. Dolphin, W. White and G. Rumi) who acted as relay swimmers during the night. Also on board were Mercedes' parents, Heinrich and Anna, her sister Doloranda, V. Hewson from Folkestone, several friends and Stanley Devon – a London-based news photographer, who had paid £3 to the pilot for a place on the boat.

At first the swim went well, despite the lowering water temperature and Mercedes having suffered painful jellyfish stings in both of her arms, but towards the end, when just 2 miles from the English coast, it was evident to those accompanying her that she was losing strength and struggling to stay awake. Despite her repeated protests of 'I will do it', 'I am going to do it', they feared she might collapse at any minute and sink into the inky darkness, and so Hirst and the others decided to stop the swim. As Hirst told the *Herald* (20 September 1926), 'After the moon had gone it was impossible to see the swimmer from a distance of more than three yards. We had a big responsibility, and with the danger of Miss Gleitze suddenly collapsing, the risk of continuing was too great.' Because of her refusal to give up, drastic action was taken, and at 3.58 on Sunday morning a rope with a slip knot was thrown over the swimmer's hands as she feebly made a stroke, and then drawn tight.

It was reported that when Mercedes was taken out of the water her body was like an iceberg, and she was so numbed with the cold that she imagined she was grasping imaginary objects in her hands. Because of her debilitated condition Harry Sharp immediately steered a course for Dover, the nearest port, and Mercedes was taken to the Hotel de Paris. Her powers of recovery were exceptional though, and after a hot bath and a massage she was soon back to her normal self. After a few hours' rest she returned by taxi to her lodgings in Folkestone.

The *Dover Standard* reported:

> After a highly credible attempt Mercedes Gleitze was beaten by the coldness of the water when only two miles from St Margaret's Bay. The pilot followed the 'Grisnez course' and maintained such perfect position that the full flood was caught, and Miss Gleitze made very rapid progress towards the South Foreland. After about nine hours she was feeling the effects of the cold water, but still persevered. When within two miles of the coast, and when Miss Gleitze had been in the water 10 hours 51 minutes, it was evident that the low temperature had so sapped her strength that a landing was not possible, and despite prolonged protests on her part she was taken out of the water at 3.58 a.m.
>
> The wonderful courage and fortitude displayed by Miss Gleitze was a marvel to all who had accompanied her, and it was sheer grit which carried her on for the last hour and a half. That she would succeed one day there is not the slightest doubt. Proper facilities for training have been her drawback so far, but with the interest certain members of the Amateur S.C. are now taking in her swims, she will have opportunities for training which she had not previous enjoyed.
>
> Miss Gleitze has financed her Channel attempts from her savings as a shorthand writer and foreign correspondent in the employ of a London firm.[16]

Despite the failure of this latest attempt, Mercedes did establish a record by a British woman, reaching within 2 miles of St Margaret's Bay in 10 hours 51 minutes.

In his autobiography, *Glorious*, Stanley Devon says of Mercedes: 'She was a London typist, young, brown-haired, blue-eyed, and beautiful. She was pre-eminently news. Unlike the American swimmers, she had nothing behind her but beauty, courage, and her typist's earnings.'

And in the 1995 biography by Ruth Boyd, *A Focus on Fleet Street*, Devon credits Mercedes with turning his career around. Under instructions from his editor to cover Norman Derham's cross-Channel swim in September 1926, Devon arrived in Dover only to discover that Derham's record swim had already been completed. He heard by chance that Mercedes was about to make an attempt, so he boarded her trainer's boat instead. When Devon returned to his office he was sacked for not completing his original assignment.

However, when the story of Mercedes' swim broke a few hours later, he was immediately reinstated. Hers was a greater human-interest story because of her refusal to give up after nearly 11 hours, resulting in her being forcibly taken out of the water. Devon had taken the only photographs, and his images were sought after by all of Fleet Street. After providing exclusive coverage of her dramatic September 1926 attempt to cross the Channel, Devon was paid a bonus of £5, with which he bought his second camera. He was subsequently rewarded with new, profitable assignments and a distinguished career as a news photographer followed. He said, 'Mercedes Gleitze changed my life. I gave up working in the darkroom.'

Sadly, Devon's pre-1932 negatives and plates were lost when the building in which they were stored was destroyed by enemy action during the Blitz on London in the Second World War, but some of the images he took of Mercedes' September 1926 attempt, are reproduced in this memoir.

Once back in London, Mercedes reportedly said she would not make a further attempt at the crossing until the following summer but would devote her spare time in the approaching winter months to improved methods of swimming and a systematic course of training under the guidance of members of the London-based Amateur Swimming Club.

However, regardless of her success so far, Mercedes had spent all her savings on her Channel attempts and had lost her job as a typist.[17] For the five attempts already made she had provided the necessary funds herself, and it was only through the generous co-operation of her pilot, Harry Sharp, that she was able to make the last two of those attempts.

To round off the 1926 season, Mercedes was invited to give a swimming display at an aquatic gala being held at the White Rock Baths in Hastings on 2 October. She was part of a programme that also included Norman Derham (who had successfully swum the English Channel the previous month) and three of Britain's Olympic divers – Isabelle (Belle) White, Eileen (Beatrice) Armstrong and Verrall Newman.

1927

In its 30 August 1927 edition, the *Gloucester Citizen* pointed out 'how women were taking up the challenge of the Channel, which only a few years ago men alone attempted'. During the 1927 season no fewer than ten women – altogether outnumbering the men – waited on the French coast for the right conditions to start the swim, including Mercedes, Mrs Weldman, Ivy Hawkes, Hilda Harding and Jane Darwin, all from the UK; the Zeitenfeld twins (Bernice and Phyllis) from the USA; M. Dorita from Switzerland; and Edith Jensen from Denmark.

First Two Attempts

After having given up her job on 1 July to concentrate on sea training, Mercedes must have been disappointed that the weather that summer had been very unsettled. Indeed, Mercedes had to wait until 28 September before making the first of two aborted attempts. After lasting 7 hours 30 minutes into this attempt, swimming from France to England, she scheduled a further attempt on 5 October, swimming the same route. This time she lasted 8 hours 30 minutes before abandoning the attempt.

Success at Last

Despite it being very late in the Channel swimming season, Mercedes decided that one more attempt could be made in the 1927 season.

Thus, on 7 October she made her eighth formal and ultimately successful attempt, taking 15 hours 15 minutes to complete the crossing. She entered the water at Cap Gris-Nez at 2.55 a.m. and waded ashore between St Margaret's Bay and the South Foreland at 6.10 p.m.

It was recorded that during the swim the sea was as calm as a millpond all the way, but it was cold, the temperature never rising above 16°C (60°F). A blanket of fog lay over the water and visibility at times was almost nil. Mercedes used breast and sidestrokes alternatively, and occasionally floated on her back to ease her muscles.

Following the triumph, Mercedes, pilot Harry Sharp and trainer George Allan were interviewed extensively.

Mercedes told journalists:

One of the people who witnessed the start was a dear Frenchman at Grisnez [M. Lucien Popieul, semaphore signalman] who stayed up late on Thursday night to see me off. He said he was not going to bed, but would stay up and follow our course with his telescope from the Signal Station until I disappeared out at sea.

It was the first time in my eight attempts that I encountered really natural conditions. When I started there was a calm sea and I derived considerable help from the neap tide, which gives a long period of slack water before the turn. The fog was very heavy, but worst of all was the intense cold which the olive oil and lard composition that was plastered thickly over my costume failed to keep out.

After two hours I began to feel very cold but I did not tell those in the boat because I feared they might make me come out. I gradually overcame the cold and continued to make good progress.

We could not tell our exact position owing to the fog but I kept on swimming by the course which I believed would lead me to the English coast … Later in the afternoon the fog and cold affected me a good deal, and for the last three hours I suffered great pain.

Mercedes also said that she suffered horribly from thirst all the time and could not eat anything solid. Nourishment during the swim consisted of hot, strong tea at two-hourly intervals, a little honey and some grapes – her trainer tied the grapes with string onto a rod and she had to fish for them. She said, 'In the excitement of trying to catch them I forgot about being cold.'

The fog guns fired at intervals from Dover Pier and the siren of the South Goodwin Lightship were the only means her pilot had of detecting their whereabouts. It is a tribute to Harry's skill that he brought his craft and the swimmer safely through the dangers of the fogbound Channel. Not only that, but several times the little party narrowly missed being run down by passing steamers. Mercedes explained:

My pilot, Mr Harry Sharp, was wonderful. He could hardly see in the fog but kept a beautiful course for me. Frequently he sounded the fathoms and then rowed away from the noise of the motorboat to listen for foghorns.

We could hear the sirens of ships in the Channel. There were times when the passing shipping came too near to us to be comfortable. One vessel, sighting me in the water, sounded her siren as she passed, which gave me great encouragement. I wish we could have taken her name.

When Harry finally shouted to Mercedes that he had heard the Dover foghorns, she knew that she was over the Goodwin Sands. The moment of landing came at a spot between Dover and St Margaret's Bay. She said:

> It would have helped a great deal if I could have seen land in the distance, but the fog was so dense that at times I could not see further than five yards ahead. When eventually I heard a loud shout from the boat, I felt a great hope surging straight through me. I let my feet go downwards gradually, and it was land. If I had not felt so weak, I should have cried with joy.

The moment her feet touched the chalk rocks on the beach, Mercedes collapsed. Her only words were, 'Thank God I am conscious!'

The spot where she waded out was shrouded in fog and deserted, and so the crew (Harry Sharp, his brother Arthur Sharp, Arthur's wife, George Allan, and one other crew member) lifted her into the rowing boat and then transferred her on to the fishing boat *Little Willie* (FE11). For Mercedes, the period after she touched solid ground was a blur, no doubt due to extreme exhaustion. She recalled:

> When I became my normal self again I was tucked up in front of the cabin bar of the fishing boat and Mrs Arthur Sharp was mothering me, as she has done in all my previous attempts. They had let me sleep for an hour. It was the sleep of exhaustion. When I woke up I was in dreadful pain and I was crying for a long time like a baby, but I could not help it. The pain was too terrible to describe.

The fishing boat with its passengers then made its way along the coast to Folkestone, arriving shortly before 10 p.m. Mercedes had recovered slightly by that time, but on 8 October *The Times* reported that she still had to be practically carried up the steps by the side of the quay from the boat to the top of the old fishmarket, where she was cheered loudly by a big crowd. After the press interviews she was taken by taxi to her lodgings in a little cottage at 214 Dover Road and put to bed.

Harry Sharp spoke about the conditions the little party faced out in the Channel:

The boom of the Dover gun and the siren of the South Goodwin Lightship were all we had to guide us. The fog was so thick that at times we could not see ahead of us at all. We could only listen for the gun and the siren each time and try to get some idea of our whereabouts by their sounds. We had the compass to tell us that we were going in the right direction, but the difficulty was to know where the land was and how near we were to it.

George Allan told reporters that in all his life he had never met anyone – man or woman – with such grit and determination. He said:

When we were near land, though we did not know it at the time, she asked me if she would reach the shore in another three hours – this after 15 hours in perishing cold water! There were times when we had no idea where we were, and from time to time soundings were taken by the crew of the fishing boat. We determined our position by the sound of the Dover fog guns and the Saracen's Head hooter. It was a great effort to keep up conversation with Miss Gleitze, but we had to in order to prevent her going to sleep. We did not see the land really until we touched it, and that was just before six o'clock, when our pilot and I were in the small boat. We were taking soundings, and suddenly Sharp, the pilot, said 'We're on the rocks,' and he shouted to Miss Gleitze to keep swimming. Ultimately our boat grounded, and Miss Gleitze, swimming less than five yards behind us, found her feet touching land.

Just before we reached land there was a good omen. A land bird came and perched on our boat. It was the crowning point of our hope, for then we knew the end was near.

Mercedes was the first British woman (and third woman) to accomplish the crossing – the first two females to succeed being Gertrude Ederle and Amelia Gade-Corson from the United States.

The morning after the swim Mercedes went for a walk 'without her hat on'.[18] She had woken up with a horrible pain in her head from the beating of the waves, but felt better after having a cup of hot, strong tea. Later that morning she was received by the Mayor of Folkestone, Alderman R.G. Wood, at the town hall, and in the afternoon, accompanied by her trainer George Allan, she caught the train to London to meet with the *News of the World* proprietor, Lord Riddell.

The newspaper had offered a prize of £1,000 to the first woman of British birth to swim the English Channel in under the time taken by Gertrude Ederle. Mercedes' time of 15 hours 15 minutes was approximately 45 minutes longer than Gertrude's, but the proprietors decided that she should be rewarded for her extraordinary grit and dogged persistence, and its editor, Sir Emsley Carr, presented her with a cheque for £500 to mark her achievement. The following statement appeared in the paper's 9 October 1927 edition:

> In recognition of her wonderful pluck and perseverance in attempting to win our £1,000 prize, although she failed to beat Miss Ederle's record, the proprietors of the *News of the World* awarded Miss Gleitze £500 as a consolation gift, and a cheque for this amount was handed to her yesterday.[19]

She was delighted with their sporting gesture, and when asked what she would do with the money, replied, 'I shall first of all pay the expenses of my pilot, £150; then I shall devote £250 to a fund for setting up a home for destitute people in London, and the remaining £100 I shall spend on myself.'

Mercedes gave a BBC radio interview on 10 October 1927 and likened the radio audience to the cliffs of England. She said she knew they were there, even though she couldn't see them. She continued, 'No doubt you have read of the little land-bird that alighted on the mast of my pilot's boat as we neared land. Nobody could possibly realise what that little bird meant to me as it seemed to deliver its welcome message through the merciless fog.'

In an interview with *The Outspan* on 25 March 1932, Mercedes said that since swimming the English Channel she had covered hundreds of miles in the water and won all sorts of trophies, but never again would she get quite the same thrill as she did after that swim.

The Vindication Swim

The euphoria of Mercedes' successful crossing of the English Channel on 7 October 1927 was all too soon to be shattered. Just a few days later, another swimmer – Dr Dorothy Cochrane Logan (swimming under the name of Mona McLellan) – claimed to have made the same crossing in 14 hours 10 minutes, accompanied by trainer Horace Carey (also a Channel aspirant). She was feted in the same way as Mercedes and was subsequently awarded the £1,000 prize offered by the *News of the World* for beating Gertrude Ederle's time. However, a few days later, after suspicions were aroused both in France and England as to the authenticity of her swim, Dr Logan was challenged. She confessed that the whole thing had been a hoax and said that she had not cashed the cheque, claiming that she had perpetrated the fraud in order to highlight the fact that – as she put it – 'anyone can say they have swum the Channel'. But by so doing, she sullied the reputations of all those who had genuinely completed the crossing.

Dr Logan was an educated woman – a Harley Street physician, and on the medical staff of King's College Hospital, London – and she must have known her hoax would tend to discredit her swimming rival's success, as well as cast doubt on others. On 22 October 1927, the *Daily Herald* published a comment that Logan had all summer in which to make her practical protest, but she had waited until the first British member of her own gender had gained the coveted place in Channel swimming records before doing so.

Mercedes knew both Dorothy Logan and Horace Carey well, and had shared a training session with them during the 1926 swimming season. Horace had, in fact, acted as her official trainer on one attempt in July of that year, and Dorothy had kept her company in the water for part of the course. Mercedes told the *Daily Sketch* on 17 October 1927 that she was greatly surprised by Logan's confession: 'I had complete faith in her. I know she is a strong swimmer with wonderful endurance.'

In response to the slight cast upon her, Mercedes stated:

So far as my semi-conscious condition at the end of the swim permitted me, I would readily have sworn any affidavit with perfect purity of conscience that my swim was honest. But such an affidavit might not dispel doubts. Therefore the best way to restore the prestige of British women Channel swimmers in the eyes of the world would be for me to make another Channel swim, which I would be most willing and happy to do at the next neap tide. After what has been said, I am determined to try to swim the Channel again this year, if I have to spend my last penny on it. My conscience is clear, but I want to repeat my performance in the presence of all the witnesses I can get.

Although very late in the season, she planned to do this as quickly as possible while she was still in training – 'Having done it once, I am sure I can do it again.'

A businessman – Mr Summers Brown, Chairman and Managing Director of Greater London Theatres & Cinemas Limited – made contact with her and agreed to give her 'this sporting opportunity to justify her late performance, by another trial costing between £50 and £100, under conditions to be arranged'.

The *Kent Evening Echo* reported that discussions had taken place within Kentish seafaring circles about whether Mercedes had the strength to withstand the lowered temperature on top of the strain of the two swims she had carried out the previous week.[20] They argued that with the arrival of the herrings at Deal comes the flow of colder water from the North Sea into the English Channel, and that to contend with that was beyond even the physical endurance of so plucky a woman as Miss Gleitze. However, her pilot, Harry Sharp, responded by saying that all she required was a calm sea: 'She possesses powers of endurance such as I have never seen in the strongest of men.'

In an interview with the *Daily Mail* on 18 October 1927 Mercedes said:

I realise my task is not an easy one owing to weather conditions at this time of the year. I want there to be no doubt about what I have claimed to do. While I was discussing the details of my project, a telephone message was received stating that Dr Dorothy Logan hoped that developments over the weekend had not influenced me and that she hoped I would abandon the attempt. I sent back a message that my plans had been fixed.

On the same day, Mercedes travelled from London by boat-train and crossed to Boulogne on the SS *Riviera*. From there she proceeded to Cap Gris-Nez to await the arrival of her pilot, Harry Sharp, her trainer, George Allan, and the rest of her supporting party.

Before leaving London, Mercedes declared that she was not daunted by the opinion of experts that it was too late in the season. 'I am fit enough,' she asserted, 'except that I have a chest cold, but that does not matter. It is the heart which tells the tale, and my heart is as sound as a bell.'[21]

Goodwill accompanied Mercedes en route to Cap Gris-Nez. When Mercedes arrived at Victoria Station, everyone – travellers, guards and porters alike – 'pressed up to Miss Gleitze to offer their good wishes', and tourists bound for the Continent on the SS *Riviera* bombarded her for permission to take photographs.[22] She told the *Daily Express* special representative:

> I am confident in my powers to stand up to the scepticism of those who say I cannot stay in the water for more than a few hours.
>
> I have been made happy by the fact that a number of distinguished people have written to me since I announced my intention of devoting any money I might win through my swim to the purpose of providing a home for destitutes, telling me of their willingness to help me in this project.
>
> Mr Arthur Evans, the distinguished surgeon [and archaeologist], is getting up a special meeting for me with an MP in the chair, when my project will be discussed, and Lady Conan Doyle has asked me to attend a meeting to discuss the matter next Monday.

Journalists from Britain, Europe and the USA gathered at the Lighthouse Hotel to cover the event and so, on 21 October, exactly two weeks after her successful crossing, Mercedes again entered the water at Cap Gris-Nez to prove she was capable of completing the distance.

The Folkestone fishing smack *Little Willie* (FE11) and the Boulogne tug *Alsace* followed Mercedes during her swim, and those on board these two vessels included Mr Harry Sharp (pilot), Dr W.E. Cheeseman (from St Thomas' Hospital), Dr Philip Frossard (of Queen Anne Street, London), Mr Sydney Hirst (secretary of the Amateur Swimming Club), Mr Thomas Dodd (representing Mr Summers Brown), Miss Nora Baker (a female companion), Mr Arthur Sharp (crew), a group of jazz musicians and a large party of journalists. Her trainer, George Allan, was in the stern of the small rowing boat (rowed by Mr Arthur Saunders), which stayed close to the swimmer the whole of the time.

Because of the wide publicity given to it, the vindication swim proved to be a spectacular affair. Tramp steamers and steam trawlers passed by and blew sirens of encouragement. The *Daily Herald* on 22 October 1927 reported that news of her progress was being constantly transmitted by wireless around the world by steamers and aeroplanes that had sighted her as they were crossing the Channel.

The cold was intense and during the swim the observers were visibly affected by it. The group of shivering press men was reduced by half, and the jazz musicians were so overcome by seasickness that they, along with the affected press men, had to be transferred to the more stable tug. Despite having coughing fits (a consequence of the chill Mercedes had contracted in the foggy conditions of her previous successful swim) there was no complaint from the swimmer – just a request for community singing to help her along.

In the event, after 10 hours 30 minutes in seas that, at times, were registering a temperature as low as 53°F (11.7°C), George Allan decided – on the advice of the medical men on board – that the swim must be abandoned. At this point, Mercedes had been battling for 3 hours against being carried down the Channel by an ebb tide against which she could offer little resistance and was on the verge of unconsciousness.

When Mercedes saw the short ladder being let down from the stern of the small rowing boat she swam away and had to be chased. A twisted towel was thrown over her head and underneath her arms, and after a struggle and protests from her to 'let me go on', the trainer and pilot pulled her aboard. The end came when she was approximately 8 miles east-south-east of Dover.

News of the events at sea, sent via carrier pigeons,[23] preceded her return and a large crowd gathered on the quay at Folkestone to welcome her back. As she stepped ashore the crowd followed her and shouted, 'Well done, Mercedes!', and, 'Never mind, Miss Gleitze, better luck next time!'

Back at the hotel Mercedes faced questions from the press, and she told them, 'It is a terrible disappointment, just terrible. But I do not think it would be sportsmanlike to go into hysterics or to cry because my swim was a failure. I am just going to bear up and smile to all the world.'[24]

Asked by *The Scotsman* (22 October 1927) if she thought her attempt had vindicated her in the light of Dr Logan's hoax, Mercedes replied:

I think those who followed me and saw every phase of the endeavour can answer that. I did so want to get across, but I am not in the slightest discouraged. I don't think it would be wise to make another attempt this year as the water is so cold. When I first entered the water I was cut by the iciness of it. As time went on it felt colder and colder.

Her sponsor for the vindication swim, Mr Summers Brown, told the *Daily Herald* (22 October 1927) that he would back any new effort by her in the summer of 1928.

Although the vindication swim had failed, it was hailed by *The Guardian* on 22 October 1927 as 'A Gallant Failure'. On the same day the *Daily Express* spoke of 'The most courageous long-distance swim ever undertaken'. The *Western Daily Press* called it 'A Glorious Failure' and referred to it as 'a Swim of Honour'. The *United Press Association* said, 'Universal sympathy had been shown her because she had undertaken a vindication of her honour' and 'no swim ever attracted such attention'. The *Daily Herald* commented, 'We believe that the public is as satisfied that Miss Gleitze did swim the Channel as it is united in admiration of her courage and her endurance.'

Captain W.R. Fairbairn, Chief Reporter of the *Lincolnshire Standard*, wrote to her:

You will no doubt remember me as the representative of the *Kent Evening Echo* who accompanied you on a previous Channel attempt, and who dispatched the pigeons from the tug telling Folkestone of the swim's progress.

I see that the question relating to your successful swim is being raised just now and it occurred to me that you might be asked why there were no pressmen on board on that occasion. I should like to be able to assure you that on that occasion it was not your fault, for Mr Sharp, your pilot, came to see me personally at the *Kent Evening Echo* office on the day that you set out for France, told me you were going to start from the other side, and asked me to come. I consulted the Editor who decided that as there was a short staff just then I should not go. My point is that we were given every opportunity.

On the suggestion of the *Daily Mirror*, both Mercedes and her trainer, George Allan, signed a statutory declaration in the presence of a Commissioner of Oaths, that her Channel swim on 7 October 1927 was a bona fide one.

Harry Sharp, her pilot, reacted angrily when asked to do the same. Firstly, he said he was very offended at having his word doubted, and secondly he declared:

If I put my name to a legal document of that description I should have to answer any questions put to me about the course I took on

7 October. Now, that course is my own secret – the result of several years' study, and I am not going to reveal it to anyone.

Nevertheless, it was subsequently acknowledged by the newly formed Channel Swimming Association that Mercedes had exonerated herself, and her record as the first British woman to swim the English Channel stood.

Consequences of the Hoax

On 7 November 1927 Dr Dorothy Logan was found guilty and fined £100 plus 10 guineas in costs at Mansion House Police Court for an offence under the Perjury Act, namely, 'That in a certain statutory declaration you unlawfully, knowingly and wilfully made certain statements false in material particular.'

Dr Logan's trainer, and later husband, Mr Horace Carey, who had signed a separate affidavit confirming Dr Logan's claim that she had swum the Channel, was given a lesser fine of £50 plus 5 guineas in costs, as the court felt he had been under Dr Logan's influence when he colluded in the fraud.

Dr Logan was also summoned to appear before the General Medical Council (GMC) on 23 May 1928 to explain her actions, but in the event the GMC decided that although the charge had been proved, she had been punished enough and her name should not be erased from the register, but reminded Dr Logan:

> … of the responsibility which rests on every citizen, and in an especial degree upon a member of an honourable profession as a registered medical practitioner, to refrain from appending your signature to any statement if you cannot vouch for its contents being true.

Not surprisingly, the controversy caused by Dr Logan gave Mercedes far more press coverage than a successful Channel swimmer would normally receive. The story of the hoax was reported in many countries, and, because of the way Mercedes responded to the challenge, it helped to raise her profile in a sympathetic way.

5

A SEA CAREER AND THE STRAIT OF GIBRALTAR

After the trauma of the vindication Channel swim, Mercedes returned to her little flat in Pimlico. She knew that in order to make a success of what she termed 'my sea career' she had to quickly identify another major body of water to cross. She decided to look for new waters that had never been swum by man or woman, and on 1 November 1927 she announced to the press that the Strait of Gibraltar would be her next venture.

Four months earlier, in July 1927, she had made a life-changing decision to leave the security of a steady job and become a professional long-distance swimmer. Her place in sporting history as the first British woman to swim the English Channel was now established. However, it was still a high-risk decision because it was such a unique occupation. She didn't have any financial backing, but the 'business plan' must have appeared viable to her.

During the weeks leading up to her successful Channel crossing, Mercedes had been living on her rapidly diminishing savings. The £500 prize money so generously given to her by the *News of the World* provided the means to settle the expenses incurred in her Channel attempts and to expand her fundraising activities. She had already made a start in this latter respect by selling signed postcards of herself, making personal appearances, and planning the publication of a fundraising magazine – the printing costs of which she hoped to cover by selling advertising space. So that these projects would not stall during her absence in Gibraltar, she secured the employment of an assistant and a part-time secretary to oversee them in her fundraising office, which she had recently set up at her London address.

Alongside her welfare work, during the month of November she also had to make all the arrangements associated with her proposed second major open-water swim. Competing in her native country was relatively easy when compared to organising an event abroad, especially in those days, but Mercedes' intention received coverage in most of the national newspapers and this resulted in an offer from the Rotterdam Lloyd steamer SS *Slamat* for her to travel as their guest. A suite and cabin were reserved for her for the four-day journey to Tangier.

After liaising with the authorities in Gibraltar and Morocco about her planned swim, she was informed that she was to be the guest of the Grand Hotel Valentina in Tangier – the proposed starting place. The hotel manager would also put her in touch with local boatmen, pilots, medical people and members of the local community willing to witness her attempt. And so, on 2 December 1927, with everything in place, the former 'London typist' packed her case and started out on her journey to Morocco.

The Strait of Gibraltar

In the run-up to this new venture, the media coverage of Mercedes' proposed swim had brought an unwelcome intervention from Millie Hudson (another British female open-water swimmer of note, and 1924 Olympic bronze medallist in a diving event), who had made a very credible but unsuccessful attempt to swim the English Channel in 1927. Miss Hudson had read about Mercedes' plans and informed the press that she was going to challenge her to a race across the Strait.

But Mercedes refused to participate in a contest. She responded:

How can I possibly accept Miss Hudson's challenge. My own arrangements for the swim are all complete – my course has been mapped out and my contracts signed. I cannot possibly accept such a challenge at such a late hour. Anyway my acceptance would make the affair look too much like a stunt, and that is the last thing I desire. If Miss Hudson wishes to attempt the swim, then nobody, and least of all myself, can prevent her, but I certainly refuse to make it a race.[25]

Miss Hudson retaliated by declaring that she intended to pursue Mercedes. She told the *Daily Express* (1 December 1927):

Miss Gleitze, I understand, is proceeding to Tangier on Friday, and is to be the guest of the Grand Hotel Valentina. Well, I shall go on Friday afternoon by the same ship as Miss Gleitze and am to be a guest at the Hotel Cecil. When Miss Gleitze enters the water I shall go in at the same time, and we will see who can cross to Gibraltar first.

On 1 December 1927 the *Daily Mirror* also reported that Miss Hudson was determined to race Mercedes across the Strait. Its report went on to say that although Mercedes had stated that she could not accept Miss Hudson's challenge, the latter had decided to leave for Tangier on the same day and intended to make an effort to swim the Strait, as though an agreed contest was actually in progress. The *Daily Mirror* had also interviewed Mercedes, who informed them that she was undertaking the swim with the sole object of adding to the sum with which she hopes to fund an institute to support people who are temporarily 'down and out'. She added, 'To talk about a race in waters which have never been explored [by a swimmer], and which are known to all seafaring experts as extremely dangerous in more ways than one, would be contrary to common sense.'

This exchange between the two swimmers was manna for the press. All the main national papers picked up on the story. On 2 December, journalists were watching and waiting to see what would happen when Mercedes and Millie arrived at Waterloo Station to board the same train on their journey to Tangier. Coverage was similar in all the papers, with headlines reading 'Piquant Situation', 'Chilly Meeting of Rival Swimmers', 'Station Scene', 'Miss Gleitze Rejects a Handshake Offer', 'Rival Girl Swimmers at Variance' and 'Sand Watch on Miss Gleitze'.

Reports of the time describe the scene on the platform:

Overtures by Miss Millie Hudson were rebuffed three times by Miss Mercedes Gleitze at Waterloo Station yesterday. Miss Gleitze had refused to associate herself with a challenge from Miss Hudson to race across the Strait of Gibraltar.

An attempt by photographers to get them to pose together for a picture was unsuccessful. Miss Hudson expressed her willingness but the overture met with no response on the part of Miss Gleitze. As Miss Gleitze was walking along the platform Miss Hudson rushed forward and kissed her on the cheek, but the greeting was not returned. Later while Miss Gleitze was leaning from the carriage window Miss Hudson went forward with outstretched hands, but Miss Gleitze withdrew into the compartment. A few minutes later Miss Gleitze was again at the carriage window and a similar incident occurred.

Approached by a press representative for an explanation Miss Gleitze replied: 'I am going on this swim on behalf of my fund for destitute men and women, not for publicity. That is all.'

When de-training at Southampton another attempt to photograph them together was made, but again without success.

'I am very much hurt by Miss Gleitze's refusal to shake hands with me,' said Miss Hudson. 'It is very unsportsmanlike on her part, because, after all, we are friends.'

Asked to explain her attitude towards Miss Hudson, Miss Gleitze said: 'All these rumours of rivalry are very petty. As I have said before, if anyone else wants to copy my ideas and follow my example they have my good wishes. I don't think that can be called an unsportsmanlike attitude.'

Miss Hudson's resolution to shadow Mercedes was blatant. She told journalists:

We shall stay at different hotels but I have made arrangements to have a day and night watch kept on the sands so that I shall know immediately Miss Gleitze enters the water. When she does, I mean to go after her. Whether she likes it or not, I intend we shall both swim the Strait together.

On 2 December 1927, both Mercedes and Millie Hudson set sail from Southampton on SS *Slamat*, which was due to arrive in Tangier on 6 December. They occupied adjoining cabins, and it was reported that mediators would make another attempt to bring them together during the voyage.

In the event, Mercedes decided to confront the situation herself. In a letter sent to the *Daily Express* just after she arrived in Tangier, she described what had taken place on board SS *Slamat* between herself and Millie Hudson:

I am now all prepared for my swim from Tangier across the Strait of Gibraltar and I am only waiting for a favourable day on which to start. Before I set out, I should like everyone to understand what exactly are the relations between Miss Hudson and myself.

There was a lot of talk in the newspapers because I would not kiss her at Waterloo Station when I left for Tangier. I had made all my arrangements regarding pilots, boats, doctors and all other necessities for the swim. Then I saw in the papers that Miss Hudson intended entering the water the same time as I did, and make use of my organisation for the swim – the expenses of which were being borne by my fund. Consequently when she rushed up to me at Waterloo Station and wanted to kiss me, I could not bring myself to do so, as I felt that it would not be sincere and genuine on my part.

It was only fair that I should have an explanation for her. On the *Slamat* I asked her to come to my cabin. She came along and sat down on my bed. Then we talked like two sisters, hand in hand, and I explained everything to her. She quite saw my point of view and promised that her swim would be entirely independent of mine, and that she would not take advantage of the course and the pilot's services that my fund was paying for. We have been good friends ever since and we have had tea and dinner together. I should like it to be clearly understood that I told Miss Hudson that, as she had chosen to follow me to Tangier, her personal safety during the swim must be entirely her own responsibility, just as my own safety is entirely my own concern.

I was suffering from bronchitis when I landed in Tangier as the result of my last Channel swim. My doctor for the cross Strait swim (Dr Drake) has regularly examined me and is now giving me ultra-violet ray treatment for it. He is astonished at the physical improvement that I have made during my short stay in Tangier. I get up at 7.30 every morning, do an hour's gymnastics on the Swedish principle with my trainer, Mr H. P. Parr, and then have massage to make my muscles supple and strong. I was very lucky to be able to obtain the services of such an expert gymnastic trainer as Mr Parr. Then I have breakfast, and from 10.00 till 11.00 I give interviews to representatives of the press. Then I play my gramophone for half an hour or so for a mental rest and have luncheon. I have a siesta after lunch and then go to my doctor and have ultra violet ray treatment from him.

I am usually invited out to tea. I went to tea yesterday with Mrs Gurney, the wife of the Consul General, and I am going to tea with the French Consul General shortly. I have an hour and a half's walk with my trainer, an hour's gymnastics and massage, and then dinner. I go to bed very soon after dinner – between 8.00 and 9.00. I am not on any special diet except that I have several spoonfuls of honey on rising and before going to bed. I do not touch alcohol or smoke.

I feel very fit in Tangier and sleep splendidly. The air of Tangier is wonderful, so keen and refreshing – just like a perfect spring day in England. It is slightly colder than I thought it would be, as I thought that Morocco was a land of continual blazing sunshine. I adore Tangier and was very surprised to find such a picturesque and essentially Eastern town so near England. The Moors are so very interesting and unusual. They wear strange and most attractive clothes and I feel that I have wandered into scenes from the Old Testament. I love the little Moorish babies. They are hitched up with striped cotton scarves on their mothers' backs and seem absolutely happy – although they look most uncomfortable. They look so sweet with their little bare legs dangling, their solemn little faces, their huge black eyes and their shaven crowns.

The Moorish shops are too quaint for words. They are tiny little places about the size of large cupboards in which there is just room for the goods of the shops and their owners. When the latter want to leave their shops they have to climb over the counters.

The donkeys are sweet and very numerous. They say that nearly all the transport of the town is still done by these dear little animals. They go trotting along under the most enormous loads which you would think would break their backs.

The great market place is wonderfully interesting. Hundreds of Moorish tribesmen and tribeswomen squatting on the ground with piles of eggs, fruits, vegetables, chickens tied together by their legs, charcoal and other produce from the mountains in front of them, and crowds of Moors haggling and bargaining with the vendors.

One corner of the market place is devoted to the snake charmers and story tellers, such wild and quaint looking Moors. The snake charmers look quite terrifying with their long matted hair and fierce expressions. I saw one man bite off a snake's head and swallow it. It was horrid.

The town is very pretty with its white walls, narrow winding lanes and general air of mystery and of the East. I could spend hours wandering round it and exploring the native shops. I hope to be able to do this at my leisure when I have finished my swim. I will be wearing a gold signet ring on my swim. This was given me by a member of the Health and Strength League. I hope that it will bring me luck during the swim.

I feel all ready for the swim and very cheerful, thanks to the splendid way I have been looked after by Captain and Mrs Davin, the owners of the Grand Hotel Valentine, and the training that I have received from Mr Parr. For the honour of Great Britain and for the sake of my Institute for London's Poor, I will do my very best to make a success of my swim.[26]

The Challenge Ahead

To swim the Strait of Gibraltar was a far more arduous task than swimming the English Channel, in spite of the shorter distance. Initial research into the risks involved in the crossing of the Strait revealed to Mercedes that navigation was notoriously difficult, partly on account of the frequent land winds from both sides, and partly due to the swift and variable currents between the Mediterranean and Atlantic seas, which make it impossible to swim a direct course.

Additional perils were the numerous whirlpools or vortexes on both sides of the Strait, which could prove fatal if Mercedes were sucked into one. These whirlpools, although not great in circumference, have been known to catch slow-moving vessels by the bows and swing them completely around. Another hazard was the possibility of attacks from sharks and whales. She could also have encountered harbour porpoises and tunny fish in the Strait. (In a later interview with the Australian newspaper *The Northern Star* on 18 April 1931, she related how some dolphins joined her for part of the swim across the Strait. These sportive creatures swam by and near her, and also underneath her. 'I did not mind them at all,' she said. 'I regarded them as friends.')

Mercedes was not deterred, and on 1 November 1927 she told the *Daily Express* correspondent covering her swim that she would have to find out about all the dangers and take the necessary precautions. Asked if she would start from the African side of the Strait or the Spanish side, she said it would

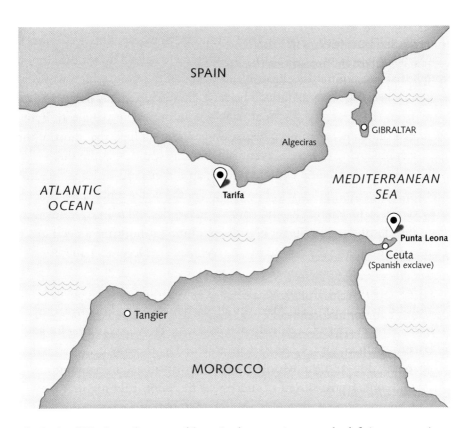

The Strait of Gibraltar – first successful crossing by any swimmer, and a defining moment in Mercedes' new swimming career.

depend upon conditions at the time. The decision was eventually made to attempt the crossing from the African side, and training started in earnest in the waters off Tangier during the early part of December. The *Daily Express* correspondent reported on 13 December 1927 that sea conditions were not yet favourable, but it was hoped that they would come right in a few days' time. The difficulty, he pointed out, was not the distance to be swum, but the currents, amongst the trickiest in the world. He wrote that favourable currents, the skill and judgement of the pilots, and, of course, the pluck and endurance of the swimmer should result in Mercedes landing on the coast of Spain near the sleepy old town of Tarifa.

The first attempt, on Friday, 16 December 1927, was from Africa to Spain. The starting point was from the mouth of the Jew's River in Tangier. Mercedes entered the water at 2.30 a.m. A slight haze hanging over the sea gave promise of a warm day, but she had not been in the water for more than

4 hours when an easterly wind (the levanter) sprang up. This was entirely unexpected and counteracted the favourable currents. The sea became so rough that she was battling against the waves all the time, which was very fatiguing. Feeding became difficult because she was repeatedly being washed away from the boat, and the boat itself was in imminent danger of being swamped on many occasions. The sea was running so high that most of the men accompanying Mercedes eventually became seasick – as did she.

The levanter continued without signs of abatement and, realising the situation was hopeless, Mercedes, after 8 hours in the water, reluctantly gave up the attempt at 10.40 p.m., having covered 12½ miles and being 7 miles away from her destination in Spain. Her disappointment must have been great. However, afterwards, she related to *The Scotsman* (17 December 1927):

As we re-entered the bay we passed the steamship *Arcadian* leaving, and she gave us a rousing British cheer, which went straight to my heart. I much appreciated being met by a large crowd, including Judge Barne and three Vice-Consuls. I am touched by the way in which the Spanish pilots and the Moorish sailors insist on accompanying me again. I am very reassured of success, as the pilots told me that they were so impressed with my swimming that there is no need to worry about tides or currents. So long as we can get fine weather, all will be well. I had no trouble over sharks – I knew we had anti-shark devices. A school of porpoises passed us. There must have been at least 100 of them. Some swam straight at me and dived under me, but I was not frightened, although they looked rather terrifying dashing at one.[27]

Mercedes' second attempt, on Monday, 2 January 1928, was again from the African side. She entered the water west of Tangier at 2 a.m. Conditions were favourable and by noon she was well over halfway across. Then, a strong west wind blew up, it became distinctly chilly and choppy waves troubled her greatly. She struggled gamely on and by 1.30 p.m. she was within 1 mile of Tarifa, the southernmost point of Spain. At this stage, in circumventing the currents, it was estimated that she must have swum more than 27 miles. People on the Spanish and Gibraltar shores sighted her and made arrangements for her to land at Tarifa. But it was in this last mile that the long strain told. Buffeted by the waves, perished by the cold and baffled by contrary tides, her strength gave out. She wanted to go on, but had obviously reached the limit of her endurance, and after thirteen hours in the water she was obliged to acknowledge herself beaten. However, this second attempt by Mercedes showed that although the cross-currents were exceedingly trying, given better conditions they could evidently be conquered.

Three more days in the first half of January were earmarked for Mercedes to try again, but on each occasion she was advised to abandon the attempt because storms were predicted over the Strait and she returned to Tangier without entering the water.

Peril in the Night
The third attempt, on Wednesday, 25 January 1928, turned out to be a life-threatening episode. She started the swim at midnight from Cape Spartel on the African coast. She had been in the water for five hours when she suddenly heard a great noise of rushing water and found that she was in a whirlpool. It was pitch dark. In desperation, she clutched with her hand as she felt herself sinking and managed to grab the side of the rowing boat, which had also been drawn into the vortex. It was immediately realised that she had disqualified herself by touching the boat, so she was quickly pulled out of the sea and the attempt was abandoned. She told the *Daily Express* representative in the accompanying tug, 'I think I would have been sucked under and drowned had I not luckily grabbed the side of the boat. It was a terrifying experience in the dark night.'[28]

Mercedes was very upset at yet another failed attempt, but knew she was extremely lucky to have escaped death. It appears that the experience took a toll on her general health. One newspaper report stated that Mercedes was unwell and confined to bed for ten days, and another stated she was unlikely to make another attempt at the crossing. The length of the convalescence indicates that she may have been suffering from a bout of bronchitis (in her case, a chronic, lifelong condition). However, when she had recovered her equilibrium she announced that she was going to persevere with her objective, but before doing so she was going to return home for a short while to reassess the swim. She booked a passage on SS *Orama*, which left for England on 12 February.

Change of Direction
Ten days later, on 22 February, Mercedes returned to Gibraltar ready to try again, but this time from the European side – the opposite direction to her

three previous efforts. While preparing for her next attempt she stayed at the 'Villaneuva', described as 'a little whitewashed cottage facing the sea, and withdrawal from the madding crowd'. Local fisherman referred to her as 'the woman who does things that men do not'.[29]

The fourth attempt, on Sunday, 11 March 1928, was from Tarifa on the Spanish coast to Ceuta – a Spanish exclave on the north coast of Africa surrounded by Morocco.

The Guardian reported, on 12 March 1928:

Gathered to see her off at midday on Sunday 11 March were the civil, naval and military authorities and almost the whole population of Tarifa. Hundreds of women members of the Rock Sporting Club of Gibraltar were also there. The weather was cold and the sky overcast, but the sea was very calm. She was escorted by Spanish smacks, the tender *Alert* (placed at her disposal by the Cunard Line), and a rowing boat with tea, coffee, Bovril and milk on board, as well as a gramophone to cheer her on her way.

This turned out to be her best attempt so far, as she reached to within 1½ miles of Ceuta after only seven hours in the water. However, it was not to be. The sea became very rough and the currents were sweeping her unrelentingly in the direction of the Mediterranean. Mercedes was again forced to abandon the swim when only 1¼ miles from her destination.

The near success of this fourth attempt must have heartened Mercedes and strengthened her belief that she could accomplish the crossing, but she had to mark time waiting for the right sea conditions before she could try again.

The starting point for her fifth attempt on Monday, 2 April 1928, was again from Tarifa on the Spanish coast. She was a little over 1 mile from the African coast before having to abandon the swim – again because of the wayward currents. The distance she covered on this diagonal course before giving up was 18 miles. Swimming in a straight line was impossible due to the strong currents, and the diagonal course added 8 miles to the distance.

Success
Just three days later, Mercedes made her sixth and ultimately successful attempt. She left the 'Villanueva' in Tarifa at 6.20 a.m. and motored to the

lighthouse near a place called Playa de Poniente on the Fortress Isla de las Palomas (from where she had commenced earlier attempts). She started the swim at 7.50 a.m. in the presence of up to seventy witnesses, including the town's mayor and the military commandant of the Garrison of Tarifa – the latter being in charge of the organisation and timing of the swim. She was accompanied by two sailing vessels (the *Joven Manuel*, owned by Don Benito Flores Alvarex, Municipal Judge of Tarifa, and the *Victor Hugo*, owned by Don Jesus Vallejo Ezquerre), together with a rowing boat – those in the latter being responsible for feeding Mercedes, playing the gramophone and singing to her. She was ravenously hungry the whole of the time on this occasion, eating at intervals ham sandwiches and omelettes, and drinking orange juice, tea and coffee. The water temperature during the swim ranged between 51°F and 57°F (10.6–13.9°C).

During the first hours of the swim, following the directions of her pilot (Don Fernando Gurrea Castro, skipper of the *Victor Hugo*), she battled strenuously against the currents, which at the beginning carried her towards the west, and afterwards caused her to drift back towards Spain. However, she persevered and after two hours she observed the Moroccan mountains covered with mist. Several ships passing in the opposite direction sounded their sirens in greeting. After 9 hours in the water, she was about 7 or 8 miles from the Spanish coast before finally meeting with a favourable current.

Mercedes – as well as the witnesses in the accompanying boats – had then to battle with torrential rain, and about 500m from the coast of Africa a heavy swell arose that, on previous attempts, had caused her to give up. Thankfully, on this occasion, it lasted only a short time, and she successfully completed the crossing, wading out of the sea on to a stony beach at Punta Leona, the northernmost point of Morocco, at 8.40 p.m. Because of the drift caused by the currents, the total distance covered was approximately 23 or 24 miles, in a time of 12 hours 50 minutes.

When she set foot on the African continent the people aboard the accompanying boats cried out, 'Cheers for England, Spain and Miss Gleitze!', which deeply touched her. She then picked up pieces of rock and sand, and after spending 2 minutes on the beach she boarded the SS *Victor Hugo*, which carried her back to Tarifa, arriving there around midnight.

Her feat won her great admiration in Gibraltar in the face of repeated disappointments. She was met by hundreds of townspeople and a band playing the British National Anthem. Mercedes expressed her gratitude to the people of Tarifa, and also to the members of the Rock Sporting Club for the keenest assistance at all times with the swim. She added that she much appreciated the help that had been so freely accorded her by the Spanish authorities during her preparations for her attempts to cross the Strait.

All her witnesses signed a declaration verifying the truth of the crossing as swum by Mercedes. This document was to be sent first to Madrid and then to Algeciras for endorsement before being forwarded to England, but in the meantime, she carried on her person a separate statement signed by the Military Governor of Tarifa, verifying the swim.

Mercedes gave her own perspective of the crossing while in South Africa:

I made five attempts to swim the Strait of Gibraltar from Tangiers before I eventually succeeded. It was my sixth and successful effort, however, that sticks in my memory. This time I started from Tarifa and landed at Punta Leona, Morocco, after thirteen hours in the water and swimming about twenty-four miles, although the distance across is only nine miles. Two tugs and an open boat accompanied me, and halfway across I was caught in the current where the Atlantic and Mediterranean oceans meet.

I made slow headway and to make matters worse it commenced to rain and storm. The Spaniards in the open boat had a wretched time and eventually they shouted to me and asked whether I would give up if conditions got worse. 'Certainly not,' I replied. They communicated my answer to the tugs and I wondered if the three boats would turn and leave me alone. However, to my relief they started to cheer and this encouraged me greatly.

I struck out more strongly and I was soon out of the danger zone. The Spaniards kept up their encouraging shouting and even tried to sing 'Tipperary' to me. One tug steamed ahead and came back with the report that the shore was close at hand, and presently I was wading up to land. The first man to greet me was the Governor of Tarifa, who had come across in one of the tugs.

We all went back to Tarifa and although it was Passion Week and music was therefore forbidden, they opened a café and gathered together a few musicians who played 'God Save the King' for me, as a mark of honour.[30]

There was cause for celebration amongst Mercedes' friends, and a party was thrown to mark her recent success. Little did anyone in the group realise that the jollity would attract the attention of the incumbent Duke of Kent, who was visiting Gibraltar at the time. Indeed, as Mercedes confided in me in later life, he suddenly gatecrashed the party with a group of friends and told her that he had come to find out what was going on.

Millie Hudson's Reaction
Millie Hudson had made her only attempt at the crossing on 2 January, the same day as Mercedes' second attempt, but starting at a different point east of Tangier. Millie, too, was eventually troubled by rough seas and gave up 4½ miles from Tarifa after an 8-hour 30-minute swim.

The newspapers reported that Millie, after hearing the news in April of Mercedes' success, travelled back to England on the liner SS *Insulinde*. Speaking at Waterloo Station, she told *The Guardian*:

As the weather was bad after my first attempt [in January] I returned to London. I went to Tangier again a fortnight ago, and hearing on Saturday that Miss Gleitze had swum the Strait I decided to come back. There was nothing else for me to do. I shall make another attempt from the Tangier side. The municipality of Tangier is organising a fund to give a prize of 100,000 francs [£800] to the first person who swims across from their coast. When the municipality's arrangements are complete I shall return and compete for the prize.[31]

In the meantime, Mercedes was journeying back to England by train via Madrid and Paris, because travelling overland was quicker than by sea. She had a pending engagement (a fundraising ball at the Crystal Palace) and had given the organisers a guarantee that she would be back in England by 9 April. This meant that she had to forfeit her prearranged passage home by sea, and travel back without her main luggage, which was still in the hotel in Tangier.

An Englishman's Word
En route home, she arrived at Algeciras Station accompanied by the Spaniards who had been with her on her swim and who had come to bid her farewell. At the station, a *Daily Mail* special correspondent

interviewed her in their presence and brought up the question of witnesses. He reported that Mercedes was 'vigorously indignant' to the suggestion that the testimony of one Englishman would be of more value than anything else. She said, 'What can people want more than the word of seventy persons that I did my swim? I swam every inch of the way.'

She then introduced the journalist to some of the Spanish witnesses in the group, including the Military Commandant of Tarifa, Don Francisco Martin Bueno, who declared, 'Before God and my honour she swam every yard.'[32]

News of her successful swim had been relayed back to England. Reuters' news agency was informed that the following telegrams dated from Tarifa on Good Friday had been received by the Lord Mayor of London. One was from Aleade (Chief Magistrate of Tarifa): 'Your compatriot Miss Mercedes Gleitze yesterday swam across the Strait of Gibraltar. This town, which I have the honour to represent, sends you cordial congratulations on her behalf and respectfully salutes her.' Another was from Don Francisco Martin Bueno (Military Commandant of Tarifa): 'I beg to inform you that Miss Mercedes Gleitze yesterday succeeded in swimming the Strait of Gibraltar. I send to you and your great city heartiest congratulations.'

In London, Mercedes was mobbed at Victoria Station. On 10 April, the *Daily Mirror* reported that police had to clear a path through the cheering crowds so that she could reach her taxi, and she was finally lifted through the door of the cab while the people fought to reach her.

She was delighted and overwhelmed with the reception given to her by friends and supporters, but on arrival at her hotel she again had to answer questions as to why there were no English witnesses to the swim. The *Daily Mirror* asked, 'Do you not consider it desirable that you should have had some accredited Englishman on board the accompanying boats?' Mercedes replied:

There was in fact one Englishman on board – a seventeen-year-old boy named Henry Solis, whose father is the proprietor of a wine business over there. There were no other Englishmen available, but surely, though, the word of 70 Spaniards, including the Military Governor of Tarifa, is good enough! I have an affidavit signed by him to the effect that the swim was genuine, and another signed by 30 Spaniards, so I do not see why any Englishmen were vitally necessary. Although the swim was finished by lamp light, I could be clearly seen.[33]

Reported on the same day, *The Guardian* then asked her about a cable-gram received from Lottie Schoemmell, an American swimmer of note, conveying congratulations on the Gibraltar swim, and challenging her to a race across the English Channel in September. Miss Schoemmell had also suggested that other American swimmers – Miss Ederle, Mrs Corson and Miss Barrett – should be invited to join in. However, Mercedes was single-minded about her objectives and unafraid to turn down challenges from other swimmers. Her answer was explicit:

> I want it to be understood that I do not claim to be a fast swimmer, nor have I any desire to go in for racing. Why should I? My aim is to specialise in tests of endurance, such as the Gibraltar swim. One of my ambitions is to swim across the Hellespont, and I have only been deterred up to now by the expense. My one desire at the moment is to reimburse the fund I am accumulating for a home for destitute people to the extent that it has been depleted by my last expenses.

On 11 April, a reception was held for Mercedes at the Kit Cat restaurant in London. After the suppertime cabaret, the Master of Ceremonies read out several telegrams. One was from the Spanish Ambassador: 'I heartily join in the congratulations on brilliant feat of Miss Gleitze in her triumph over Strait by swimming from conquering side sustained by protection of her Spanish name (Mercedes).' Another was from Lord Lonsdale, regretting his inability to be present to welcome Miss Gleitze 'after her triumphant and magnificent success. I hope it may be only one of the many achievements of her life, and that she will live for many years to enjoy it and to set an example of the wonderful endurance and strength of mind she has shown.' Mercedes was then introduced by an official of the Amateur Swimming Association to the gathering of sporting and theatrical celebrities, which included Captain Malcolm Campbell and his family.

As soon as the notarised Act of Requisition document authenticating her successful crossing of the Strait was received from the British Consulate, Mercedes had it translated from the Spanish by Flowerdew & Company of Chancery Lane, London, and forwarded copies to the national newspapers. After what must have been an intensely distressing experience when her successful crossing of the English Channel was cast into doubt by the fraud perpetrated by Dr Dorothy Logan and her partner Horace Carey, Mercedes would never again perform a swim without having a detailed, authenticated record of it produced by people of good repute. The notarised Act of Requisition document and other records relating to the swim can be accessed at www.mercedesgleitze.uk.

Jabez Wolffe

There was a shabby attempt by Jabez Wolffe (a provocative open-water swimmer/trainer, who had himself made over twenty unsuccessful attempts to swim the English Channel) to undermine her feat. In a letter to the editor of the *Daily Mail* on 11 April 1928, Wolffe wrote, 'The claim of Mercedes Gleitze to have swum the Strait of Gibraltar without press representation makes it her second unofficial swim, the first being across the Channel … Perhaps her next unofficial swim will be across the Atlantic!'

However, Mercedes had already stated to the press, 'None but the malicious can question the swim. I was accompanied by two fishing smacks and rowing boats, those in the latter feeding me, playing a gramophone and singing.' She emphasised the point later by saying, 'The fact that there was no [adult] English witness can only in my opinion increase the validity of my swim, because the Spaniards would on no account have given the honour of the achievement to Great Britain had there been the slightest doubt regarding the swim.'

Mercedes had succeeded in becoming the first person ever to conquer the Strait of Gibraltar, and her sea career was up and running. The purpose of the swim was not just to accomplish the feat but also to heighten her profile, and there was no doubt she had succeeded in that as well.

6

BLACKPOOL TOWER CIRCUS CONTRACT

On her return from Gibraltar, when asked by the press what her next project would be, Mercedes told them that she would like to make an attempt to swim across the North Channel between Ireland and Scotland.

Unfortunately, at this point in time her financial affairs were not in good order. When she left England for Gibraltar, the money she had put aside for the care of destitute men and women stood at just over £400. This included part of her prize money from the *News of the World*, the fees she earned for public appearances and the sales of signed postcards. However, her prolonged Strait of Gibraltar project, lasting over four months, had cost between £150 and £200. And, apart from the heavy expenses associated with this swim, on her return to London she wrote to a friend telling her that she had been 'badly bled by people who were only interested in me from the money point of view'.

It must have been with a certain amount of relief that one of the offers Mercedes received at that moment in time was a contract of employment from the proprietors of the Blackpool Tower Company, to give swimming displays at the Tower Circus during the 1928 summer season. She accepted the offer gladly as it was a chance to replenish her charitable fund, and so she made arrangements to travel north to commence work.

The Blackpool Tower Circus was then – and still is – a very popular venue with holidaymakers, and her swimming event drew in 2,000 spectators at each of the twice-daily sessions (2.30 p.m. and 7.30 p.m.). Because her performances were so well received, her original contract was extended to 25 October 1928.

Despite ongoing worries about issues surrounding the funding of her proposed charity, Mercedes enjoyed her time at the Blackpool Tower very much. She wrote to Mr Lisle (a friend in Ireland) that when she first arrived in Blackpool she felt 'frightfully miserable and homesick for London and my own little flat', but went on to say that she quickly acclimatised after moving into her new accommodation at 4 Lowry Terrace.

During her time in Blackpool, Mercedes shared the bill with the town's own Lucy Morton, Britain's first Olympic gold medal winner in the 200m breaststroke event at the 1924 Paris Olympics, and she made friends not only with her fellow human performers, but also with the animals – ten lions, two tigers, four elephants, eight bears and a puma. In a letter dated 26 June 1928 to Mr William Hope-Jones, her friend and mentor, she related, 'Before my afternoon performance I woke up Buddha and Lizzi [two tigers]. Buddha came close to the iron bars – I put my hands through and stroked his lovely face.'

In between her two daily performances at the Tower Circus, she kept up her open-water swimming training – initially under the supervision of Mr R.L. Swarbrick (Superintendent of Blackpool's Corporation Baths in Cocker Street), and, later on, employing a Mr Gregory who had the skills to double up both as a swimming coach and a gymnastics coach. Mercedes went on to tell Hope-Jones about her participation in a form of exercise that was a forerunner to what is now known as aerobics, but which she called 'Rhythmics'.

The general public was first made aware of 'exercise to music' in the 1960s via a book by Americans Dr Kenneth Cooper MD (an exercise physiologist) and Colonel Pauline Potts (a physical therapist), and its popularity increased in the 1980s via sales of numerous exercise videos. But Mercedes was using this form of exercise in Blackpool (under instruction from her trainer, Mr Gregory, and his wife) as far back as 1928 to keep her body in good condition for her sea career. She wrote to Hope-Jones:

Had a nice time at the gym again. Did sixteen each of all the club movements I knew to music. Started on my rhythmics and, with the instructor's wife, danced a series of rhythmic arm and leg movements.

He says I shall be an expert at rythmics presently. I hope he is right, as I love movements which are graceful and feminine.

In the same letter, she said:

For the first time in my life I feel really happy, the cause of it being that the Official Trustee of Charitable Funds has consented to guard any Institute monies I may send him until building commences. As you know, I have been aiming at having this done ever since last October, and the fact of it taking such a long, long time to get the right Trustee and the right kind of Deed drawn up, approved, signed and sealed, worried me.

The relief Mercedes felt at finally getting her proposed charity onto a proper footing was echoed in the postscript of the following letter that she wrote on 18 June 1928 to a teacher friend at East Hove Higher Grade School:

Dear Miss Yeomanson,

When last I wrote to you I promised a longer letter as soon as I had more time to spare. I have been fortunate in obtaining a 21 weeks' engagement in Blackpool and shall not be seeing London again until about the 25th October.

My work for the Blackpool Tower Company is very interesting and very easy. Twice a day I have to give a swimming exhibition in front of a daily total of 4,000 people and I enjoy it very much. First I am introduced by the Stage Manager to the audience, then I make a short speech, then I dive into the pool and give an exhibition of over arm side stroke, breast stroke, trudgeon stroke, half arm back stroke, full arm back stroke, swimming with arms folded on chest, floating, and drinking from a cup given to me by two 'fishermen' in a rowing boat.

I have a nice dressing room, and yesterday I had the honour of shaking hands with eleven journalists representing different Irish newspapers, who had witnessed my performance and descended to my room to question me about my forthcoming attempt to swim across the Irish Channel.

I am now in strict training for this swim which includes the following:

1) I do a full hour's practice, swimming every morning from 8.30 to 9.30.
2) Every day after my 5 o'clock performance at the Tower, I go to the gymnasium and do a full hour's Swedish Drill.
3) Every day I do at least one hour's walking.
4) Every other day I get osteopathy treatment [with Dr McKeon].

I feel very fit physically and am full of confidence. I am now expecting telegraphic instructions from my pilot at Portpatrick to proceed to the Scottish coast to commence my swim. From all the arrangements that have been made for me it seems that Scottish and Irish people are taking a very keen interest in my proposed attempt to swim the Irish Channel, and as soon as I leave Blackpool [an authorised contract break] for Stranraer I shall be presented in the latter town to Councillors and other important Scottish folk, and I believe they have arranged for me to lay a wreath on the War Memorial. I am therefore keenly looking forward to the wire calling me to Scotland.

Please give my kind regards to the other teachers in the school, also to the girls and boys. You can rely upon me doing my very best to win for Brighton and England this further swimming honour.

With love, I remain,

Yours sincerely, Mercedes

PS: You will be pleased to hear that I have now succeeded in establishing the Fund for my proposed Institute on a legal basis and have signed a deed which constitutes a Declaration of Trust between the Official Trustee of Charitable Funds, Lord Fermoy and myself.

Now that the legal issues in connection with the setting up of her charitable fund had been completed, Mercedes was able to concentrate on the organisation of her next major open-water challenge – the North Channel.

7

THE NEXT ENDEAVOUR: THE NORTH CHANNEL

One must not be afraid of big, open stretches of water; one must be in complete harmony with nature. What is required most of all is the ability to expend just the minimum amount of energy. As with most things, the more swimming one does the more one feels able to do.

Beginners often find it difficult at first to breathe correctly. Personally I have never experienced any difficulty in this direction, as an angry sea does not frighten me. I never become panicky, and therefore do not get breathless.

Courage and endurance – these are the qualities which long-distance swimming develops.

Mercedes Gleitze 'Swim your Way to Health' published in the South African *Rand Daily Mail*, 5 May 1932

Mercedes was the first person ever to make an attempt to swim across the North Channel (known in Irish and Scottish Gaelic as *Sruth na Maoile).* This strait separates north-eastern Ireland and south-western Scotland, and its waters ebb and flow into the Atlantic Ocean. During 1928 she made four attempts over a 22½-mile course from Donaghadee to Portpatrick.

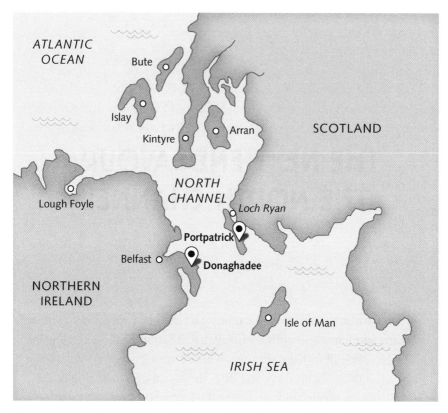

The North Channel – such inhospitable waters for swimmers and sailors alike.

The North Channel turned out to be Mercedes' most gruelling challenge and during her many attempts (both in 1928 and 1929) she had to battle with temperatures as low as 44°F (6.7°C) as well as heavy Atlantic swells creating waves as high as 15ft – not to mention sea leeches, stinging jellyfish and the sighting of a shark. She had a narrow escape when, on one of the attempts, she was caught in a tidal race and a hurricane. So wild were the conditions that a passing passenger liner, SS *Killarney*, turned from its course to stand by in case she and her crew needed help.

The First Attempt (Saturday, 23 June 1928)

On her return from Gibraltar in April 1928, Mercedes had made it known that she would like to make the North Channel her next big swim, and she began making tentative arrangements. When negotiating her summer contract with the Blackpool Tower Company, she had a clause inserted allowing her a leave of absence of two days to make an attempt on the crossing when conditions were right. There was a great and real interest both in Scotland and Ireland after she announced her plans, and while she was in Blackpool a large group of Irish journalists representing various publications travelled over to ask when she would be making the attempt, and in which direction.

This was going to be her biggest undertaking to date. The North Channel was, and still is today, one of the most difficult crossings for a swimmer to make. This is borne out by the fact that, at the time of writing, only nineteen individuals have completed solo swims across this strait compared to the many hundreds of swimmers who have crossed the English Channel.

Mercedes' initial plan was to swim from Donaghadee on the Irish coast to Portpatrick in Scotland (just over 22 miles as the crow flies). The tides running between these two sea ports are extraordinarily strong, and there are numerous cross-currents which make it difficult even for rowing boats to make headway. The chief threat, however, would be from the temperature of the water, that was considerably colder than that experienced in either of her two previous major swims across the English Channel and the Strait of Gibraltar.

Hugh Muir (late of the London Fire Brigade) was to be her official pilot on this occasion, and he travelled in advance to Donaghadee on 9 June 1928 and co-ordinated arrangements on the Scottish side with Mr Milroy (Portpatrick & District Burns Club and Portpatrick Bowling Club). While in Donaghadee, Mercedes was to be the guest of Margaret Ruddell of the Royal Hotel, and on the Scottish side Mrs Paterson of Fernhill, Portpatrick, would be her hostess.

The plan was, once Mercedes received word by telegram from Muir that tides and currents were favourable, she would then travel from Blackpool to Stranraer in Scotland by express train and, if prevailing winds continued, it was expected that she would take a boat across from Portpatrick to Donaghadee, from where she would commence the swim shortly before high tide so as to gain full advantage of the 6 hours' ebb that sweeps northward. She would then have to battle against the flood tide and would hope to reach the Scottish coast on the succeeding ebb.

The main obstacles would be the six different currents from the Atlantic and the Firth of Clyde that meet off Corsewall Point – and, of course, the low temperature of the water (caused by the melting icebergs in the Baltic Sea that flow into this channel that, together with its great depth, gives it its intense cold).

The anticipated telegram arrived and, on Thursday, 21 June, wearing a brown coat and close-fitting hat to match and carrying a small suitcase, Mercedes left Blackpool for Stranraer. A large, enthusiastic crowd was waiting to greet her at Stranraer Station and she was accorded a civic welcome by Provost Dyer, who wished her success in her venture. She then proceeded to Portpatrick and was received by Mr McMaster of the Parish Council, who invited her to inspect the Boy Scouts and Girl Guides, and to lay a wreath on the war memorial.

Mercedes realised that if an attempt were to be made, it would have to be the following morning (Friday, 22 June), as she was under contract to give an exhibition at Blackpool the day after. However, the view was held at Portpatrick that stormy weather, fuelled by strong south-west winds and a high-running sea, would make an attempt impossible at the planned time. She immediately made an application to the Blackpool authorities for extended leave of absence, and this was granted until Monday. She then spent the day visiting places of interest and declared that if this present attempt had to be abandoned, she would keep on trying.

The following day, although a fair south-westerly breeze was blowing, conditions had improved enough to make the attempt viable. Amid cheers and cries of 'Good Luck!' from the crowds on the pier, Mercedes left Portpatrick at 9.30 on Saturday morning, 23 June 1928, in the fishing trawler *Thompson*. It was reported that she slept most of the way to Donaghadee. On nearing the harbour, the *Thompson* was soon surrounded by a flotilla of small boats flying flags. Donaghadee Harbour, also decorated with flags, was thronged with a cheering crowd, and when Mercedes stepped ashore she received a tumultuous reception.

Mr McWhinney, the town clerk (who, with Mr Milroy on the Scottish side, helped to organise the swim), introduced her to members of the Urban District Council. She was then taken to the Royal Hotel, where she was met by her hostess, Margaret Ruddell. The Marchioness of Londonderry DBE, accompanied by Viscount Castlereagh and his three sisters, Lady Margaret, Lady Helen and Lady Mary Stewart, called on her at the hotel to wish her good luck.

After resting for two hours, shortly after 3 p.m. Mercedes was taken by car to Robbie's Point, about 1 mile south of Donaghadee Harbour. She disrobed in one of the shelters and was covered in a thick coating of protective grease. At 3.40 p.m. she waved her hand to the crowd, entered the water and struck out for the Scottish coast.

The wind had dropped, but the water was bitterly cold. Heavy rain had fallen just before and during the early part of the swim, and this had a calming effect on the water. Numerous small craft accompanied her on the initial stage of her swim and their occupants kept cheering her on. She covered the first mile in 25 minutes. At 4.45 p.m. she received her first nourishment, and at this point the accompanying craft turned back, leaving just two boats – the *Thompson* carrying press representatives, and the pilot boat containing her pilot, Hugh Muir, his niece, Nettie Muir, and Dr McVeagh. Alex Riddell from *The Northern Whig & Belfast Post* and McVeagh took turns at the gramophone. At 5.30 p.m. Mercedes had passed the danger zone of the Copeland Islands and disappeared into the mist. In the vicinity of the Copelands four tides meet, and it was with the idea that she should encounter that particular obstacle while still fresh, that her pilot started her from the County Down shore.

About 2 miles north of Donaghadee, after coming abreast the Copeland Head, it was observed that the flood tide, which was running at about 3 miles an hour, was carrying Mercedes well to the north. She carried on strongly, following this northerly direction until the ebb tide began shortly after 10 p.m. At this stage she was about 9 miles south of the Maidens lighthouses, and had swum about 19 miles using breaststroke, with brief spells of sidestroke. Boats put out frequently from the Irish coast, with the occupants singing and shouting encouragement.

The water was so intensely cold that hot liquid refreshments were given to Mercedes more frequently than at the usual 1-hourly intervals. Despite the freezing conditions, she remained cheerful and responded to her favourite records, which were being played on the gramophone carried by the pilot boat. The sea temperature at that point was 44°F (6.7°C). Although swimming strongly, it was evident to Dr McVeagh that the intense cold was beginning to have an effect on Mercedes. She continued steadily, however, and it was a striking tribute to her strength and endurance that she kept up an average of thirty-three strokes per minute. At 10.30 p.m. she requested the company to sing 'Home, Sweet Home', to which they immediately responded. At 11 p.m. she was showing signs of extreme exposure. At 11.25 p.m. Dr McVeagh advised her to give up, but she indicated that she wished to complete at least 8 hours in the water. However, the doctor was adamant, and she was brought aboard. When placed in the warm cabin of the *Thompson* she was exhausted and benumbed, but with the help of her doctor and Miss Muir she recovered before reaching Portpatrick.

The *Thompson* put into Portpatrick harbour at 1.30 on Sunday morning to the accompaniment of cheers and cries of 'Well done!' from the crowd that had gathered to greet her, despite the early hour. Mercedes had been in the water for 7 hours 45 minutes and, due to the underlying currents, had swum approximately 23 miles in a zigzag fashion. However, when she abandoned the swim she was just 11 miles out of Donaghadee (the distance in a straight line between Donaghadee and Portpatrick being 22 miles).

Although Mercedes' objective was not accomplished, eyewitnesses were filled with admiration for the courage she displayed, as she no doubt would have continued but for the intervention of her medical advisor. Her failure can be attributed to the temperature of the water. She was just about to receive the benefit of the ebb tide when she was taken out of the water.

When she arrived back in Blackpool on Monday afternoon, she informed a representative from *The Scotsman* (26 June 1928) that now she had the experience, she felt absolutely confident that the swim could be accomplished. She said that arrangements were already in hand for a second attempt during the third week of July and that every detail would be carefully considered on both sides. She added that she was very delighted by her enthusiastic reception at Portpatrick and Donaghadee.

Excerpts taken from letters to friends after the failed swim underline her commitment to pursuing her dream, despite the ordeal that she had just been through:

My first attempt to conquer the Irish Channel has taken place but was unsuccessful on account of the extreme cold of the water, the temperature of which varied between 44 and 48 degrees. I am not disheartened, and my Scottish and Irish friends have already made preparations for my second attempt in July.

I was obliged to give in on doctor's instructions. Having got over the first shock of the terrible chilliness of the Irish Channel, I feel confident that when next time I try I shall be able to endure the cold for many more hours, and in addition I am sure we shall then have some sunshine which will help considerably. I can assure you that I shall do my best to succeed and thereby win for England another swimming honour, viz that of being the first person to swim across the Irish Channel.

It seems that such a long distance swim is hardening me more and more, and I feel confident that my 8 hours' immersion in 44 degrees will help me to overcome all difficulties on my next trial. Everybody was so very good to me both in Ireland and Scotland, and I am dying to be there again.

The Second Attempt (Thursday, 26 July 1928)

A full description of the swim published in *The Scotsman* on 27 July 1928 recorded that Mercedes motored from Lismoyle to the Royal Hotel, Donaghadee, arriving at 2.30 a.m. The Urban District Council had fitted the pier with electric lights so that the many people who had gathered could see her start. She entered a beautifully calm sea at 3 a.m., although there was a slight breeze blowing west by north.

Mercedes was accompanied by the yacht MV *Kathleen* and a pilot boat carrying, amongst others, two pilots (Andrew White and Robert Bunting), Dr McVeagh and Nettie Muir, her attendant – the latter two having been with her on her first attempt in June. The pilots from both the Scottish and Irish sides were familiar with the tides and swift-running currents. At 3.30 a.m. she had completed the first mile and was swimming strongly in what witnesses described as ideal conditions.

When daylight broke the Mull of Galloway was plainly discernible, and Killingringan, 10½ miles north of Portpatrick, was easily recognised. She received her first ration of nourishment at 4 a.m. and thereafter at intervals of one hour. Later, however, because of the drop in temperature, it would be necessary to supply her with these at more frequent intervals.

There had been a drizzle of rain early on, which set up a slight mist, but as the day advanced conditions improved. The temperature of the water was taken several times during the course of the swim. At times it was about 12 degrees higher than on the occasion of her first attempt in June, but taken together with the low readings it averaged 51.5°F (10.8°C). It was realised by those accompanying her that the full intensity of the cold would not be experienced until she was about midway, where there is a very deep gully in the bed of the channel. In addition to the cold, there was the added danger that she might be forced to leave the water because of basking sharks, several of which had been seen in the channel recently on their way to the fishing banks off Ballantrae and the herring grounds in Loch Fyne. One of these monsters was actually observed in the course of the swim and was approximately 10ft long.

At 7.30 a.m. she was 4 miles out, but by 8.30 a.m. she had made only half a mile more, owing to the direction of the current. She continued steadily for 2 hours 30 minutes and at 11 a.m., in response to an enquiry, Mercedes stated that she would be glad of company in the water. So Constable Archie McVicker, a strong swimmer who had himself swum from Donaghadee to Copeland Head (a distance of 2 miles), joined her in the sea. Constable McVicker accompanied Mercedes on her swim for an hour. On being taken out, he was evidently suffering from being in the cold water.

Mercedes continued swimming strongly, encouraged by the singing of her favourite songs from the boat, amongst which were 'Souvenirs', 'Moonlight and Roses' and 'Home, Sweet Home'. She remarked at that stage that she was feeling very fit.

At 11.30 Mercedes was given hot coffee and she was 3 miles east by north of Copeland Island. At 12 the tide slackened, and here she made very good progress. About 12.30 p.m. she had gained 1¾ miles in the last hour, being 12 miles from Portpatrick on a direct course. By 2.30 p.m., still swimming strongly, she was 10¾ miles from Killingringan.

Just before 4 p.m. she spoke of the coldness of the water and advised Constable McVicker not to enter the water again, as he had intended. By this time, a number of boats had arrived from Donaghadee and a request was made for the occupants to sing her favourite hymns, 'Abide with Me' and 'Lead, Kindly Light'. Mercedes was pleasantly surprised when the Reverend H. Daunt of Donaghadee voluntarily took to the water to accompany her shortly after 4 p.m. and his sporting action brought loud applause from the spectators. He was compelled, however, to give up after 15 minutes.

At 4.30 p.m. her pilot and her doctor, observing signs of distress in Mercedes caused by the bitterly cold temperature of the water, advised her to abandon the attempt, but she refused and expressed the desire to at least complete 14 hours in the water. At 5 p.m. she had accomplished this and reluctantly gave up her plucky endeavour. The North Channel had once more proved itself the victor.

On arrival at Portpatrick at 8 that evening, Mercedes received a rousing welcome from over 1,000 people assembled on the pier from a wide area. She expressed her determination to accomplish the conquest of the channel in spite of the many difficulties she had encountered. The low temperature, the absence of any gleam of sunshine whatsoever, and the obscurity of the coast – which was shrouded in a typical Scottish mist – had all contributed to her failure.

Mercedes left Stranraer early the following morning and within an hour of her arrival at the Blackpool Tower, after a tiring train journey, she was giving a swimming demonstration in the Circus. She received another rousing reception that afternoon from the audience and again at the evening performance for her courageous attempt.

She told the *Gazette & Herald* representative who interviewed her in Blackpool:

The water was terribly cold, and it was the cold that defeated me, not the currents. A temperature of 51 degrees is very low for a long distance swim, but my 14 hours-long swim has hardened me for my next attempt, and I think I shall be able to stand the cold for about 20 hours – which is the time in which I estimate I can accomplish the swim. Last time I was only able to stand the cold for 8 hours, and but for that first attempt I should not have been able to stay in the water for 14 hours on Thursday.

I had a wonderful reception both at Portpatrick and Donaghadee. On Tuesday, when I arrived at Donaghadee in a motor launch, the crowd was so great that the police had to fight every inch of the way to get me to my hotel, and it was the same when I started the swim, although it was three o'clock on Thursday morning.

I could not start early on Wednesday morning as I intended because I was unable to get any sleep on account of the enthusiasm of the crowds outside the hotel, and just before midnight on Tuesday I was smuggled out of the hotel and taken by motor car to the private residence of a councillor about two miles away so that I could rest.

Both in Ireland and Scotland I have been treated with amazing kindness. The committees in both countries have been wonderful, and owing to their kind assistance my swims have not cost me anything. So confident are they that I shall succeed, they have promised me the same generous assistance in September.

As I was swimming across, my Irish friends hired pleasure boats and came out in parties to sing and cheer me on my way. I shall never forget the wonderful kindness I have received.

A poem was written to Mercedes by 'C.C.S. of Donaghadee' about her attempt:

Bravo! little woman
Yours the courage bold
That stirred the heart of yeoman
And pioneer of old
Yours the quiet power,
Leagued with smile serene,
That stands above the hour
Of petty wish and dream.

Not for you to ponder
If you should or could,
Or let intention wander
'Neath fickle Chance's mood.
Armed with heart and reason
And charm, now gift so rare,
You dare the Channel freezing,
With figure lithe and fair.

A God-speed to your venture,
Thus spake the Northmen's voice,
And those who thought to censure
In praising found rejoice.
As to those cold steel waters,
You leapt with fearless heart,

While dawn–light dimly shatters
The clouds of night apart.

What if the cold sea sunders
Your purpose hour by hour,
Your dauntless spirit thunders
And at defeat gains power.
'Til Neptune, long resisting,
Falls victim to your Art,
And Hercules, insisting
On strength, plucks out his heart.[34]

Mercedes had earlier told her organising committee that she wanted to try again at the beginning of August but was obliged to inform them that she had been unable to secure a leave of absence from Blackpool for another attempt during that period. It had been explained to her by the Tower authorities that there would be thousands of people in Blackpool – it being bank holiday week – who would be anxious to see her performance. It was therefore arranged that the next attempt at the crossing would be made on the first favourable day after 23 August, when the tides would be more suitable.

The Third Attempt (Sunday, 26 August 1928)

Thomas Milroy, a member of the Portpatrick organising committee, had telegraphed her the day before telling her to proceed to Ireland via Heysham. She was met in Belfast by her hostess, Mrs Ward of Lismoyle, and completed the journey to her hotel in Donaghadee. Sir William Turner (Lord Mayor of Belfast) called on her and wished her every success. She was then asked by her pilot, Andrew White, to christen his new motorboat – the chosen name of the boat being *Mercedes*.

While this third attempt was being set up, Mercedes wrote to the committee:

The singing of the banjoist, Mr Patterson, lessened the hardship of my last swim a great deal, and I was greatly relieved to receive his offer to sing to me again. During the latter stages of the swim I am sure that my witnesses will be kind enough to sing hymns to me and I should be glad if you would take several hymn books on board. Some of my favourite hymns are Lead, Kindly Light, Nearer My God to Thee, Son of My Soul, and Art Thou Weary, Art Thou Languid?

About 1,500 people assembled to see her off as she entered the water at Donaghadee at 5.25 a.m. Conditions were extremely favourable, there being no wind and a calm sea. She struck out using sidestroke. As before, a number of motor and row boats accompanied the swimmer. In the official rowing boat were the same two pilots, Andrew White and Robert Bunting, Dr McVeagh, her medical advisor and Nettie Muir, her constant attendant. Amongst the party on the official motor launch, MV *Kathleen*, were Constable McVicker of Donaghadee, who also had accompanied her on the last attempt, the launch owner, W.H. Roberts, and Mr Patterson, the banjoist from the Pierrot Troupe.

The first mile was covered in 27 minutes and by 2 p.m. she was near mid-channel. The wind then veered to the south and the water became choppy with a heavy swell. Constable McVicker (as on the last occasion) entered the water at 5.27 p.m. and swam with Mercedes for half an hour, an animated conversation being kept up by the two swimmers. The temperature of the water was 55°F (12.8°C) – 4 degrees higher than on the July swim. Mercedes was being fed by Nettie Muir every hour on coffee and Bovril, and Mr Patterson played his banjo and led the singing of her favourite songs.

At 6 p.m. Mercedes was about 7 miles off the Scottish coast. At that point, she was caught by the ebb tide at 7.50 p.m. and driven back about 2 miles. At 8 p.m. there was a torrential downpour of rain, while a thunderstorm raged along the Scottish coast, but the pilot brought her on an excellent course, clear of the infamous and treacherous Rambarry currents.

She swam on pluckily, but shortly after 9 p.m. Dr McVeagh and the attendants on the accompanying launch advised Mercedes to abandon the swim. She stubbornly refused and the doctor and others repeatedly entreated her to give up the effort. Finally, at 9.30 p.m., she was seized by her pilot and forcibly lifted from the water in a state of collapse. She had by then been in the water for 15 hours, completed 16 miles of the distance and was within 5 miles of the Scottish coast – so far, this had been the best of her three attempts.

The motorboat reached Portpatrick shortly after 10 p.m. in the gathering darkness. Thousands of people from all over the south of Scotland had spent the afternoon at Portpatrick and had continued to wait in the dark for Mercedes to be brought back in the launch. They gave her a great reception when she arrived. 'I shall never give up,' she told a reporter as she was being taken to the shore. 'I did not want to give up tonight.'

When she arrived back in Blackpool she reaffirmed her intention to try again to the *Gazette & Herald*:

No! I have not yet given up hope of swimming the Irish Channel. I think I could have done it on Sunday if only they had let me continue. To begin with the sea was calm, but presently it became choppy and rain fell in torrents for a time. Despite adverse conditions I covered more distance in the same time than I did on the last occasion. And that notwithstanding a heavy sea, with the swell against me. Several times my doctor urged me to come out. My reply was to swim away from the boat. They were however so insistent they sent rowing boats after me and finally dragged me from the water. The battle with the waves had made many inroads upon my strength, but I was quite eager to swim on, and I had sufficient strength left to do so.

Apart from the massive disappointment she must have felt at not completing the crossing, this latest attempt did take a physical toll on Mercedes. After her first two tries she had recovered very quickly, but in letters to two friends (Nettie Muir and Mr Milroy) she wrote that it had taken her a long time to recuperate from the August swim as she had seriously injured the muscles in both her legs. At performance times, the attendants at the Blackpool Tower had to practically carry her from her dressing room to the pool, and it wasn't until a fortnight after the North Channel attempt that she was able to walk without pain. However, recover she did.

The Fourth Attempt (Monday, 5 November 1928)

When she started her swim, Mercedes was confident of success, as she had been advised that the water was warmer in November than at other times of the year. She was given a hearty send-off at 3.30 in the afternoon and struck out strongly into the channel. Amongst those accompanying her in two motorboats and a rowing boat were her pilot Andrew White, the ever-constant Nettie Muir and Constable McVicker, Mrs Blackler, and three journalists. There was no doctor with them this time, but as usual a gramophone and records were taken to cheer her on.

However, less than 5 hours later she returned to Irish soil, defeated again by the coldness of the water. The *Belfast Telegraph* and the *Belfast Newsletter* both reported on the prevailing conditions on 6 November 1928:

At first the sea was fairly calm despite the sharp breeze, and Mercedes, her body covered with olive oil and lard, made good progress. Conditions altered, however, and she was caught by a strong ebb tide. To those watching it seemed as if she would be beaten even before she reached the Copeland Islands, which lie about three and a half miles from the pier. However, she ploughed her way through the breakers with a powerful breaststroke, which she maintained from the start until practically the finish at a steady rate of 32 to the minute – an amazing performance in itself. But as the evening wore on the sea became more threatening. At times she was lost to view amongst the waves, and flashes of lightning showed her struggling gamely against the overwhelming odds.

At seven o'clock Mercedes called out to her pilot, Andrew White, and admitted that she was in agony from the biting wind and icy sea. She had in addition been suffering uncomplainingly from a cramp in her left leg which had been breaking her resistance for some time. With great difficulty she managed to say to Andrew, 'The cold is terrible. It is killing me. Will people understand if I give up? I am willing to go on if you think I have not yet justified the interest that has been shown in me.'[35]

Andrew assured her that they were all amazed she had stuck it for so long and said that no one would misunderstand if she decided to come out now. He told her that she had done more to justify herself in the eyes of those who were interested in her progress than she had done in any of her other swims.

The boats were drawn up alongside the swimmer. Constable McVicker left the newly christened motorboat *Mercedes* to board the rowing boat, and with other members of the crew helped Mercedes out of the sea. She was then transferred to the *Mercedes* and carried into a little cabin where brandy, hot-water bottles, coffee, massage and other fermentations were utilised to restore her frozen circulation and 'bring back life to the girl who had, but a comparatively short time before, left Donaghadee a cheerful, smiling figure, supremely confident of her ability to accomplish the task which even her pilot had pronounced impossible'.[36]

Andrew White, in view of Mercedes' condition, realised that it was vital to get her to shelter as soon as possible, and so they turned for Donaghadee instead of going on to Portpatrick as had been originally planned. The County Down port was reached at about 8.30 p.m. and a large crowd, drawn by flares set alight in the approaching boats, had gathered to give Mercedes a rousing reception. The *Belfast Telegraph* reported on 6 November:

> The cheers indicated the general appreciation of a courageous effort, and when the prostrate girl, wrapped in blankets, was carried up the pier steps to a waiting motor car, there was a warmth in the resounding cheers that can only come from Ulster men and women who had been raised to a high pitch of enthusiasm by a great sporting effort.

She was taken to the Royal Hotel and handed over to the care of Margaret Ruddell and Mrs Crawford who, after just a couple of hours, managed to restore her to her usual smiling self. There was a steady stream of well-wishers at the hotel to compliment her on the effort she had made, and while all messages were appreciatively received, the one that brought tears to her eyes was from W.H. Roberts, the owner of the pilot boat, who assured her that she could yet succeed, and that if she returned next summer his yacht would be at her disposal.

Tribute was also paid to those who had accompanied Mercedes on the attempt, most of whom (apart from the pilot and his crew) were victims of seasickness. The *Belfast Telegraph* wrote on 6 November:

> It was agreed by everyone who had witnessed her herculean struggle that the plucky girl swimmer had taken part in the finest endurance test of her series in the Irish Sea. Only those who were in the accompanying boats can possibly realise what a fight it meant to last those 3½ hours while being tossed about most part of the time like a

cork on mighty rollers, which seemed bent upon carrying her in the wrong direction to dash her helpless against the Copelands.

In this latest effort Mercedes had covered nearly 12 miles by reason of the zigzag course she was forced to take because of the buffetings of a strong ebb tide, but when she was obliged to surrender she had actually only reached a point about 6 miles in a straight line from Donaghadee Harbour. After being in its waters for 3½ hours, the icy North Channel was – for the fourth time – declared the winner.

Mercedes said afterwards, 'I endured acute pain. The wind cut through my chest like a knife and benumbed my limbs. I fought vainly to shake it off. I did my best, but the conditions were too bad. This is my last attempt this year.'[37]

Although this fourth attempt did draw a line under the efforts of 1928, this would not be the end of Mercedes' attempts to conquer the North Sea.

8

FUNDRAISING AND A PRESS ATTACK

The year 1928 had proved to be one of highs and lows for Mercedes. The good times included her Gibraltar Strait success and five happy months giving swimming exhibitions at the Blackpool Tower Circus. During that period she had also fitted into her busy schedule her first four attempts at crossing the North Channel. But during those same months she also had to deal with a situation that had evolved in connection with her fundraising activities.

In October of that year, Mercedes had just fulfilled her summer contract with the Blackpool Tower Company, and the open-water swimming season was also drawing to a close. This freed her up to concentrate on her welfare work and also to defend herself against an unwarranted attack by an 'exposé' magazine.

It is not just a modern phenomenon that the lives of the rich or famous bring significant money to certain sections of the press, and it is an undeniable fact that profits are higher if articles denigrate rather than celebrate people in the news. In her day, Mercedes must have been one of the first high-profile female swimmers to be targeted – by the *John Bull* magazine. References to an unpleasant article in that publication were found in Mercedes' archives. However, after digging deeper, the source of the smear and her response to it were revealed. She was accused of irregularities relating to her charitable fundraising, but these allegations of inappropriate payments were subsequently shown to be unfounded.

After her successful English Channel swim in October 1927, Mercedes carried out specific fundraising exercises on behalf of her future charity (mainly, the sale of signed photographs of herself, personal appearances and a proposed fundraising magazine), and the money raised was added to the larger amount she herself had put aside for the fund from her swimming earnings in a dedicated savings account.

She had told a representative of *The Guardian* as far back as 1 November 1927: 'My charity work is at present a private concern, but I have taken steps to create a public fund. I have instructed my solicitor to draw up a deed and appoint a trustee.' When Mercedes left for Gibraltar the following month, she had already deposited a little over £400 into her dedicated savings account.

On her return to England on 9 April 1928, she immediately informed the media that in order to cover her expenses in Tangier and Spain she had been obliged to use some of the funding she had set aside for the charity (the bulk of which was her own private money). The following statement by Mercedes appeared in a number of newspapers the following day, including *The Guardian*, the *Daily Express* and the *Scotsman*:

One of my ambitions is to swim across the Hellespont, and I have only been deterred up to now by the expense. My one desire at the moment is to reimburse the fund I am accumulating for a home for destitute people to the extent that it has been depleted by my last expenses.

Her six attempts on the Gibraltar Strait had been carried out over a period of just over four months, and the venture, although successful, had cost her between £150 and £200. Mercedes had settled all the bills incurred, including extended accommodation at the Hotel Valentino in Tangier, her outgoings in Spain and her training and travel expenses, and the receipts were lodged at her office in London.

Apart from the above, on her return to London she found that other debts in connection with the printing of a fundraising magazine and the administration of her office had accumulated in her absence. She had left her financial affairs in the care of an employee while she was in Gibraltar, and they had been seriously mismanaged.

All this happened before she was able to transfer her savings to an official charitable trust fund account, soon to be set up. On her instructions, solicitors had been negotiating the establishment of an official fund and the appointment of trustees with the Charity Commissioners during her absence in Gibraltar. These negotiations, which started in November 1927, had of necessity taken time, but were to come to fruition in June 1928.

Over the five or six weeks following her return from Gibraltar, Mercedes had to fulfil engagements emanating from her recent swimming successes. At this point in time she could not have been fully aware of the extent of the mismanagement, because she left that same employee running the office when she relocated to Blackpool in late May. This meant she had to monitor the financial disorder from afar.

Her first step was to enlist the help of a business friend from Birmingham, C.B. Roe. On 4 June 1928, she wrote and asked him to act as supervisor during her absence from London and to regularly inspect the books to make sure they were written up to date. These books included the post-card ledger, petty cash book, post book, salary book, office expenses book, telephone record book and the account book recording monies handed to the Charity Commission.

Additionally, on 17 June, in order to publicly refute the accusations that had been circulating about her fundraising (which had been picked up by some of the national newspapers), she wrote a letter to Arthur Beverley Baxter, Managing Editor of the *Daily Express*. In her letter she informed him that 'a National Women's Organisation who were interested in my career and who were anxious that, as a woman, I should make a success of everything I undertake' had warned her that 'a certain man [unnamed], who was at the time known to be very hard up for money', was trying to sell a 'story' about her to the *Daily Mail*.

Mercedes told Mr Beverley Baxter:

After receiving this friendly warning I thought to myself: 'If the *Daily Mail* is interested in making enquiries about my activities I shall call on them so as to give them a chance to ask me questions'. The very next day (my last day in London) I called on the News Editor of the *Daily Mail*. He asked me no questions.

She continued:

From the above it seems that I have made my name too valuable and that it is absolutely essential for me, in the interest of my work, to seek moral protection so as to prevent people with dishonest intentions from 'making discoveries' for the purpose of filling their pockets.

It will be obvious to you from the enclosed correspondence that my heart and soul belong to England's poor.

She asked Mr Beverley Baxter to help her challenge the rumours by 'appointing a Chartered Accountant to collect all books, receipts, accounts, agreements, etc. necessary for him to make out a balance sheet of monies received and spent by myself since October 1927 to date'.

This was a proposed business arrangement with the *Daily Express*, because she went on to write:

The terms regarding appointment of this accountant to be as follows:
(a) If I succeed in swimming the Irish Channel, you will defray the cost.
(b) If I fail, I will pay him.
(c) In return for getting an Accountant to make out this balance sheet I give the *Daily Express* the right to publish any information about my welfare work and my proposed Institute for London's Poor they may like.

Mercedes also enclosed a signed letter of authority giving the *Daily Express* 'the power to obtain any first-hand information about my work which you may like'.

Mr Beverley Baxter wrote back on 20 June 1928:

All I can do is offer you my blessing. It is not in our power to appoint anyone – in other words it is quite outside the usual activities of a newspaper. It seems to me that the best thing you can do is to put yourself in the hands of an honest and competent solicitor and if you would like me to recommend one I can do that. In the meantime we are looking forward to your successful swim and will treat you with the same generosity as before.

This was the second time in Mercedes' career that instead of being able to fully enjoy the success of a pioneering swim, she was challenged – this time about her fundraising. However, as with her response to the slight cast by Dr Dorothy Logan on the validity of her successful English Channel swim, she did not lose heart. With the help of C.B. Roe and two other close friends and advisors (Harry Bradburn and William Hope-Jones) she fought to clear her name.

On 30 June 1928, Mercedes appointed a London-based chartered accountant recommended by Hope-Jones and instructed him to make out a balance sheet showing monies received and spent by herself from October 1927 to June 1928. In October 1928, with the books in order, and all outstanding debts associated with the running of the office either discharged or being cleared over an agreed period of time, Mercedes gave up the tenancy of her flat in Belgrave Road from where the office had operated, which she could no longer afford to rent. Her loyal friends, Harry Bradburn and his wife, generously offered her a room in their house in Staines in which to store her personal possessions.

But that was not the end of the matter. During that same month (October 1928) allegations were published in the *John Bull* magazine claiming that she used money intended for her charity to buy clothes and to pay quarantine fees for a dog given to her by her trainer on one of her attempted crossings of the English Channel. However, the purchase of clothes was a necessary expense for her to carry out personal appearances at functions relating to her swimming career and welfare work while away from home, and the quarantine fees were the result of an unplanned act of kindness, viz:

Purchase of clothes: The Gibraltar Strait swim took place on 5 April 1928. The following day Mercedes had to hurriedly take the train home from Spain as she had guaranteed to be in London on Easter Monday, 9 April, for a fundraising dance at Crystal Palace. In order to meet this guarantee she had no time to go to Tangier first to collect her luggage containing all her clothes. She also had a number of other social engagements to fulfil on her return to London, such as the Kit-Cat Club dinner and other personal appearances, and the only clothes she had were the ones she had travelled to London with (which she had worn to train in for about four weeks whilst in Spain), so it was necessary to get an appropriate new outfit immediately. She had asked one of the assistants at her office to negotiate with Christophers

Dressmaking House in Wigmore Street for the items she needed, and he informed her that Christophers had agreed to supply her with her requirements on three months' credit. Later, because her finances were in such a poor way, she renegotiated repayment for the clothing at £3 per week, amounts she knew she could honour thanks to a contract of employment with the Blackpool Tower Authority.

Dog's quarantine: In September 1927, Mr George Allan (Mercedes' trainer) bought a young Alsatian puppy at Boulogne. Bill Burgess, the Channel swimmer/coach, had recommended that particular breed to him, and Mr Allan took the puppy to Cap Gris-Nez where Mercedes was awaiting favourable weather for a Channel swim attempt that month. The puppy was left in her charge and followed her everywhere on all her long country walks. When she made her next (unsuccessful) attempt, she took it on board her pilot boat which was anchored at Cap Gris-Nez, and instructed her pilot, Mr Harry Sharp, that immediately they entered Folkstone Harbour he should hand the dog over to the customs officials, explain that she had no licence to bring him into England, and request that they tell her what steps she had to take about the matter. Mercedes had become fond of the puppy and George Allan had passed ownership of it to her. At Folkestone, the dog was duly transferred to Ashford Dogs' Home for its six months' period of quarantine. Mercedes had asked the customs officials whether any charge would be made for putting the dog into quarantine, and they categorically assured her that there would be no charge, which she (somewhat naively) took to be the case. On her return from Gibraltar the quarantine period had expired, and she received an account from Ashford Dogs' Home for £24, representing a charge of 15 shillings a week for its upkeep. Although she complained strongly about the incorrect information given to her at the time, she realised she had to settle the bill. In the event, the Ashford Dogs' Home generously waived 50 per cent of the charge, and this was followed by an equally generous offer from a Lincolnshire newspaper to pay the outstanding balance of £12 on her behalf. In June 1928, Mercedes collected her dog, but as she was now under contract at the Blackpool Tower Circus for the summer and unable to care for it, her married sister, Stella Seaton, gave it a home. [38]

It transpired that the *John Bull* article was the result of an action by her rogue employee who, having been exposed by Mercedes and her advisors for mismanagement of her affairs, had contacted the magazine with malicious accusations in order to deflect attention from his own poor professional conduct.

Mercedes' advisors, Bradburn and Hope-Jones, both interviewed the employee, who subsequently signed a confession admitting to maladministration of office matters. He also admitted selling the story to *John Bull* for £10 after having failed to secure a deal with the *Daily Mail* earlier in the year. This signed confession was taken by Mercedes to solicitors, Messrs Jesson, Topham & Hall for their opinion. She wrote to Bradburn on 19 October 1928:

> Mr Topham's opinion is that whilst it clears me as far as my own conscience is concerned, it does not put me right as regards the public – the latter not knowing of its existence. He suggests that you should take it to *John Bull*, let the editor read it and see if he won't put a modified article in a future edition of his journal, failing which a definite decision re libel action could be made.

Unfortunately, there is no further information in the archives detailing what happened after that. However, a likely scenario is that if the *John Bull* editor had refused her request, Mercedes would have realised that to take on the proprietors of a newspaper in order to obtain redress would involve her in expensive litigation. It could be likened to a 'David and Goliath' battle – a virtually penniless woman versus a wealthy publishing company. The money she earned at the Blackpool Tower Circus was being used to make good outstanding office and swimming debts as well as legal fees relating to the institution of her charity – all of which she managed to clear gradually over the following twelve months. She also had her current living expenses to find, and costs relating to her planned attempts on the North Channel that summer. Additionally, she was committed to reimbursing the fund she had previously put aside for the charity. It must therefore be assumed that, because of financial constraints, she decided to let the *John Bull* libel rest, and move on.

In a letter to Hope-Jones, Mercedes told him, 'I now know that in order to make a success of my life I must remain free and unattached.' From that point on, she handled all financial transactions herself. She led a completely peripatetic life and became a seasoned traveller.

In the latter part of 1928 she had given up her flat in London and, from then on, she moved from one swimming venue straight to another, staying mainly in local bed and breakfast accommodation. She arranged for her mail to be forwarded around the country to wherever she might be swimming, care of Corporation baths, boarding houses, hotels, the GPO (General Post Office), or at stores where she might be employed doing promotional work.

She must have found this nomadic lifestyle manageable and safe, because in January 1929 she contacted Thomas Wallis & Co. Ltd, of Holborn Circus, London, from whom she had purchased office furniture on an instalment plan, giving them the authority to collect their goods from Harry Bradburn's house in Staines. Her monthly payments on the furniture were up to date, but she had decided that the travelling associated with her sea career made it impracticable to find and furnish a permanent home. Messrs Thomas Wallis were sympathetic and wrote to her saying, 'We have only the most pleasant recollections of our business transaction with you.'

When her charity was formally established by a Declaration of Trust on 20 June 1928 there remained a balance of £113 8s 2d in Mercedes' dedicated savings account. This sum was handed over to the Official Trustees of Charitable Funds in London, and while under contract with the Blackpool Tower Circus she was able to add to it. By August 1928 she had already raised it to £200, increasing it to £351 13s 6d by September 1929. As of 1 July 1930, mainly thanks of the success of the programme of endurance swims, Mercedes had deposited £878 13s 4d with the Charity Commission, and the fund continued to grow.

In order to re-state to the public her position with regard to fundraising, she asked the *Derby Express* in March 1930 and the *Leicester Mercury* in May 1930 to inform their readers that her endurance swims were being carried out in her own name and not that of her proposed charity. She explained, 'I am entirely dependent on swimming for my living, and like everybody else I earn what I can. When I can spare some for my fund, I send it to the Charity Commissioners entirely of my own accord.'

When organising her tax affairs she informed the Inspector of Taxes:

Unfortunately I have no permanent address as my swimming career necessitates me travelling from sea to sea and place to place, but as nearly all my movements are given publicity, it is easy to trace my whereabouts. A letter addressed to me c/o Corporation Baths or c/o the GPO in whatever town I happen to be, usually reaches me.

And in a letter to the Bradford branch of the Inland Revenue, written in June 1930 while on the Isle of Man, she described how expensive it was to live a nomadic life and eat out in station restaurants and hotels. She informed the Inspector of Taxes that her profits for the first three months' aquatic work in 1930 (income from endurance swims) amounted to £429 13s 10d, which she had paid over to the Official Trustee of Charitable Funds, but:

… in order to make this profit I had to spend £74 travelling to twelve different towns for personal interviews with Corporation Officials, and £100.6.2d (after my agreements had been fixed) during the course of fulfilment of my contracts. This £100.6.2d includes: 1) travelling expenses, 2) hotel expenses, 3) equipment, and 4) training expenses.

These four items constitute an essential part of my career. I have been travelling continuously since January 1st in the execution of my work. As you know, the charge for food and tips on trains, in station restaurants and hotels, is five shillings per meal, which means that whilst engaged in contracts I am compelled to spend nearly a pound a day on food - unless I disregard my duty to the people I have signed contracts with and miss my regular meals. You will readily understand that success as far as my career is concerned is entirely dependent upon perfect health and absolute physical fitness, my work being so hard that very often during the course of its fulfilment I am on the verge of unconsciousness.

If I lived a private life – as was the case during my typist days – I could easily live on 30/- or two pounds a week as far as food and lodgings are concerned. Travelling requirements on this score are absolutely out of proportion to normal everyday requirements, for which reason they constitute essentially an important factor in my unavoidable business expenditure.

To give you but a brief understanding of 'incidental travelling expenditure' I would mention that since leaving your town about a week ago, I have had to spend 30/- on luggage transport alone (fees – left-luggage office 6/-; luggage transfer to different stations 2/-; taxis and train to boat, and boat to hotel 8/-; boat porters' fees (Liverpool to Isle of Man) 8/-; tips to station porters at different changing centres 6/- = 30/-). This merely is an illustration.

For your information, please note that I have no banking account in either bank or post office, or at any other savings source – also I possess no home, being single, and cannot therefore invest surplus money on household articles. All the money I retain is the necessary sum to take me from contract to contract.

It appears that the national and local press eventually disregarded the smear by *John Bull* magazine, and Mercedes continued to enjoy positive media coverage throughout her career. This reaction also applied to the public, as was made evident by the overwhelming support and encouragement given to her by the many thousands of spectators who attended her swimming events. There was no wrongdoing by Mercedes, just the inexperience of a young woman who trusted people. She learnt from this experience, and throughout the rest of her career she kept her accounts under her own control and in good order.

9

CLOSED SEASON
ACTIVITIES

Winter in Manchester

Having given up her lodgings in London, after the close of the 1928 season, *The Guardian* reported:

> Miss Gleitze, Mill-Hand Miss Mercedes Gleitze, of swimming fame, is putting the winter 'closed season' to good use by gaining personal experience of the conditions under which various classes of working girls live and earn their living. Lodging unpretentiously somewhere in the Hulme district of Manchester, she has spent a week as an assistant behind the counter of a big Manchester Store, and is now at work in a spinning mill. Before her well-known swimming exploits Miss Gleitze was employed as a typist.[39]

Her first contact with Manchester had been via a letter she received from Councillor J. Mathewson Watson, Chairman of the White Heather Fund for Blind Children,[40] while she was with the Blackpool Tower Circus. Councillor Watson asked her to give a swimming exhibition on behalf of their charity.

From November 1928 until the beginning of April 1929, Mercedes lodged at the home of Mr and Mrs J. Froggert, 14 Eagle Street, Hulme. During her stay in Manchester, she secured work on a loom and then at the weaving mill at Brunswick Mill in Bradford Road, which belonged to Henry Bannerman & Sons Ltd of Ancoats, Manchester.

A journalist went to the Bannerman mills to cover the story. He was taken by the manager to the noisy room where the spinning was in progress and reported, 'Miss Gleitze, with no shoes and stockings, which is the custom, was attending the spinning machinery.'[41] Mercedes commented later that she enjoyed working amongst the girls in the mills, and found the factory conditions good and the work less strenuous than working in a shop.

On 2 February 1929, she wrote to a friend, 'I am living in the slums of Manchester with the poor I love, studying their mode of life, and am thoroughly enjoying my experience.'

While wintering in Manchester, Mercedes supported the White Heather Fund's charitable events and although she moved on when the swimming season started in pursuit of fresh waters to conquer, she kept in touch with Miss Ethel Williams, the honorary secretary of the fund. They were like-minded women with a strong interest in social welfare. On 25 June 1929 she wrote to her Manchester friend:

Dear Ethel,

Do you remember the evening we spent at the All Saints Cinema gazing at Irish scenery on the screen? I am on my way back to this dear country to tackle the Irish Channel once again – successfully this year, I hope.

The people at Boston were wonderfully kind to me and it is due to the support I received from them that The Wash swim I contemplated whilst at Manchester is now achieved.

I hope you are keeping well and that you are as happy as ever. Also that Mr Watson is enjoying good health.

Am travelling via Holyhead, Wales – an awfully tiring journey: change at Nottingham–Derby–Crewe–Chester–Holyhead–Dublin–Belfast–Donaghadee.

Love and best wishes,

Mercedes

In a later letter to Ethel she wrote:

I have addressed to you c/o Mrs Froggert a case containing 21 boxes of chocolates and 3 bars of chocolate. They were all given to me by people who have witnessed my different swims, and as they are more than I can make use of, I would be very grateful if you would kindly distribute one box to each house in Eagle Street.

Spring in Nottingham

In April 1929, after leaving Manchester, Mercedes paid a shorter visit to Nottingham with the same purpose in mind, lodging with Mr and Mrs Midwinter. Although she had hoped for the visit to be away from the eyes of the media, a local reporter for the *Nottingham Evening Post* tracked her down as she was about to enter one of the city's largest hosiery mills in search of a temporary job for two weeks to cover her stay there. She told him that she was in the area to gain more background knowledge of the levels of poverty existing in Britain. With the strong leaning she had towards welfare work, she wanted to write about the conditions poor people had to endure. She commented that it was fortunate that the local authorities in Nottingham were gradually demolishing the worst of the slum housing associated with extreme poverty and disease.

10

THE 1929 SEASON

During her winter sojourn in the north of England, Mercedes planned a series of cold-water swims, commencing in May 1929, in waters known for their low temperatures. Her intention was to acclimatise her body in advance of a further attempt the following August in the icy waters of the Irish Sea. But the loughs and estuaries she selected for these preparatory swims were also waterways that had never been swum before, and she naturally wanted the honour of being the first person to cross them.

In the event Mercedes successfully carried out seven innovative swims during 1929 in British waterways (the Wash, Lough Neagh twice, Loch Ryan, the Firth of Forth and Lough Foyle twice), four more assaults on her nemesis, the North Channel, and an unplanned sojourn on Sanda Island in the Mull of Kintyre.

The Wash

The Wash is a square-mouthed bay on the east coast of England where Norfolk meets Lincolnshire. It is one of the largest estuaries in the UK, and its waters ebb and flow into the North Sea. Nobody had ever attempted to swim across this bay before. Some of the local pilots prophesied failure and warned that the currents were worse than those in the English Channel. They also expressed the opinion that Mercedes could be thrown onto a sandbank, thus voiding the swim. However, she was determined to prove them wrong.

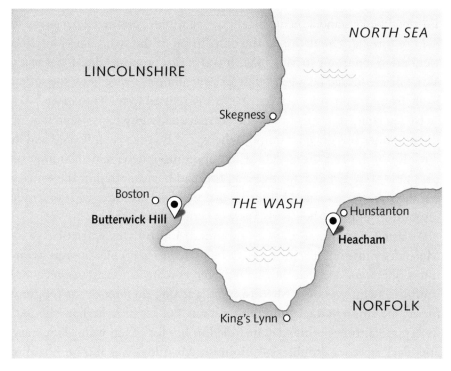

The Wash – another pioneering swim, with three friendly seals for company.

She travelled from Nottingham to Lincolnshire at the end of April 1929 to set up a base and enlist support for an attempt on this estuary, and once they knew her intention was serious, a dedicated group of people in Boston formed a committee to organise the swim. It included not just seafaring people, but volunteers from many different professions. Captain W.R. Fairbairn, chief reporter on the *Lincolnshire Standard*, knew Mercedes from her English Channel days when he was a journalist working for the *Kent Evening Echo*, and he had accompanied her on some of her early Channel attempts. In the Wash venture, he took on a main role on the organising committee and was on standby duty to let Mercedes know when the conditions were favourable. He also accompanied her on all three Wash attempts.

A *Daily Mirror* journalist reported that 2 gallons of milk and a cocktail bar would be on the accompanying boat – the milk for the swimmer and the cocktail bar for the amusement of her friends. Other items on board consisted of 1lb of lard, twenty-four bath towels, eight hot-water bottles, a dozen blankets and a medicine chest – all things considered necessary to help restore her circulation at the conclusion of the swim. The journalist went on to report on 16 May 1929, 'It was at first proposed that, if necessary, Miss Gleitze should be given a dose of strychnine to revive her if she suffers badly from the intense cold, but she firmly refused to resort to drugs.'

To determine the strength of the currents, an empty basket representing the swimmer was dragged through the water. By the way it floated and its direction and speed, the assistance and opposition she would encounter on her swim were gauged. A huge dog fish had been spotted in the estuary, but the fishermen assured Mercedes that these sea creatures were of a mild disposition and that their bark was worse than their bite.

As usual, a gramophone was provided, and for this particular swim Mercedes chose ten specific tunes to be played to her while she was swimming. She requested that they be repeated as many times as was necessary until the swim was over. She displayed a strong preference for religious music, and amongst the hymns this time was 'For Those in Peril on the Sea'. Two popular tunes of the day included in her list of ten were 'Tipperary' and 'Pack up your Troubles'. A violinist (Mr Addy) was also on board to vary the repertoire.

After settling in at the Plummers Hotel on the Freiston shoreline, Mercedes carried out some initial test swims, and a date of 8 May 1929 was set for an attempt from Skegness to Hunstanton. However, the evening before, she received a note from Captain Fairbairn saying:

> A general gale warning was issued this evening and we have had to call the swim off. I am sorry, but the outlook suggested that it may be a day or two before we can start. Make the best of it, and we will talk it over at 12 noon tomorrow.

In the event, her first two tries on 16 May and 10 June (5 hours 30 minutes and 11 hours 30 minutes respectively) – both starting from the Cut End at the mouth of the River Witham, Frieston, Lincolnshire – were abandoned due to wayward currents, low water temperatures (never above 52°F (11.1°C)) and the swimmer suffering from extreme cold and stomach cramps.

Success

Mercedes finally triumphed on 20 June 1929. She covered 25 miles, swimming from the foreshore at Butterwick Hill, south-east of Boston in Lincolnshire, to Heacham in Norfolk. The distance across the planned course was 16 miles as the crow flies, but the strong currents added a further 9 miles to the swim. Entertainingly, three seals followed her nearly all the way and she amused herself by watching them. She wrote to her mother afterwards, 'I expect they were wondering what kind of a fish I was!'

After the swim Mercedes wrote to Mr Rysdale, the proprietor of the Plummers Hotel, to thank him for his generous hospitality and for looking after her personal needs so well during the trying days leading up to her successful swim. Rysdale had also helped with the organisation and she told him how pleased she was to see him on Hunstanton Pier waiting to greet her. She went on to thank him 'for supplying the bottle of "60 over proof" which was rubbed into my limbs after my swims. I am sure this was responsible for me recovering within twenty minutes instead of within an hour of being carried to the cabin!'

To mark her achievement, a brass commemorative plaque commissioned by Heacham Parish Council was affixed to a shelter on the North Beach. The plaque was swept away in the devastating east coast floods of 1953, but eventually washed back onto the beach with other wreckage. It now hangs in the Parish Council office at Heacham. A new plaque commemorating Mercedes' successful crossing was commissioned by the local authority in 2004 on the seventy-fifth anniversary of her swim and is affixed to a wall on Heacham's North Beach near the spot where she waded ashore at the end of the crossing.

Although Mercedes had tried to obtain sponsorship for her swim across the Wash, she had been unsuccessful. However, her travel expenses to Ireland for her next swim had been covered by Southport Corporation, where she had performed exhibitions swims in between her first two attempts on the Wash, and during her time in Boston her accommodation and food had been generously provided by the proprietors of the Plummers Hotel, as well as by local supporters. She also received an additional gift of £1 to help with incidental expenses, and a thank-you letter, dated 29 June 1929, which she wrote to Councillor Coppin reads:

Dear Councillor,

Just before leaving Boston, Mr Reynolds, Captain of the Boston Swimming Club, handed me a one pound note saying that you had asked him to give it to me to refund me for the expenses I incurred in connection with my swims. It was very considerate of you indeed to think of me in this way and I thank you most sincerely for your kindness.

I have used your pound to reimburse myself for travelling expense in connection with my swims, as explained in the attached tabulation.

You may rest assured that I shall always remember with gratitude the great kindness, sporting interest, help and support extended to me by the town of Boston, and whenever I am congratulated upon my recent Wash success, I bear in mind the fact that had it not been for Boston I would not have accomplished the feat.

I have now another equally severe task in front of me, e.g. that of swimming the North Channel – or trying to at any rate. The sun has been shining quite brilliantly since my arrival and I am hoping the rays are warming the water nicely, so that when the call comes for my start, the temperature of the water won't be quite as reminiscent of the North Pole and ice bergs.

With best wishes,
Yours very truly,

Mercedes Gleitze.

Tabulation   £ s d

Fare from Nottingham to Boston to swim the Wash	6.9
Tip to porter, Boston	6
Fare to Belfast from Nottingham to swim Lough Neagh	
and the North Channel	1.16.3
Tip to porter	
Nottingham	4
– Derby	6
– Crewe	6
– Chester	6
– Holyhead	6
Tip to stewardess on board ship	6
Berth on board ship	2.0
Tip to porter, Dublin (no change left)	3½
Wire to Mr Caughey, Belfast	1.6
Tip to railway official for sending it	6
Tip to porter, Belfast	6
Luggage deposit fee, Belfast	6
Incidentals: Stamps for letters to Irish people	
in connection with swim	1.0½

£2.11.8d

....

Received from Southport Corporation for fare to Ireland: £1.12.8d
Received from Councillor Coppin to cover expenses: £1.00.0d

£2.12.8d

The full story of the swim produced by Captain W.R. Fairbairn can be accessed at www.mercedesgleitze.uk.

After the swim, Mercedes left Boston for Northern Ireland – still with her sights set on the North Channel, but first of all to carry out a swim across Lough Neagh.

Lough Neagh – Breadthways

Lough Neagh in Northern Ireland is the largest lake in the United Kingdom and measures approximately 19 miles by 12 miles. Mercedes was the first person to complete both crossings of this body of water – breadthways and lengthways. There are no currents of any description in this freshwater lough, so there is no tidal help, nor any tidal setbacks.

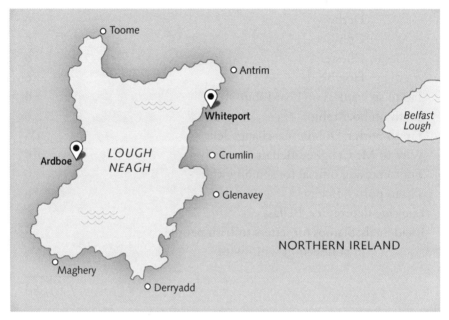

A breadthways swim across Lough Neagh – adverse winds caused Mercedes to finish the swim at Whiteport, a small stony beach south of Antrim (the planned landing place).

This was Mercedes' second major swim in 1929, but the idea was first proposed in June 1928 by John Murphy, a member of the family of Patrick Murphy & Sons of Ballymena who owned the Massereene Arms Hotel in Antrim. Initial negotiations are described in the following letter Mercedes wrote to him on 30 June that year. It is reproduced in full because it illustrates her developing skills as a business woman, as well as the confidence that she – a young woman just 5ft 2in in height – had in her own ability to carry out back-to-back major swims with little respite in between:

Dear Mr Murphy,

Since my recent attempt to swim across the Irish Channel I have been inundated with invitations to give swimming exhibitions, etc., in various towns, but none of the propositions are as attractive as the offer you have made. Long-distance swimming being my special line, I should simply love to undertake a swim across Lough Neagh, especially if I could derive some financial benefit out of such a swim. The trouble with all the invitations I am getting is that I am tied down by contract to give two shows per day at the Blackpool Tower Circus, and in nearly every case I have to turn the offers down. In your case, however, something might be done, as leave has been granted me by contract during the month of July to make a new attempt to swim across the Irish Channel and, provided you could do all the organisatory work connected with such a long-distance swim, I could arrange when leaving Blackpool for the Irish coast to leave on a Saturday evening and do the swim lengthways across Lough Neagh starting early Sunday morning, which would leave me two more days to devote to the Irish Channel.

Owing to the large experience I have had in long-distance swimming I suffer from no after effects the day following a long-distance swim and, provided I have a night's rest in between, would be perfectly fit for the Irish Sea.[42] I should be glad if you would kindly go into the matter and see whether it would be possible for you or the Ulster Association to pay me a remuneration of say £100 in the event of my swimming from shore to shore, as well as return journey Blackpool paid. If I swim the lake only half way or three quarter way (which I do not think will be likely) I do not require any remuneration, but merely my return journey paid. In return for your paying me £100 if I successfully do the swim, you retain the right to refund yourself by getting paying witnesses on any motorboats you might have for the occasion, sell article rights, etc, and in addition you have of course the publicity value.

If in case something to the above effect could be arranged, please fix a date either for the last but one or last Sunday in July, but before deciding which Sunday you choose, please find out whether spring or neap tides are running at that particular time. To do my Irish Channel swim successfully I must have a neap tide, and it would be advisable therefore to choose a Sunday on which a neap tide is running. Once a definite decision has been come to regarding the matter you could go straight ahead with any advertising you may care to do.

Again thanking you for your kind offer, I remain yours truly, Mercedes Gleitze

The response from Murphy was positive, but it was soon apparent that it would take longer than the two weeks available to set up this major event and so the proposed swim did not take place until the following year. When the time came in July 1929, the challenge had been extended to swimming the lough both breadthways and lengthways, which Mercedes was happy to do.

Although she was now in control of her own agenda, Mercedes still made arrangements to swim both Lough Neagh breadthways and the North Channel with only a few days' rest in between. Lough Neagh was to be first, and on 8 July 1929, to test the waters, she swam across Antrim Bay. J. Barr of Antrim assisted her with this warm-up swim. It took her 3 hours 30 minutes to reach the opposite shore. Two rowing boats accompanied her, one containing four policemen, who sang 'Tipperary' and 'My Wild Irish Rose' to her. Although it was only a trial swim, there were crowds waiting for her at the landing place.

On 10 July, while marking time, she wrote to D. Cooper, an organiser of her recent Wash swim:

I am at present on the shores of Lough Neagh awaiting an opportunity to swim it. The chances of doing it seem very remote as the lake is in a terrible state of upheaval and no boat would venture out, so I have to bide my time like I had to with the Wash.

Spent the evening in conference with my organisers and lake experts. We agree about everything excepting the landing place – they want me to land at Antrim for the convenience of the crowds who will be awaiting results, and for my personal comfort because all other parts of the coast are covered with stones – and I want to land near Whitehead [Whiteport] for geographical reasons and in the interest of the swim. We are at loggerheads about it but I expect the landing, if I am lucky enough to get to it when the swim does take place, will prove mutually satisfactory.

On the same day Mercedes also wrote to Jasper Sharpe, a witness on her Wash swim, 'I have been feeling sick all day – headache and throat ache and homesick for a swim. In the afternoon I went to the library to feed my mind on the winning-through spirit of tennis players.' This kind of motivation is still used by athletes today, for example Andy Murray's ambition to meet Lennox Lewis and his employment of Ivan Lendl as his tennis coach in order to 'feed off' their winning spirits.

The next day brought better conditions. A letter dated 11 July to Mr Manning, another supporter in Boston, relates:

This afternoon my Antrim friends took me for a ride to Larne. We had tea there and then drove home through an Irish glen, the first one I have seen. The scenery here is positively bewitching. On arrival back at Antrim I found to my delight that the gale which had been raging on the lake for several days had subsided, so with the help of friends I quickly got things on the move to enable the start of my proposed Lough Neagh swim tomorrow morning. It was rather a rush getting everything fixed up and assembling all the necessary people.

The Swim

Conditions the following morning remained settled, and so the breadth-ways swim across Lough Neagh took place on Friday, 12 July 1929. Afterwards, in a letter to Mr Reynolds at the Boston Amateur Swimming Club, she wrote:

I wish you had been with me today in Lough Neagh. I commenced the swim at 8.37 am at Ardboe and successfully finished at Whitehead [Whiteport] Bay at 10.25 p.m. (13 hrs 8 mins). Being fresh water I had to swim every inch of the way. During the whole day different motor-boats and vessels came out from different parts of the shore to keep me company. I also had a solicitor, a doctor and pressmen on the official boat.

The arrangements were as perfect as they were in the Wash. Towards the end, the sea – I mean the lake – got rough owing to a strong breeze springing up, and for every stroke I swam the waves pushed me back a yard. We were steering for Antrim where the wind hailed from, so there was nothing to do but to choose a different landing spot so as not to have to fight a contrary breeze. We headed for Whitehead [Whiteport], and although it is a desolate shore, a crowd of several hundreds gathered to witness my landings. It took me 25 minutes from the time I touched ground to get to dry land, having to crawl over 20 yards of stones. It was rather an ordeal and twice I thought I could never manage it, but I did, and a policeman and doctor carried me off in a car to a nearby house for treatment, after which I was taken by car to Antrim where the street was crowded with people awaiting my arrival. Some policemen waiting at my hotel door carried me to the bathroom, where another doctor and two women were waiting to attend to me. Half an hour later, however, I was completely restored to normal health and ready for my next long-distance swim. I am not quite sure where that will be, but I read in the *Daily Express* that I am going to swim Loch Ryan in Scotland tomorrow! I have not made any arrangements for this but it seems my Scottish friends have. Anyhow I am due to go to Scotland tomorrow to stand by for the neap tides for my Irish Channel swim.

In another letter addressed to 'The Singer on Lough Neagh', she wrote:

I am so grateful to you for the great interest you took in my endeavour to swim Lough Neagh and for the splendid help you rendered not only with your singing but also with your practical assistance on the boat and upon landing. It was ever so good of you to walk beside me from the time of touching ground until I reached dry soil. On long-distance swims the moment of landing – though it ought to be the happiest – is always the most trying part of the undertaking, and the fact of having able friends close at hand to supervise the landing is always a source of gratification.

The distance across Lough Neagh on this breadthways swim, taking into account the altered course, was approximately 18 miles, which she completed in 13 hours and 48 minutes. Mercedes remarked afterwards that so far this was her most pleasant swim because of the higher temperature of the water. [43]

The second, lengthways, part of the Lough Neagh challenge was to happen later on that year, but in the meantime, her next scheduled swim took place in Scotland and she quickly travelled from Antrim to Stranraer to finalise arrangements.

Loch Ryan

On Saturday, 13 July, one day after her breadthways crossing of Lough Neagh and three days in advance of a planned further attempt on the North Channel, she made arrangements to swim across Loch Ryan. Not only was this a worthwhile crossing in its own right, but it was also part of her plan to use the very low temperatures in this Scottish loch to help acclimatise her body to what she knew she must endure if she were to real-ise her ambition to conquer the icy waters of the Irish Sea. After the event, she stated that the waters of Loch Ryan were colder than those of Lough Neagh and in her other practice swims off the Irish coast.

The Stranraer local authority enthusiastically supported the event and played a main part in its organisation. The George Hotel in Stranraer was her base, and she was looked after by Councillors McConnell and W. MacRobert. Before, during and after the swim the latter's daughter, Sheila, together with Barbara Ford (the artist) and Mercedes' companion from North Channel attempts, Nettie Muir, acted as lady attendants. Their brief also included feeding Mercedes and operating the gramophone during the swim. Hugh Muir (her pilot on her first Irish Channel attempt in 1928) was in the pilot boat, and he and Augustus Carnochan (the Procurator Fiscal in Stranraer) took turns at the oars and steered the course.

On the day, MacRobert drove her to Cairnryan Lighthouse at the entrance of Loch Ryan – the picturesque starting point of the swim – and with the help of her lady attendants she completed the preparation for her swim in the lighthouse. At 3.43 p.m. Mercedes walked across the shingle and, after fixing a veil over her hair and face, she entered the water to the cheers of the crowd that had gathered to see her off.

The conditions were ideal, the water was smooth, and the sun shone. She used sidestroke for the first few yards, and then changed to her favourite breaststroke. She maintained this all the way to the finish on an average of thirty-three strokes to the minute. Hot milk and light refreshments were provided every half an hour. Strong currents were experienced between Cairnryan and the buoy of the Scaur, where the tide runs out swiftly

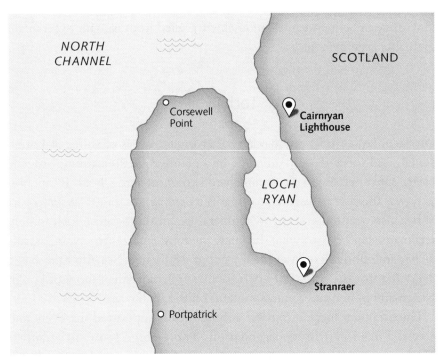

A cold but stamina-building swim in Scotland's Loch Ryan.

towards the mouth of the loch, but she had the advantage of the flood tide until within about an hour of the finish.

Mercedes waded ashore at Stranraer Harbour at 7.21 p.m., having completed the crossing of 6 miles in 3 hours 38 minutes. A fleet of about ten motorboats crammed with spectators and at least a dozen rowing boats had followed her, and when she reached the harbour she found that over 5,000 people had gathered to see her swim in.

When Mercedes was in the coldest part of the loch near the buoy on the Scaur (a large sandbank, which runs out more than halfway across the loch from the Kirkcolm shore), the mail steamer SS *Princess Maud* hove round the Cairnryan Light. In order to warn the captain of the swimmer's presence, a motorboat was detailed to give a sign. A little girl in an accompanying motor skiff was wearing a red beret, and this was borrowed and waved on a boat hook at the captain on the bridge of the steamer. He noted the situation and passed Mercedes at a slow speed, thus averting a potentially heavy backwash that could have tipped her accompanying crew into the sea.

The Firth of Forth

After her successful crossing of Loch Ryan, Mercedes travelled from Stranraer to Donaghadee to prepare for a further attempt on the North Channel, arranged for 16 July 1929. However, the weather again interfered with her plans, and in a letter to Mr Mitchell – a friend in Boston who had helped during her swim across the Wash the previous month – she explained how she felt:

16th July 1929. My swim across the Irish Channel was to have started at 4.30 this morning, but at 2.30 am, to my dismay, I was woken up and informed that the weather had changed, the sea had got up rough and that my swim was off. So all arrangements had to be cancelled and the attempt postponed until the next neap tides – today being the last favourable day as far as currents are concerned.

Although willing to submit to postponement of the Irish Channel swim I did not feel at all inclined to submit to ten days' inactivity as far as a long-distance venture is concerned, so I decided to go to Glasgow by bus to investigate the possibility of swimming the Firth of Forth. At the bus terminal I was met by a Glasgow *Daily Express* lady reporter who took me to tea, then to the *Daily Express* office to consult maps, then to supper and then to the station to catch the train to Edinburgh. At the end of this trip I was met by the Edinburgh *Daily Express* representative who took me to the newspaper's office to collect further Firth of Forth information. By tomorrow evening I shall probably know whether or not I shall be able to get the necessary local support to enable my Firth of Forth project to fructify. In the meantime I am putting up at the local YWCA for the night and I feel fagged out from my day's travelling.

The Firth of Forth had already proved a difficult waterway for long-distance swimmers, partly because of the very strong currents of the Firth, and partly because, even in the height of summer, the temperature of the water is always low. Matthew Webb (of Channel swimming fame) had once tried but had to abandon his attempt because of the cold. The temperature of the water during Mercedes' successful attempt on 28 July was 54°F (12.2°C) and never higher than 57°F (13.9°C) , and she was suffering badly from the cold on completion of the swim.

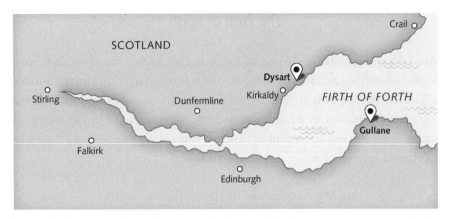

The Firth of Forth – a demanding swim, with the North Sea's strong currents, adverse winds and low temperatures ebbing and flowing into the estuary.

The only recorded crossing at the time was that of W.E. Barnie, who swam from Burntisland to Granton on 31 August 1924, a distance of 5 miles between the two points, 4 hours 30 minutes. The water on that occasion was recorded as calm. Mercedes selected a longer crossing from Port Seton to Kinghorn Ness, about 13 miles to the north-west in a straight line.

First Attempt
The immediate and enthusiastic support given by the local authority for the proposed swim matched that of all the other regions where she had performed. Alexander N. Cameron, instructor at the Nautical College, Leith, acted as course director and pilot. Thomas Bunyan, the Edinburgh Baths superintendent (who was later to help Mercedes set up her record-breaking endurance swim at the Infirmary Road Baths), acted as organiser as well as masseur and official witness. Mr and Mrs G.W. Ferguson hosted her during her stay in Edinburgh.

Mercedes wrote to friends in Ireland after her first try at the crossing on 21 July:

I attempted the Forth swim today and failed after eight hours in the water on account of adverse weather conditions. The sea was as rough as could be and in addition we had a contrary wind. The Edinburgh officials were splendid about it and have asked me to stay on so as to have a go at the Firth under proper weather conditions.

She also wrote to Hugh Muir, her friend and organiser in Portpatrick who was helping her with her attempts on the North Channel. 'To keep in good form I am trying to swim the Firth of Forth. It had a tremendous sea and adverse wind the last time I tried but I shall have another go, for the only way to achieve success is to fight for it.'

An Edinburgh friend, A.R. Evans, sent a sympathetic note to Mercedes to tell her:

I had you under observation through my telescope for quite a bit but could see you were having a rough passage owing to the short choppy sea. That is the worst of westerly winds in the middle reaches of the Forth — they kick up a sea quite out of proportion to their own velocity.

Second Attempt
Mercedes' successful crossing of the Firth, lasting 11 hours 20 minutes, took place a week later on 28 July 1929, and an authenticated witness account was produced by Alexander Cameron. It covered both Mercedes' first attempt at the crossing and her successful second one. With the witness statement is a certified log of the swim charted on Admiralty Chart No. 114a.[44]

A Magic Moment
At the end of the swim, Mercedes was rather overwhelmed by the reception given to her. She said, 'It was a cold, wretched swim which took me nearly eleven and a half hours, but when I waded out near a colliery on the Fifeshire coast I found about 12,000 people waiting to cheer me, and they certainly treated me royally.' In later writings, she recalled:

My favourite Scottish song is 'Rolling Home to Bonnie Scotland'. I love the song, not merely because of its beauty, but because it brings back to me a wonderful memory — the last fighting hour of my successful swim across the Firth of Forth when, in the depth of darkness, about 50 rowing boats brought out to me from my prospective landing shore, full of well-wishing, singing and cheering Scotsmen, accompanied me in the last laps of my swim.

It was a scene like a page from a fairy-tale book which nothing can ever efface from my mind. Pitch darkness — the mast lights of my pilot boat – a yard in front of me the guiding lantern of my attendant rowing boat – to the left and to the right of me, in fact all around me, the flickering, star-like lights of the 50 rowing boats – just darkness and twinkling hurricane lamps – and voices, voices producing melody – the tune of 'Rolling Home to Bonnie Scotland'.[45]

Immediately after her successful crossing, Mercedes wrote to Thomas Bunyan:

Please accept my very best thanks for organizing my two Firth of Forth swims. If it had not been for your great kindness and your wonderful help I should have returned to Ireland the day of my arrival in Edinburgh, and the Forth would never have made my acquaintance – which would have been a great pity. I felt very proud and honoured to have you on board as one of my officiating witnesses.

She then journeyed to the Glens of Antrim Hotel in Cushendall to prepare for yet another attempt at the North Channel.

The North Channel Again

A Swimmer's Perspective
An article written by Mercedes and published in *The Lincolnshire Standard* on 21 June 1929 set the scene for Mercedes' renewed assault on the North Channel. In it she recalled her 1928 experiences in those waters and gave an insight into what a long-distance swimmer must expect to face when swimming across seas.

LONG-DISTANCE SWIMMING. IS IT EASY?
Last year I made four attempts to swim the Irish Channel. Thousands of Irish people witnessed my starts and hundreds in boats watched me cover mile after mile of freezing water. Owing to the flow of water from melting ice-bergs coming from the north, the temperature, even in mid-summer, is always extremely low. Many of my lady-witnesses cried unrestrained tears at the cold I had to endure – others prayed for my success.

Our constitution not being the same as that of creatures of the sea upon whose element long-distance swimmers encroach, and consequently not being able to adapt ourselves to the severities of the sea, excessive cold, etc. – we have to pay the penalty. I have paid many a time. On one occasion I had been swimming for 14 hours 50 minutes – my position being only five miles from Portpatrick (my goal) – when my doctor gave orders that I should be taken out. I was not 'finished'. Far from it. I wished to continue my swim and struggled vigorously with the doctor and two fishermen, who seized my arms to lift me out, until overpowered. They carried me to the cabin where I lay for at least an hour in a semi-conscious condition, just moaning with the pain caused by the returning circulation. My doctor and lady attendants who had spent the time dipping towels into boiling water and wrapping them round my limbs and shoulders to make me warm, were getting desperate, and I heard the doctor's voice appealingly shout, 'Miss Gleitze, speak to us, speak to us, you are not swimming now, it is all over.' But I was still too paralysed to talk.

As on this occasion, so have I, on many others, suffered whilst in the quest of aquatic achievements. My swims in the Irish Channel last season have proved to me conclusively that it is by no means impossible to conquer this stretch of sea. This Channel, it is true, is notoriously rough, and the currents obviously very strong, but these difficulties are not such that they cannot be overcome. The greatest enemy in my estimation is the cold, and I am hoping that on my next attempt to conquer the Irish Channel I shall be able to overcome this adversity and successfully complete my task.

In order to acclimatise myself to cold water, last month I decided to devote the last two weeks in May to an attempt to swim the Wash. Although the temperature of the water in the Wash during the month in question will still be very low, it can scarcely be any lower than the temperature of the Irish Channel in mid-summer, and I consider this a good way of hardening and preparing myself for the severe task of conquering the Irish Channel.

I have often wondered why it is that, while there are thousands of excellent swimmers in the sporting world, there are comparatively few who have the necessary stamina, strength and endurance to take up long-distance swimming.

Apart from ability to swim, I think the main essentials are a strong heart, good lungs and generally a strong and healthy constitution. Another important factor is will power: the will to endure the cold; to put up with the discomfort of choppy waves; to ignore the sting of jelly fish; to be disconcerned at the nearness of porpoises, dolphins and even sharks; to bear the pain of aching shoulder, knee and shin muscles; to remain floating in the water with your arm or leg seized with cramp – and yet continue the swim; to remain unperturbed when a large steamer, having passed too near, causes a nasty wash, and a series of mountainous waves jostle you up and down; to bear up when you cannot have the hot drinks you asked for, longed for and sorely need – a raging gale having put the 'kitchen' out of function by upsetting the stove and spilling the food; not to be upset if the goggles 'go wrong', but to slide them off the head and take the force of the spray; not to become dejected if every witness is laid out on the deck, a victim of seasickness; to fight for consciousness when an attack of sleepiness threatens to send you to the land of oblivion; and last but not least, to have the courage to say 'I want to carry on' when asked to give up, though every part of your body may be aching and you have spent endless hours visualising blankets and hot water bottles and been positively longing for a lie-down on terra firma.

A New Attempt

While waiting for accommodating tides in the North Channel, Mercedes wrote her thank-you letters to the people in Boston, without whose help she would not have been able to organise her swim across the Wash. In one letter, to Mr Rysdale, proprietor of Plummer's Hotel in Lincolnshire, she said:

I am writing from the Queen's Hotel, Belfast, where the owner, Mr Campbell, has offered me hospitality, and shall stay here only a little while pending developments in connection with my swim …

An organ grinder down below has just started a series of tunes, 'In Old Nebraska' being one of them. This was sung to me a good many times in the Irish Channel last year …

The organ has switched on to 'Without you Sweetheart', and my feelings are about the same – sitting in a Belfast hotel without my sea.

But I have just got to wait for the right tides and not fret for want of an early swim.

In another to Councillor Coppin in Boston, she wrote:

Had a consultation with the pilot I had for my last two swims last year and gleaned from him that the most suitable time for my attempt would be either on the 14th, 15th or 16th July. The tides will be slackest on these three days. So I am downing weapons till that date and taking things easy. The pilot I shall probably have for my attempt [Hugh Muir] will be the one who steered my course on my first Irish Channel attempt and he is coming up specially from London to do that job. He has set his heart on getting me across and is giving me his services in an honorary capacity. He is a native of Portpatrick and his niece [Nettie Muir] last year was my lady attendant on all four of my swims.

Miss Margaret Ruddell of the Royal Hotel was telling me that two days before Donaghadee heard that I was coming she came across a man leaning against the sea wall watching the waves roll in, in gale-like fury. All of a sudden he looked at Miss Ruddell and said 'Miss Gleitze must be coming, this is her weather!' A few days after that the *Northern Whig* rang through and informed Miss Ruddell that I was on my way. Seeing my Donaghadee friends yesterday made me turn my thoughts back to the day in November of last year. I had failed in my fourth attempt and was leaning out of the train in Donaghadee Station gazing at a crowd of Irish friends who had come to see me off. All of a sudden they started singing 'God be with you till we meet again'. My Irish friends and I have now met again!

Change of Course
The previous year, Mercedes had made four attempts on the North Channel from Northern Ireland to Scotland. However, after fresh discussions, her committee agreed to her suggestion to choose a different starting point this year. The course she had chosen was in the reverse direction, from the Scottish coast across to Northern Ireland, and interim arrangements were made with organisers on both sides of the water.

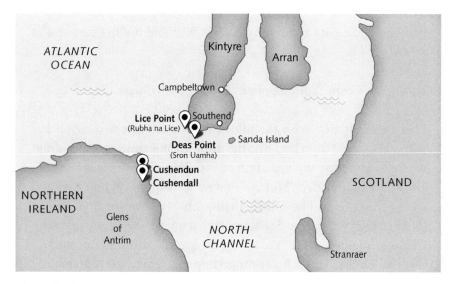

The Mull of Kintyre – an alternative course across the North Channel.

The first attempt of 1929 had been planned for 16 July, from Knock Bay, north of Portpatrick, to the Donaghadee coastline, but it was aborted due to dangerous conditions at sea. All arrangements were cancelled, and the swim postponed until the next neap tides. Eventually, on Saturday, 10 August, the rearranged attempt took place, from Scotland to Northern Ireland, over a different, shorter course: the starting point was from Lice Point (*Rubha na Lice*) on the rounded, south-western headland of the Mull of Kintyre. Mercedes pushed off from a submerged boulder where the rock rises sheer from the water and began her swim.

The water was exceptionally cold, and after swimming for over 10 hours her numbed limbs would carry her no further. When taken into the pilot boat she was in a state of collapse and was eventually carried to the Glens of Antrim Hotel in Cushendall by a stretcher party, where arrangements had already been put in hand by Kathleen DeLargy to aid her recovery.

Lough Foyle – Both Ways

The lakes and rivers that shape Lough Foyle create a natural boundary between County Derry in Northern Ireland and County Donegal in the Irish Republic. The management of the lough falls under the jurisdiction

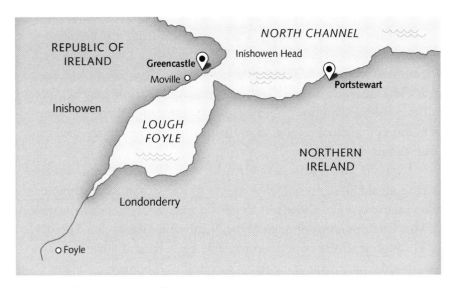

Across the wide-open mouth of Lough Foyle – both ways.

of the Loughs Agency, which is a cross-border government body. Lough Foyle is almost landlocked, but Mercedes planned to make this double swim close to its mouth – from Portstewart to Moville and from Moville to Portstewart – a feat unaccomplished by any other swimmer.

Mr Frank Martin, the incumbent town clerk at Portstewart Urban Council, was mainly responsible for engaging Mercedes in the first instance. He considered she would be a star attraction for the Portstewart holiday season, and his foresight turned out to be correct. On the Greencastle (Moville) to Portstewart crossing on 17 August 1929, when she waded ashore at Bearnville Port near the salmon fishery, the press reported that it seemed that the whole countryside had turned out to see her finish. She was told it was the biggest crowd ever seen in these parts, and the assistance of the police was necessary to clear a way for her to reach the waiting car.

The reverse crossing from Portstewart to Greencastle, just north of Moville, took place on 20 August 1929, and a special correspondent who covered the swim wrote in the *Northern Constitution* of 24 August 1929:

I followed, borne mechanically onwards in the watery wake of Miss Gleitze, and I tell you all that you cannot conceive the magnitude of the performance who did not cover the course with her. There has been a tendency in some circles to decry all long-distance swimming acts, and, frankly, I fell into the Gleitze aquatic procession prepared to be unimpressed. In the event I was astounded, enthused, chastened. That battle towards the Tironenail coast, seen at close quarters, of nine stone of humanity against gravity, tide, time, cold, exhaustion, ennui, partook of the epic: there was a suggestion of spiritual combat in it, the spectacle of a supreme courage, an august determination.

I watched the sixty-odd petrol-fliers as they streaked down the Dundonald Straights on Saturday. As a display of pluck, endurance, and tenacity, their show was to me a wan affair in comparison with Miss Gleitze's grim conquest of the North-West Passage on Tuesday. Through it all she continued to smile bravely, and never failed to respond to an encouraging remark from the accompanying boats.

The longshore critics may question the interest or vitality of the feat, but the feeling of all who saw it enacted was one of profound admiration. The staff in charge of our boat was of the Clan Bacon, who are not readily aroused to marine enthusiasm. Their verdict was that Miss Gleitze was a pebble for gameness. Bob Miller is not given to exaggerating his own or anyone else's activities in the main. He considers the swim a classic performance.

In view of these authoritative opinions the critics should hide their diminished forms. Probably the majority of them could not swim across the Ormeau Baths![46]

Interviewing Mercedes at the Montague Hotel after the swim, the same special correspondent remarked:

Miss Gleitze is not exactly an easy proposition to interview. She does not smoke or join her interlocutor in a drink, and this gives an impression of reserve and reticence. My experience of celebrities is that they never give out the vital stuff until after the third![47]

The North Channel, Attempt Two

Mercedes' next attempt at the North Channel crossing from Lice Point took place on Friday, 30 August 1929. William Brown of Cushendall and Alex Murray of Waterford were in charge of the boat, Maurice Finlay being responsible for the engine.

Mercedes entered the water in the Mull of Kintyre at 9.12 a.m. Progress was satisfactory from the outset as she was able to make good use of the current, and the prospect of reaching the Irish coast appeared to be excellent. It was raining slightly and foggy when she entered the water, but shortly after 10 a.m. the fog closed in and the Irish coast was completely blotted out for the remainder of the day. She continued to swim strongly, but as time went on and the fog became denser it was felt that to continue would be futile. At 3.30 p.m. she was taken out of the water. Her condition after this swim, which had lasted 6 hours 30 minutes, was not as bad as on the previous attempt, and under the administration of Dr Joseph McCambridge of Cushendall she soon recovered physically.

At this stage the steering gear of the boat failed, and it drifted for a considerable distance on the fast tide before things were put right. The weather conditions became so bad that it was deemed advisable to make for Ballycastle Harbour instead of proceeding direct to Cushendall.

The frustration Mercedes must have felt would have been acute, because she was only about 4 miles off Fair Head on the Irish coast when the dense fog forced her to abandon the swim. However, later on the journey from Ballycastle to Cushendall she expressed her determination to make another attempt in September. She was given a great reception in Ballycastle and, as usual, a large crowd of Cushendall folk waited on the quayside to welcome her back, despite this latest failure.

Lough Neagh – Lengthways

After the breadthways swim of Lough Neagh on 12 July 1929, Mercedes travelled to Scotland and completed open-water swims there. During this time she kept in touch with John Murphy at the Massereene Arms Hotel about the proposed lengthways crossing of Lough Neagh and gave him a preliminary date of 27 July. She wrote:

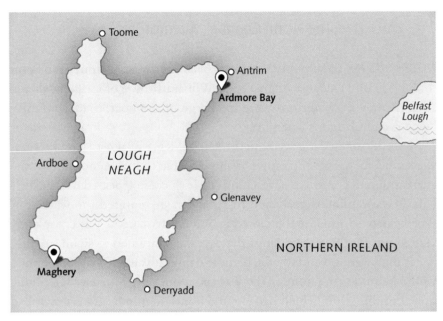

Lough Neagh – Mercedes' longest open-water swim (20 hours 1 minute) in Britain's largest inland body of water. A freshwater lough, but still subject to adverse weather conditions.

I was delighted to note from your letter that you propose form-ing a Committee for this swim. I am looking forward immensely to tackling it and, providing the same kind of records are played to me on the gramophone and the same repertoire is rendered by the same vocalists I had before, I see no reason at all why I should not succeed.

To enable me to spend a restful night before the swim I shall take the 7.30 p.m. Larne boat from Stranraer on the 26th July, and should be ever so grateful if you could kindly meet me on arrival of the ship at Larne on that day, or get a friend to do so if you should be pre-vented. In the meantime I leave all arrangements for my swim in your hands, and feel confident that everything will turn out O.K.

However, in the event, the swim had to be postponed until September. Open-water swims are notoriously difficult to arrange. Weather conditions are ungovernable and can change dramatically in moments without any prior warning. Even today, would-be open-water swimmers have to play the waiting game.

In a letter dated 24 July, Mercedes explains to John Murphy:

The Edinburgh swimming officials who are looking after me here, and who are in charge of my Firth of Forth attempt, have asked me to stay on a little while so as to get a really good chance to accomplish this latter swim. I am sure you don't mind postponing arrangements in connection with my contemplated Lough Neagh lengthways swim. Please explain the position to everyone concerned. I shall be in Antrim at the very latest on the evening of August 4th so as to be in time for the Cushendall Regatta on August 5th, and we could then discuss the new date for the Lough Neagh enterprise.

As promised, Mercedes travelled to Antrim on 3 August and a meeting of the swimming committee was set up at the Massereene Hotel the next day to discuss the question of date and other details of the lengthways swim. As she had already made arrangements for further attempts on the North Channel during the month of August, a date was eventually set for the Lough Neagh swim to take place on Sunday, 8 September. The planned place of departure was from Maghery in County Armagh and the destination was Ardmore Bay in County Antrim. It took Mercedes 20 hours and 1 minute to swim the length of this lough, and it turned out to be her longest open-water swim.[48]

Persevering on the North Channel

On Sunday, 15, and Monday, 16 September respectively, Mercedes made her third and fourth attempts that year at crossing the North Channel – this time starting from Deas Point (*Sron Uamha*) on the southernmost tip of the Kintyre headland. The following article, written by G.B. Newe of Cushendall, who was on board her accompanying vessel, covered both attempts:

A Gallant Failure: Hard luck! There is no other way to describe Miss Gleitze's last attempt on the North Channel. After swimming 11 hours and 20 minutes and covering in that time 40 miles, Miss Gleitze was forced to give up when only 1½ miles from the Irish coast.

Miss Gleitze, who was stopping at Cushendun Hotel, left Red Bay pier on Friday 13th inst. for Cambelltown in order to make an attempt on the channel from Dee's Point on the Mull of Cantyre. Weather conditions remained bad on Saturday 14th, and it was decided to wait over until Sunday morning. Miss Gleitze was a guest of the Royal Hotel, Campbelltown, who made all of us comfortable during our stay.

Sunday, 15th September 1929: At 5 a.m. on Sunday morning we left Campbelltown, reaching Dee's Point about 8.30 a.m. With some difficulty we got ashore and Miss Gleitze entered the water at 9.20 a.m. Conditions were then favourable. After being in the water for two hours a strong gale suddenly sprang up and lashed the waves into fury. It became so bad as to be positively dangerous, and with difficulty Miss Gleitze was taken from the water. This constituted a danger for the occupants of the small boat, which included the writer, but the splendid seamanship of Charles McCambridge and his brother James and John McNeill made things comparatively safe. During the exciting moments the S.S. *Killarney* stood by, for which we are grateful.

We were obliged to make Southend as quickly as possible, where we had to remain the night. Here we were treated well and can never speak too highly of the people of Southend and the obliging coastguards there. The local Town Hall was placed at our disposal and we had the experience of sleeping on the floor for the night.

The experience was rather enjoyable except for our ship's doctor, who was in a bad way owing to not having a shave or pyjamas or change of collar. The hotel at Southend realised his discomfiture and provided him with a razor. Having shaved he proceeded to look for shamrocks, giving it as his opinion that shamrocks grew in Scotland!

Monday, 16th September 1929: In the morning we were treated to ham and eggs – a royal feast. Leaving Southend at 11 o'clock, Miss Gleitze entered the water at 12.50 midday. It was exciting getting on the rocks at Dee's Point owing to the huge swell coming in on the beach. Several times we were wet with spray. When leaving the rocks after Miss Gleitze had taken to the water the doctor almost fell in, but was rescued in good time. Everything went well for hours and we made wonderful progress, Miss Gleitze being in the best of form.

The temperature of the water was 56°F (13.3°C), being four degrees warmer than on the two previous attempts.

About 7.40 p.m. a trawler passed (No. 101), and the motor launch got some fresh water from her to replenish a fast diminishing supply. About 8.25 p.m. Miss Gleitze asked for brandy, which relieved the cold for a time. We were approaching the Irish shore steadily and everyone was in good form. About 11 p.m., however, the swimmer became semi-conscious, and at 12.10 a.m. the doctor decided that she must leave the water. She had been in the sea for eleven hours twenty minutes, having covered a distance of forty miles and being only one and a half miles from Irish land – just below Torr Head.

Medical attention was speedily given, and although in a very exhausted state Miss Gleitze recovered pretty well before we reached Ballycastle harbour. It was necessary to make Ballycastle, as the strong ebb tide prevented us getting round Torr. At Ballycastle we remained anchored until about 7 a.m., as the heavy swell made landing impossible. Miss Gleitze was then conveyed to Cushendun Hotel by motor, where she is recovering rapidly. There was intense excitement in Cushendall and Cushendun, and everyone remained up most of the night to get news of us. It is estimated about 800 had collected at various points to cheer us up. The Rev. J.H. King of Killylea, Captain G. Robinson of Ballycastle, and Captain Harrison, also of Ballycastle, worked hard with the cars all night scouring the coast for news.[49]

Marooned on Sanda Island

During 1928 and 1929, Mercedes had made a total of eight attempts to swim across the North Channel. The failure of her last attempt was made more painful by the fact that she swam to within just 1½ miles of the Irish coastline before the decision was made by her doctor to take her out of the water – but she was not done yet. The longing in her to complete the crossing drove her to organise one last try before the winter set in, and on 25 September 1929 she crossed over by boat with a supporting party, again making for the planned starting point on the Mull of Kintyre. Amongst the group on board was a representative of the *Ballymena Observer* (W. Weir), and the following article, dated

Friday, 4 October 1929, is his first-hand description of what happened to
the party of twelve on the motorboat *Little Mary* that night (the article
refers to her 'fourth attempt' in 1929, but if it had materialised, it would
have been her fifth that year):

Stranded on the Island of Sanda
Thrilling Adventures on Motorboat in the North Channel
Miss Gleitze's Fourth Channel Swim Abandoned

Real thrills are few and far between, but our representative had more
than he bargained for last week when he accompanied a party from
Cushendun to the Mull of Cantyre to witness a Channel swim by
Miss Mercedes Gleitze from Scotland to Ireland.

A party of twelve, which included Miss Gleitze, the skipper of the
motor boat Mr Kennedy from Carnlough, and a dare-devil crew con-
sisting of a pilot and mechanic and the rowers of the boat that was
to accompany the swimmer, set off at 11.10 p.m. on board the motor
boat *Little Mary*, which formerly belonged to the late Dick Wilson.

The conditions were said to be favourable, and certainly the water
was smooth as the motor boat, with the rowing boat in tow, set off
from Cushendun bound for the Mull of Cantyre in the moonlight,
and we felt our importance as we left the shore, cheered by the
Cushendunites. But the feeling of importance disappeared slowly but
sadly as the smooth water began to ruffle and a fresh wind sprang up.
Miss Gleitze was in the forecastle – there was just room for her and
the engine of the boat – and the rest of us were parked together in a
central pit. Waves broke over the little boat's bow and scattered themselves amongst the passengers, and the further we went the bigger
grew the waves, and the more grew the discomfort of the voyag-
ers. It was being realised that there was little likelihood of the swim
taking place, but a vote decided us to go on to the Mull, and gaily we
went along, buffeted about like a cork, with more than an occasional
drenching of spray.

It was said to have been Miss Gleitze's fourth attempt to swim the
North Channel during her stay in Mrs McBride's Hotel, and those in
charge thought they would let her see the difficulties of entering the
water from the Mull during a swell. We were nearing the Mull and

could see the bold outline of its rugged rocks when the motor engine gave out, and we went drifting along. We all realised the danger of drifting on to the rocks, but happily the tide was carrying us to the right, towards Southend, but still too close to the rocky coast to be comfortable. A large passenger steamer aware of our danger stood by in case we signalled for assistance, but the crew aboard our boat knew their business.

Eventually the motor was repaired, and as everyone now felt the impossibility of swimming in such angry waters we turned at 2.30 a.m. in the direction of Cushendun, and now began a battle royal between the waves and the motor boat for supremacy. We were having a really bad time, and the row boat behind with two passengers had a much worse one. If we were getting spray, they were getting waves, and there was always the danger of the bows being smashed in by the heavy seas. Signals of distress from the two men in

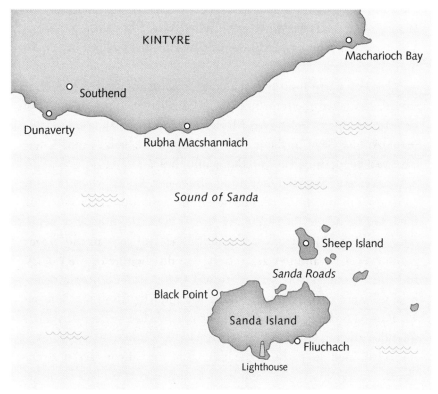

Sanda Island – a refuge from the hostile waters of the North Channel.

the boat had already been made when suddenly our motor ceased just as we were hit by a great wave. On rushed the row boat, and its bows actually ran over the top of the stern of the motor boat, fortunately doing no damage. More motor trouble, and we again began drifting in a very angry sea.

On the outward journey we could see the lighthouses on Rathlin, the Mull, and the Island of Sanda; the latter two are the big peaks we so often see on clear days from the Antrim coast, and there was some little comfort in those lights. But homeward bound, we first lost sight of the Mull, our main guiding light, and when the motor gave up for the second time all the surrounding lights failed us, and for a few moments we felt alone and at the mercy of the waves. Another successful repair job by our Ballycastle mechanic and the motor commenced throbbing again, and in the distance we soon picked up the Sanda Lighthouse. The seas were getting bigger with the wind increasing to gale force, and it was decided to run for shelter to the Island of Sanda. It certainly was a relief to us all to drop anchor at 3.30 a.m. in a calm bay, and how we got into that bay even the pilot himself does not know.

A landing party soon found a comfortable spot, where rugs were spread, and when the remainder of the party arrived we enjoyed our first meal at 4 a.m. from Mrs McBride's hamper, to the accompaniment of 'The Gay Cabaliero', 'Jack is every inch a Sailor', and 'Where have you been, Billy Boy', on the gramophone.

We were on Sanda right enough but none knew whether there were any inhabitants besides those on the lighthouse, which was on the opposite side of the island and the road was too difficult to negotiate in the dark, so exploration parties set out in search of home comforts. A large house was discovered in the sheltered corner of the bay, and two of us were sent off to pay a visit to the homestead, and here we were heartily welcomed by Mr and Mrs Alexander Russell. Mr Russell is the proprietor of the island and runs a sheep farm. It is splendid grazing land, and he says it pays much better than cultivation. He joined the party on the beach, and cordially invited us to the house, where Mrs Russell and her servants very soon had us sitting down to a real hearty breakfast. That was the beginning of a generous kindness that was extended to the party during their stay on the island. Mr and Mrs Russell are Scots, and the very best of the Irish might equal but could not beat them in extending hospitality. Every member of the stranded party must have felt they were intruding, but both Mr and Mrs Russell succeeded in making them part of the household …

Having explored the island, we had to think seriously of the future, and as it was impossible to set off on our homeward journey that day we had to provide supplies. Mr Russell's intention was to take sheep in his yawl to Ayr market, but the stormy weather prevented the trip. He was short of stores for his own use, and decided to set sail for Campbelltown, keeping as close to the coast as possible, and we decided to go along also for stores, leaving Miss Gleitze and two others of our party on the island …

We returned to the island on Friday forenoon after a pleasant trip on a smooth sea and decided to make for Ireland in the afternoon, but when we got in sight of the bay there was no trace of the motor boat; only the row boat remained at anchor. When we got on shore we were told that the two men we had left on the island had set off for home on the motor boat at twelve o'clock. We were in a worse position than ever, with only a row boat to cross the North Channel.

Mr Russell had become very keen on Miss Gleitze's Channel swim, and he had invited her to remain for a few days with them after our return so that he could organise a swim from Scotland and conduct her across. He had an expert knowledge of the currents on the Scottish side, and he had great faith that she would succeed. But with our motor boat gone, a different programme had to be arranged, and the latest idea was for Miss Gleitze to attempt the swim if conditions were favourable, accompanied by Mr Russell's yawl and the Cushendun row boat, and the alternative course was for Mr Russell to bring the party on his yawl to within rowing distance off the Irish coast.

The last night (Friday) spent on Sanda was a wonderful night. Our gramophone was produced and our records used. Mr and Mrs Russell and their son Jim and Uncle Sandy were there. Bob the head man, and Willie the ploughman and his wife, the servant girl, and all our own party. Pat, our cook, made the sandwiches. But the supper would not have been a success without Mrs Russell's assistance – she had to make the tea, and keep us in order. The sailor boys and every one of the Cushendun boys – and there were eight of them – had been around the world as A.P.'s or cooks. They all claimed to have been round it several times, and they talked of China and Japan, India and Africa, just as we would talk of Belfast and Dundalk. Is it any wonder that they could sing sea shanties? And there was one of them, Johnnie something, who had the real way of singing an Irish folk song, and the Ballycastle mechanic had a few good songs too; but at an interval someone produced a melodeon, and it was quietly handed to Willie the ploughboy. The visitors were not going to have it all their own way. He was asked to play 'The Road to the Isles' but he said that 'he didnae ken it'. Then a few notes were whistled and off Willie went with the tune, and tune after tune he gave us. It was a real good evening and night.

The party that accompanied Miss Gleitze from Cushendun on Wednesday night consisted of Hugh Kennedy, Carnlough; James Gault, Ballycastle; Hugh Russell, Belfast; Dan McNeill, Henry McNeill, Thomas Banks, John McNeill, Pat McNeill, Johnnie Hamilton, John Roy Hamilton, all of Cushendun; and W. Weir, *Ballymena Observer*.

A number of daily press reports which discredited the crew have been contradicted. There was no one on board seasick, but three of the party were attacked with something much more serious. When the motor gave up for the first time opposite the Mull the exhaust pipe broke and first Miss Gleitze had to be removed from the cabin violently ill with the fumes from the exhaust, and for more than half an hour she was prostrate. Then another member of the party was attacked with the same malady, but in a milder form, and finally the skipper of the boat, who had been tinkering with the engine, became sick, and it was late in the day before he recovered.[50]

In the event, Mercedes remained on Sanda for three months as a guest of the Russell family. It would have been a healing time for her after the endless battles with the unyielding Irish Sea. She spent long hours in the island's caves, planning and organising future ventures, as well as writing the beginnings of her memoirs.

Biggest Disappointment

Although Mercedes experienced other setbacks in her open-water swimming career, it is apparent from her letters and interviews that her failure to swim across this cold, turbulent stretch of water separating Scotland and Ireland was her biggest disappointment in an otherwise successful and impressive career as a professional long-distance swimmer. In an interview given during a later tour of Australia, she acknowledged, 'The North Channel was my hardest swim – the water there is intensely cold, the temperature being about 48 degrees even on a warm day. I suffered intense pain from the cold for some time, even after I came out of the water.'

However, Mercedes' legacy was to show that the North Channel *could* be crossed by a swimmer. On her final (eighth) attempt, she swam to within 1½ miles of the opposite coast before the tide took her out to sea again, and although she didn't 'touch', she demonstrated that the swim was possible. In so doing, she opened the door for others to follow and succeed where she had failed. In the ninety years since Mercedes challenged this turbulent stretch of water, at the time of writing only nineteen people have achieved solo swims across it compared to the thousands who have swum across the English Channel.

Alex Russell – A Scottish Memory (2012)
The above description by W.J. Weir of the picnic held on the beach in the early hours of 26 September 1929, after the storm-tossed party landed safely on Sanda Island, corresponds with memories recalled in 2012 by Alex Russell. Alex is the grandson of Jane and Alexander Russell, who had originally bought the island in 1920 and raised sheep on it for a living. Angus Martin, editor of *The Kintyre Antiquarian & Natural History Society Magazine*, included Alex's memories in an article he wrote about swimming across the North Channel:

Alex was brought up on Sanda, which his father, Jim Russell, had inherited. He remembers his father telling him of his first encounter with Miss Gleitze and her Irish retinue. When Jim woke up one morning, instead of the sounds of gulls and waves, he was mystified to hear music. When he looked, he saw Mercedes Gleitze and her companions picnicking on the beach to music played on a wind-up gramophone.[51]

Barnacle Bill – An Irish Memory (1932)
In 1932 the Glens of Antrim Historical Society published the following article by the author 'Barnacle Bill', in which he penned his memories of the attempts Mercedes had made to cross the North Channel during the year 1929. This engaging article – like all the Irish press coverage of her swims – is a delight to read:

Channel Swimming and Cushendall
By 'Barnacle Bill'

Cushendall, August 1929. Channel swimming craze. Mercedes Gleitze. Town excited, tremendously. Her smile, you know. Local belles exceedingly jealous. Mothers anxious. Grey-headed veterans not so anxious.

Meet Mercedes. Channel swimmer. Several endurance records. Keen to conquer North Channel. Some job, but she is determined to try. Tries four times. Failure. Plucky. Delirious on three of them. Shipwrecked on Sanda Island on fourth attempt.

Cushendall Annual Regatta. Crowds line beach and rocks. She gives diving exhibition. Tame affair. Big attraction. Big 'gate'.

Still August. A week later, in the morning. Jack Coyles in the Bay with his White Heather. Legge almost deserted. Just a few to see us away. Jolly party. Charlie McCambridge, his brother Paddy, Jim McIlroy, Ed O'Loan, Alec O'Hara, Dr J.P. O'Kane, Frederick Sims, G.B. Newe, a London Pressman.

Tins of sandwiches. Stoves, kettles, cups.

The Mull of Cantire our destination. Grim, lonely, forbidding fastness. Sea-girt. Home of seals and seagulls. Foghorn and lighthouse.

Sea becomes very rough, and we run into Southend. Decent wee place. Comfortable. Wire home for £ s d. Jolly time.

Next morning attempt begins. Mercedes all grease. All smiles, too. Jim McIlroy sings, helped by Eddie O'Loan. Gramophone. 'The Dear Little Shamrock', 'Half Way to Heaven'. Gets broken. Thrown overboard. Half way to bottom by this.

Mercedes swimming strong. Half-hour feeds. Milk – coffee – chocolate. Coffee – milk – chocolate. A sandwich in between. Plucky, yes very.

Londoner fed up. Reads Chesterton. 'The Secret of Father Brown'. Feels rotten. Sims consoles him. Brothers in adversity.

Strong tide. Nine knots an hour. More than Mercedes bargained for. Get out of our course. Should be somewhere off Glenarm. Torr our objective. After sixteen hours Doctor O'Kane takes control. After hours of sailing reach Torr. Rain. Rain. Nothing but rain. And fog. Piles of fog. Thick blankets. Shortage of cigarettes.

Home. 'It's a grand life the sea!' Some ass, doubtless.

Another trip. Meet Maurice Finlay. Tall, thin, good-natured Maurice. His crew, his two sons. His motor boat. More comfortable, handy craft. Solid. Mr W. Brown at the wheel. Decent chap, Brown. Coastguard. Alec. Murray. Stout fella, Alec. Diver by profession. Rest of crew as before, minus Sims. Plus Joe McCambridge. Joe doesn't know the squalls ahead.

Second attempt. Failure. Weather bad. Hard luck.

Third attempt. Meet Maurice again. And happy, hearty Paddy Lynn. Dr. Russell. Dr. Marquess, medico. Not over popular, Marquess. Misses the stateroom. Forgotten his toothpick. Pyjamas. Razor. Only one pair of socks. Rather tragic.

Captain James Spiers in charge. Hard as nails. Expert seaman. Windjammers. Breezy. Popular. Boss. Fears nothing on the sea.

Campbelltown overnight. Fine town. Half filled with Glensmen. And Glenswomen. At home. Marine Hotel for some of us. See the sights. A drink or two. Friday.

Third attempt Saturday morning. Captain Spiers says no. Weather unfavourable. Maybe Sunday.

Sunday it is. Fine morning. Start at daylight from Campbelltown. Mull, about 8.30 a.m. Mercedes enters. 9.30, sudden squall. Seas like mountains. SS Killarney stands by until we are safe. More hard luck. Charlie McCambridge a hero. Plucky fella, Charlie.

Southend for the night. Sleep. On the floor of the Territorial Hall. McIlroy sings. Eddie O'Loan threatens to damage him. Doctor in the hotel. Borrows a razor. Happy.

Monday. Another attempt. Weather good. Events go swimmingly. So does Mercedes. Can that be the Garron? Maybe. Ireland anyway. Swims all day. Good grub on board. Gramophone plays 'Home to our Mountains'. Most suitable.

Evening. Nothing but rolling water. Cold. Mercedes as plucky. Coffee – milk – chocolate. Milk – coffee, chocolate. A coal-boat passes by. We replenish our water supply.

Tired? Rather! Could sleep for a week. Mercedes paddling bravely. Night. Lights on the Irish shore. Cushendun? Possibly Cushendall. Home anyway. So near. And yet so far. Tide about to turn. We urge her to swim hard for half an hour to get out of it. If she does not, then failure again.

Tide turns. She is being carried out to sea again.

Failure! She is exhausted. Poor girl. No doubt about her pluck.

Somehow we reach Ballycastle Bay. Exhausted, all of us. Home to Cushendall.

The postscript reads:

The Editor accepts no responsibility for the staccato memories of Barnacle Bill. But August is the anniversary of the Channel swim. It was said the men-folk of Cushendall neglected all in their frenzied efforts to sail the North Channel and dance attendance on the swimmer. Well, that August is still a memory spoken of with bated breath around Cushendall firesides. Who Barnacle Bill is readers must guess.[52]

11

ENDURANCE SWIMS

During her career, Mercedes carried out a series of endurance swims between 1930 and 1933, raising the British endurance swimming record from 25 hours to 47 hours in the process. These endurance swims were held in corporation pools, or 'ponds', as they were often referred to in those days. She was chasing the women's world record of 54 hours 28 minutes held by an American swimmer, Myrtle Huddlestone, and there is no doubt she could have bettered that time had not family commitments intervened.

The idea of achieving the British record for endurance swimming had already embedded itself in her mind in 1928. In September of that year, while working out her contract with the Blackpool Tower Authority, she organised a swim off the Blackpool coast in an attempt to break the existing record of 25 hours (claimed by Dr Dorothy Logan in a failed attempt on the English Channel), but this attempt in Blackpool had to be abandoned after 14 hours because of a sudden considerable drop in sea temperature. However, in November 1929, during her sojourn on Sanda Island, she wrote to Edinburgh Town Council outlining an innovative plan to break the British record for endurance swimming in an indoor swimming pool and asked if they could accommodate the event in one of their corporation baths. She said that she would not be setting out to create a speed record, but rather 'to demonstrate how the mind can concentrate on the task under-taken and reveal the unquestionable art of conserving strength, hour after hour, resisting all the time Nature's call for a rest by the wayside'.

Edinburgh Town Council agreed to host the event and timed the swim to coincide with a major public holiday in Scotland – Hogmanay. However, apart from a possible new British swimming record being achieved, it was still a risky business venture. There was no precedent to follow, and nobody was sure how many people would be motivated enough to turn out in the middle of a Scottish winter, at all hours, to witness such a swim. Thomas Bunyan, the baths superintendent, had seen with his own eyes the 12,000-strong crowd that had gathered along the Fifeshire coast at the finish of Mercedes' Firth of Forth swim, and he must have convinced the committee that her attempt at the British record, albeit in a small, 26-yard-long local swimming pond, could be a crowd-puller too.

In the event, the media reported that the crowd was the largest ever seen at an aquatic promotion in that city, and a contingent of police had to be sent to take control. Every inch of standing space was occupied, the crowd encroaching on the very edge of the pond. So dense was the throng inside, that movement was almost impossible. An appeal was made on behalf of the crowd outside in the street for those who had witnessed the swim for an hour or two to leave so that others could take their places, but this appeal did not meet with much success.

After witnessing the public response to her initial endurance swim, Mercedes foresaw that she had hit upon a financial winner. The second event, held in Dublin, proved that her groundbreaking swim in Edinburgh was not an accidental success and sporting achievement in any discipline – by women as well as men – could move and inspire people from all walks of life.

Her income from open-water events was sporadic and unpredictable, and after deducting travel and living expenses there was little left in the kitty. She realised that if she could organise a series of endurance swims around the country, increasing the distance slowly but gradually, this would generate a steady income and would boost the amounts she was able to donate to her charity. And so she wrote to fifty municipal corporations all over Britain seeking permission for the use of their pools.

She submitted a basic business plan suggesting that entrance money would be divided equally between the council and herself, the council to be responsible for advertising the event, making food and drink available to her in the water at intervals and finding people of good repute to act as timekeepers and logkeepers. Timekeepers were to do 3-hour shifts (6 hours during the night) and detailed logs of the swims were to be compiled and signed by officials for Mercedes to keep as proof of her swims. She also asked if they could find a retailer who would loan them a gramophone in exchange for advertising value on the promotion leaflets. She guaranteed that she would be responsible for her own health and safety in the water, but she asked if they could secure the voluntary services of any interested nurse or doctor to attend her during the swim.

Five local authorities immediately agreed to host an event: Douglas, Dundee, Hull, Newcastle and Stafford. Dublin and Cork had already booked her, and after positive media coverage of the first swims other corporations followed with offers. Repeat performances were also secured in Leicester, Dublin and Huddersfield. Mercedes did not have a manager or agent to assist her and personally travelled all around the country to negotiate contracts with the relevant local authorities.

Admission charges in Britain and Eire averaged around 1s per adult and 6d for children, but in some poorer areas the entry fee was reduced, especially on day one of the swim. (Later, in New Zealand, Australia and South Africa, the terms were different: Mercedes was paid a set percentage of the gate and had to organise the event herself.)

At all of the endurance swims many thousands of spectators filed through the turnstyles, sometimes staying for many hours to watch her swim. Police regularly had to be called to control the crowds outside waiting their turn. For example, in Derby about 7,000 people paid to witness the swim, and in Huddersfield there were 8,033. In Sheffield, the local media wrote that never before had a swimming audience been roused to such a pitch of excitement as was shown at the Glossop Road Baths when the signal went at 11.16 p.m. indicating that Mercedes had been swimming for 36 hours. Inside, the building was packed almost to suffocation. Outside, several thousands more waited patiently for announcements, causing frequent traffic blocks, and extra police had to be summoned.[53]

In Dundee, journalists reported that scenes unprecedented in the history of swimming in that city were witnessed towards the conclusion of the swim. Nothing like this mammoth crowd had ever before been housed in the building. The seating areas were full to capacity and hundreds sat around the very edge of the pond. Many spectators sacrificed comfort to get a better view by sitting on the top of bathing cubicle doors, while others more daring perched themselves high up on the diving ladder.

Strict precautions had to be taken by the police to prevent accidents, the chief danger being that someone might be pushed into the water. It was, however, a cheery crowd, and they helped Mercedes along with their community singing.

While this was going on inside, there was an equally amazing scene outside. The queue for the 'sixpenny doors after ten o'clock' had begun to form in the late afternoon. As early as four o'clock crowds flocked down to the harbour, many armed with books and food, ready to sit it out. By ten o'clock, queues – several deep – encircled the entire building, and in addition thousands stood along the West Protection Wall and in front of the Unicorn, hoping to gain admittance. Thousands of people – as many as would have filled the building twice over – were disappointed at not gaining admission and clamoured around the main entrance, so that a special squad of police, large as it was, had a hectic time preventing them from gaining access by sheer force of numbers.

About 11.30 an attempt was made to burst open the north-west door of the pool, but the prompt action of the police averted this. About twenty people, however, were successful in reaching the roof of the building, from which vantage point they could look down on the swimmer, while others made a determined attack on a window. Altogether, a total of 8,000 people paid for admission over the two days.[54]

Apart from community singing by the watching spectators and constant music being played on the gramophone, many professional entertainers volunteered to help out at all the events – jazz bands, singers, pianists, choirs and so on. And before retiring for the night, artists performing at local theatres called in and helped to keep everyone amused.

In Newcastle upon Tyne, Florrie Forde, one of the great stars of the early twentieth-century music hall (famous for popularising the song 'The Old Bull and Bush' and many other hit tunes of that genre), was appearing at the local Hippodrome. At 10.45 p.m. Florrie came on poolside with a party of friends to see Mercedes swim and, with the permission of the Hippodrome management, she entertained everyone for 40 minutes with old-time songs. On day two of the swim, Florrie returned for a second visit, delighting everyone by again singing popular songs to the crowds.

At the Wellington event in New Zealand a quartet of Maori singers and dancers came on poolside to entertain her and Mercedes found their refrains and *hakas* (traditional posture dances) most inspiring.

Non-professionals also helped out at events. In Hull a party of local fish bobbers performed a clog dance and sang to her, and in Leicester, to help her through the difficult night-time lethargy, twenty men drew up chairs at the side of the pool and told her stories to keep her awake. When their vocal resources came to an end, the men danced up and down the edge of the pool, and some even brought tins and other noisy instruments into use.

A smoking ban was enforced on day two of the swim in Dublin and the stifling atmosphere that had built up in the Tara Street Baths dramatically improved. Cork followed suit and imposed a smoking ban from the outset.

The water temperature in indoor swimming pools, which was kept at a constant 75°–80°F (23.9–26.7°C), helped Mercedes complete her target because she didn't have to battle against her worst enemy in open waters, the cold. Her recovery time was also quicker after a swim in the warm water of indoor pools than in cold, choppy seas. In those latter conditions it sometimes took 2 hours for her blood circulation to be restored. However, fresh water – which is much more enervating than the sea – has its own drawbacks. It lacks buoyancy, and the intermittent respite she received from the movement of waves in open waters was not present.

Swimming lengths in a small pool involved frequent turns, so she avoided this by swimming in circles parallel with the edge of the pool, sometimes reversing the procedure to counter any danger of giddiness. The test is one of real endurance, as the swimmer is under an obligation not to touch the bottom or the sides of the pool, nor is floating allowed. Even when taking nourishment one must tread water – which Mercedes declared is more tiring than swimming.

The most taxing period in these endurance swims was usually between 2 a.m. and 7 a.m. when she had to overcome a great desire to sleep, and this was always more severe during the second night. The rhythmic movement of breaststroke, together with the warmth in the pool, produced drowsiness. She described it as 'a deadly lethargy'. She knew that if she gave way to sleepiness she might lose her sense of direction and touch one side of the pool, which would disqualify her. Always, however, when the first streams of daylight entered the building, she quickly revived, and swam with renewed vigour. This need for sleep was, of course, also common to open-water swims, but in that environment the turbulence of the waves and weather helped to keep her alert.

She did not find endurance swimming unduly monotonous because she was passionately fond of music, and its provision was critical to the success of all her swims. She used the rhythm, voices and lyrics of songs and hymns to inspire and stimulate her movement in the water, and this helped her to remain conscious and aware of her surroundings when swimming for periods of up to 47 hours. She frequently acknowledged her dependence on the spectators to talk to her and keep her alert and amused with sing-ing and music, especially during the long night hours. On 23 July 1932, Mercedes wrote to the manager of the Gramophone Department in West Street, Durban, who had loaned her a machine and records while in South Africa:

I don't think there is any sports person in the world who appre-ciates the gramophone to the extent that I do. My list of aquatic achievements, I am afraid, would not be half as long were it not for the inspiring influence of the music rendered by the gramophone I invariably have with me.

During all her swims she had a continuous audience, not only to sing to her but to converse with. She felt the sympathy emanating from them, which must have warmed and encouraged her. She said she also spent a lot of time thinking about life, and to help pass the time she signed autographs and sometimes read newspapers while swimming.

In an interview with *The Cape Argus* just before her 46-hour endurance swim in Cape Town's Long Street Baths in 1932, she told them:

People say to me: 'Why do you do it?' and when I tell them that I get a good deal of pleasure out of it they are surprised. I was 10 years of age when I learnt to swim, and in Brighton when father used to swim into the depths I followed him. I could always remain in the water longer than the average girl, and this gave me the necessary confidence to go in for long-distance swimming. I find swimming up and down a pool much harder than sea swimming, for there is the monotony and sleepiness to fight against.

I laugh when I think of the peculiar fancies that I sometimes have during these endurance swims. In New Zealand I had a craving for cray fish, and as none was available in the town they had to go outside to get it. In Christchurch I wanted ice-cream, and in Rotherham mince pies. In most cases, though, I have a longing for fish, and I shall probably have that here in Cape Town.

I don't swim up and down the pool as is commonly imagined, but along the length and width, keeping near the side. I swim the trudgeon stroke, the breast stroke, and the over-arm side stroke, alternating each to break the monotony and to keep the muscles in good working order. And then, by way of a change, I swim the back stroke up and down the centre of the bath. I average 32 strokes each minute, so that in 46 hours I shall have made 88,320 strokes and covered between 50 and 60 miles. While being fed I tread water. The conditions of the swim are that I must keep moving for 46 hours.

My biggest fight will be to keep awake. I don't feel uncomfortable during the swim at all until the second night. It is more a pleasure than anything else. I enjoy the music and the audience. My hard time will be between Friday evening and Saturday morning. But I shall rely on the good spirits of my audience to keep me awake. I usually start to get ravenously hungry on the second day. Sometimes I close my eyes while swimming just to relax for a few minutes. It seems to refresh me. As soon as seven o'clock comes each morning my condition changes and I seem to get back my full energy. However sleepy I may have been feeling, whenever seven o'clock comes along I am wide awake again. I cannot explain it. The last two or three hours of the swim are usually the easiest.

Before and after each of my endurance swims I am examined by a doctor. And on every occasion they have told me that my condition after the swim is exactly as it was at the start.

Mercedes never wore a swimming cap during her endurance swims. The pressure on her head would have been intolerable after a few hours. She didn't cover her body with the grease used in sea swims. Instead, she rubbed Vaseline on her hands and occasionally wound bandages around them. She also rubbed Vaseline or olive oil on her feet to reduce soreness and applied soothing drops in her eyes to counteract the effects of chlorine.

Although the media invariably reported that she was in a state of collapse after every endurance swim and had to be lifted out of the water, this 'collapse' was due to the fact that the muscles in her legs couldn't support her after being in the water for so long. She explained to the journalist 'Crawl' from the *Derby Telegraph* just before her endurance swim in that city, 'I feel well while I am swimming around, but when I attempt to climb out, then I find myself in a helpless state. I am like a child.'

Because water is so much denser than air, at the end of an endurance swim Mercedes experienced a loss of balance and a lack of sensation touching solid objects when moving from one environment to the other. Also, because of the constant friction of her costume against her skin over such a long period of time, she couldn't bear anyone touching her. At the end of each endurance swim her costume had to be cut off. This method of undressing was found to be the one least likely to cause her further pain. She said that after a long immersion in water the only thing that worried her slightly was the tenderness of her skin. However, this skin sensitivity disappeared after resting in a warm bed, and her leg muscles soon returned to their normal healthy state – as did her hands and feet, which had become ghost-like in colour during the long immersion in water. A good sleep, a massage and a rest day after each endurance swim was all she needed to recover from these trials.

Her mainly liquid nourishment during the swim seemed to sustain her, although as the swims increased in length, solid food was added to her diet. She was fed honey, Bovril, Ovaltine, chicken broth, glucose, hot milk, fruit drops, coffee and tea during the swims. Modern-day long-distance swimmers know the value of a high carbohydrate diet, whereas Mercedes used glucose and protein to produce the energy for her feats of endurance. In particular, she had tremendous faith in honey as an energy-giving food. It is reported in more than one newspaper that she always had a second breakfast the morning after the swim, and also needed to satisfy a very strong craving for lemonade, but later on in the day her food and liquid intake returned to normal.

The fact that she carried out these endurance swims with sometimes only a few days rest in between is further proof that the human body is capable of so much more than it is credited with. However, when someone attempts to push boundaries they will invariably meet with some opposition. When applying to Leeds Corporation for permission to perform an endurance swim in that city, the incumbent baths superintendent refused to accommodate her. But Mercedes didn't give up. She wrote to Tom Bunyan, the baths superintendent in Edinburgh, and asked him to support her application. She informed Tom that Mr Burgess, his counterpart in Leeds, 'seemed to be obsessed by the idea that my endurance swims are injurious to my well-being and that I have to suffer too much'. Mercedes asked Tom to:

> … help me cure his mind by writing him a letter telling him that you gave me massage treatment prior to my Firth of Forth swim, and for ten days prior to my 26 hours' endurance swim in Edinburgh, and that in your opinion my muscles are so well trained for long-distance swimming, and my general physique so well adapted for long-distance work, that it is almost as easy for me to swim continuously for 30 hours as it is for the average person to walk continuously for half an hour.

She suggested that he quote her back-to-back swims in Leicester and Sheffield, and Stafford and Liverpool, as evidence. However, although Tom wrote a very strong letter in an attempt to convert his opposite number in Leeds, he was unsuccessful.

In all, Mercedes carried out twenty-seven endurance swims at venues in Britain and Eire, as well as in New Zealand, Australia and South Africa. The local authorities and Mercedes both benefitted financially from the events and it was mainly because of the income from these endurance swims that she was able to build up her trust fund. Regrettably, however, although she held the British record for endurance swimming, family commitments eventually prevented her from achieving the world record she desired.

12

AROUND THE ISLE OF MAN

The year 1930 was an eventful one for Mercedes. It was the year in which she was able to substantially add to her charitable trust fund by introducing a new type of event (endurance swims) into her schedule, while at the same time continuing to fulfil her passion for sea swimming. It was also the year in which she married. But first there was the Isle of Man.

The Isle of Man (known in Manx as *Ellan Vannin*) is a self-governing British Crown dependency in the northern Irish Sea, almost equi-distant from England, Northern Ireland, Scotland and Wales. It is 32 miles long and 14 miles across at its widest point. The estimated distance that Mercedes would actually have to swim was approximately 100 miles, over a course well known to be a trial for any swimmer. This swim turned out to be a great success, and no doubt helped her get over the disappointment of her chilling Moray Firth experience. Details of the Moray Firth swim can be found in Appendix 4 on page 264.

In early June 1930 Mercedes journeyed to Douglas, and over Monday and Tuesday, 9 and 10 June 1930, she 'warmed up' for the event by successfully completing a further endurance swim in the Henry Bloom Noble Public Baths, raising the British record to 37 hours. And on Friday of that same week (13 June), she set out on her next battle with her old adversary, the sea.

The Manx people had responded enthusiastically to her planned swim around their island, and in no time at all a support group had been formed. William Cunningham of Carrick, Lewaigne, generously placed his yacht

Talofa Too at her disposal, and this craft, with a rowing boat hitched to its stern, served as the pilot boat. T. Lee (coxswain of the Douglas lifeboat) was the pilot, aided by his son, W. Lee, and the official observers were T.A. Quayle, W.T. Quayle, T.W. Drennan, E. Corlett, W. Grice, G. Kelly, W. Thompson and J.O. Smith. A representative from the *Isle of Man Examiner* acted as timekeeper on board, and he also compiled a daily log of the swim.

In the event, Mercedes took nine days to swim around *Ellan Vannin*, completing 56 hours of actual swimming time. Her course started and finished at Douglas Bay, and the planned stages en route were: Ramsay, Point of Ayre, Rue Point, Kirk Michael, Contrary Head, Port Erin, Kitterland and Langness. At the end of each stage of the swim, the island's traditional anthem was sung to Mercedes by the welcoming crowds.

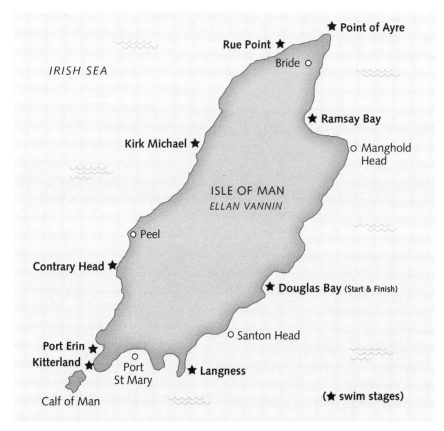

Another innovative marathon swim in set stages, this time around the Isle of Man.

At the presentation ceremony after the completion of the swim, E. Corlett, one of the official observers, spoke about the heavy weather she had come up against throughout the swim. He said that when Mercedes arrived at Ramsey at the end of the first leg she had been buffeted so much by the seas that she could hardly see out of one eye; on her way through the Sound, and especially on the stage to Peel, she had to struggle for hours against the tides, which were constantly against her; and on the last leg from Langness to Douglas, Corlett said the seas were so heavy that had anything happened she could not possibly have been taken out of the water to safety.[55]

13

AFFAIRS OF THE HEART

In 1926, a 'romance by letter' began between Mercedes and a young soldier, Private William Farrance of the East Lancashire Regiment, when he was stationed in Quetta, India (now part of Pakistan). William saw a photograph of Mercedes in an Indian newspaper and wrote to her.

It wasn't unusual for Mercedes to keep up a correspondence with some of her fans but, in this case, she must have felt there was something special about William, and she responded in kind. In the event, at some time during their exchange of letters, which took place over a period of two years, William proposed and Mercedes accepted, although they had yet to meet in person. The letters between them are not in the archives, but the story was picked up and reported widely by the media because of its human interest.

In November 1928, William's regiment returned to England, and he hurried to Blackpool to present himself to her. However, he was met with the news that Mercedes had left Blackpool for Ireland to make another attempt on the North Channel, and so William travelled to London to await her return. They eventually met on the steps of Westminster Cathedral and talked for the first time while strolling through Green Park. This initial meeting lasted about half an hour, at the end of which they made arrangements to meet again. The second meeting, however, turned out to be the final one, because shortly afterwards Mercedes asked William to release her from the engagement.

In response to questions from the press, she said that although he was an exceedingly nice man, she did not now consider herself fit to be the wife of any man on account of her passionate love of the sea. She explained:

> When I consented to marry him two years ago I did so because I thought I had as much right as any other girl to become a wife, and perhaps a mother, but now I find that the call of the sea is too great. I shall never be able to settle down as a wife until I have successfully swum the Irish Channel, the Wash and the Hellespont.

She added that she could see no point in 'letting a man make a home for me when, in my thoughts, the sea spells "home, sweet home"'.

Betrothal and Marriage

However, Mercedes' resolve to marry a second suitor was made in 1930. This 'whirlwind romance' was, if anything, even more avant-garde than her previous 'correspondence romance', and her decision to say 'no' to the first and 'yes' to the second was wholly influenced by the hunger within her to swim across uncharted waters and to realise her dream of funding a charity to help people living in poverty.

Her future husband was a Dublin-born man called Patrick Carey. He first saw her when she was featured in the *Pathé Pictorial News* at a cinema in Coventry, but he didn't see her in person until February 1930 when he went to the Tara Street Baths in Dublin to watch her perform a 28-hour endurance swim. He then travelled to Stafford Corporation pond to watch her carry out another endurance swim on 3 and 4 July, where he was one of a party on night watch.

Although he made several attempts to get into conversation with her, she didn't respond to him until seven o'clock in the morning. During the final hour of the swim, he asked her if he could have a rose out of the numerous bouquets she had been given and was delighted when she said he could. At the end of the endurance swim, Mercedes was taken straight to her hotel to recuperate, and the following morning he discovered that she had caught the 5 a.m. train to Liverpool for another event due to take place that same day. So Patrick followed her to Parkgate Swimming Pond in Neston, near Liverpool, where she was under contract to perform a 9-hour exhibition swim, and it was here, on 5 July, that they had their first proper conversation from the side of the open-air pond. However, it lasted only 2 or 3 minutes.

A few days later, on 10 July, when Mercedes arrived at Barry in South Wales to prepare for her attempt on the Bristol Channel, Patrick was waiting at the station to greet her. This was the first time he had seen her as an ordinary citizen, and not swimming around in water. He told her that he had not known which train she would be arriving on, so he had spent the evening meeting all the trains until she finally arrived on the last one.

Three days later, on 13 July, while waiting for the right conditions for her Bristol Channel attempt, they met on the beach in Barry, where he proposed to her. She told him she would let him have an answer the same evening, and when they met again at seven o'clock she consented to marry him.

When explaining her decision in a letter to a friend, she said:

I have a great admiration for Irish qualities and the Irish character, and he has inspired me with the confidence that he will prove an ideal life's companion – and, far from hindering me in my career, to which I am passionately devoted, he will help me on with it and encourage me to his utmost ability both in the practical and spiritual sense.

When reporting on her forthcoming marriage, the *Belfast Telegraph* (2 August 1930) asked Mercedes about her professed high regard for Irish people. She explained that during her extended visits over the past few years to Northern Ireland and Eire she had cemented numerous friendships, which she now cherished.

When interviewed by a journalist from the *Dover Standard* (12 August 1930) about the engagement she said, 'I accepted him because he has given me his promise that he will not in any way interfere with my swimming career.' Mercedes also extracted a promise from her future husband that she could continue to swim under her maiden name. This fact alone demonstrates that, at least while she was financially independent, Mercedes was able to retain her own identity and not be forced to conform to the existing stereotypes of women of that era. In Britain, certain categories of women had been given the vote a mere 4 years earlier, and this was still quite a radical demand for a woman to make.

On 8 August 1930, just one month after their first conversation together, Mercedes and Patrick were married at St Paul's Roman Catholic Church in Maison Dieu Road, Dover, with the Reverend Canon G.W. Grady officiating in the presence of a large congregation. The two chief bridesmaids were Bernice and Phyllis Zeitenfeld from New York (better known as the Channel Twins), who were in Dover training for an attempt on the English Channel. The little attendant was 6-year-old Patricia, daughter of Captain Tennyson Scott, the best man. Captain Scott (a friend of the groom's) acted in a dual role, as he also gave the bride away. Of note, there were no members of either the bride or the groom's family present at the wedding ceremony. This was perhaps due to the haste with which this unconventional wedding had been arranged.

As they left the church, they were faced with a battery of cameras and microphones, and a large crowd of well-wishers. They made their way by car to Admiralty Pier to catch the 1.15 p.m. boat for Calais. When the wedding party arrived at the Marine Station, Mercedes placed her wedding bouquet at the base of the memorial to the men of the South Eastern & Chatham Railway who had fallen during the First World War. The journey from the church to the docks had been so rushed that she did not have time to change out of her wedding dress and had to do this on board ship, instead of at the Grand Hotel in Dover where she had been staying.

They eventually set sail on the *Maid of Kent* en route for Constantinople. This was not to be their honeymoon. Before knowing she was going to be wed, Mercedes had put in place all the arrangements in connection with a proposed swim across the Hellespont, and the wedding ceremony was quickly slotted in so that her new husband could accompany her. They planned a belated honeymoon in the Sahara, away (temporarily) from water.

Although married to a Dubliner, Mercedes was not partisan about the political struggles in Ireland and in 1932, while in South Africa, she wrote in a letter to Jim Hughes, CID Dublin Castle:

Patrick and I have not forgotten you, and we both hope you are well and are not having too anxious a time over the present state of political affairs in Ireland.

We get all the news of happenings in Ireland out here, and it is my sincere wish that the current differences between the Irish and English Governments will be settled peacefully and amicably.

14

THE HELLESPONT

The Hellespont (the Dardanelles) is a long, narrow strait connecting the Aegean Sea to the Sea of Marmara, and it divides the Balkans in Europe from Asia Minor along the Gallipoli Peninsula. The narrow, winding shape of the strait is similar to that of a river. It is 38 miles long, approximately 3.7 miles across at its widest point and has a maximum depth of 338ft. Water flows in both directions from the Sea of Marmara to the Aegean via a surface current, and in the opposite direction via an undercurrent. The currents produced by the tidal action in the Black Sea and the Sea of Marmara are such that ships under sail must await at anchorage for the right conditions before entering the Dardanelles.

The poet Lord Byron, who also had a passion for open-water swimming, famously swam the Hellespont on 3 May 1810, and he is recorded as saying he was more proud of this one achievement than all of his poetry combined. Mercedes was the first woman to tackle the Hellespont at its widest point where the current is strongest, and also to complete the double (there and back).

With her trip to Turkey in mind, Mercedes first contacted a friend, Gilbert A. Flamant, who had spent some time in that country. He wrote to her on 9 July 1930:

During our very interesting talk while you were swimming at Stafford I promised you an address where you could get in touch with any English people in Gallipoli, and also I said I would give you a memento to my Gallipoli visit, well here are both: The Secretary, St Barnabas Pilgrimages, 7 Hobart Place, London SW1. I am certain these people will be helpful to you. The enclosed buckle is only of sentimental value and I send it as a mascot, hoping it will bring you good luck. I came across a wounded Turk during the Gallipoli Campaign in 1915 and gave him some water and a cigarette. He was so grateful that he gave me the enclosed, the only thing of value (as he thought) that he possessed. When you go to swim the Hellespont, take this with you and perhaps it will bring you good luck.

In a reply to her response to this letter, Gilbert commented:

I am glad you received my little war souvenir safely. It seems strange that it should go back to Gallipoli. As you say, perhaps it will bring you good luck. In looking up some information about the Hellespont I find that Byron accomplished the swim without the inducement of a beautiful girl to greet him on the other side!

In the meantime, Mercedes had also written the following letter to the Secretary of St Barnabas Pilgrimages:

On the 8th August I shall be going to Gallipoli via Constantinople. The purpose of my visit will be to make an attempt to swim across the Hellespont. Some friends of mine who are anxious that I should not go to a foreign country without being equipped with some useful advice from some authorities acquainted with local conditions, have given me your name and address as a likely source of information.

If you could let me have the name and address of some British authorities stationed in Gallipoli or somewhere on the shores of the Hellespont, providing of course there is a British Depot in that part of the world to which I could turn in case of need, I should be very grateful.

The secretary responded:

I think if you got into touch with Mr Whittal at Chanak he would be best able to help you over there. He is the representative at Chanak of

Messes. Walter & Gilchrist, Shippers, Constantinople, from whom you will be able to obtain Mr Whittal's address. I hope all will go well with you and that you will be successful in accomplishing your aim. I think the only British people on Gallipoli are the men of the Imperial War Graves Commission.

And so, on 8 August 1930, immediately after their marriage ceremony in Dover, she and Patrick set sail for north-west Turkey for her planned swim across the Hellespont.

There has always been a positive response from people to sporting achievement, whatever the discipline, and Mercedes found this wherever she travelled. Just eight days after leaving England, she had gathered a support group around her, which included the Governor and the Mayor of Chanuk, to help organise the swim. She decided to attempt the crossing both ways, but on separate days.

Europe to Asia

On 16 August 1930, Mercedes completed the crossing from Tenker to Kum-Kale in 2 hours 55 minutes. The water temperature was a comfortable and constant 60°F (15.6°C) throughout the swim. The following report covering the swim was written by one of the witnesses, Ruth Millington:

A chilly dawn, with the north wind chasing the smoke-like clouds across a grey-blue sky, a ruffled sea, that wonderful crispness in the air which put fresh life into our veins, this was the morning that greeted us as we all assembled on Customs Pier at Chanak to act as witnesses to Miss Gleitze's Hellespont swim from Tenker to Kum-Kale.

At 8.00 a.m. punctual we left Chanak by local motor boat, our party including the Mayor of Chanak, the Governor's daughter, two members of the Municipal Police Force, Mr Carey (the husband of Miss Gleitze), Halil Ekrem, and several other Turkish friends – in all 15 witnesses. Mr & Mrs Carey, myself and small son were the only English aboard.

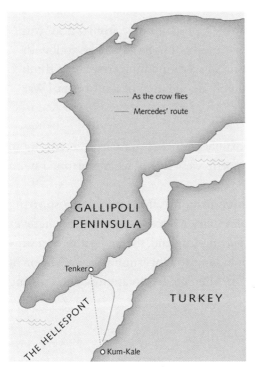

There and back across the Hellespont
– an easier swim than predicted.

We headed for Tenker on the Peninsula, arriving there at 9 a.m. Here the seas were somewhat choppy, and for a while Miss Geitze surveyed the foam-crested waves and the seas rather dubiously, strong currents travelling at the rate of four knots, but we assured her that all would be well and she entered the water at 9.10 a.m. At this point a motor launch with the Governor of Chanak, his wife and other minor officials joined us.

The fair swimmer was now battling with the strong currents and seemed to make little headway, but having once overcome these the seas appeared to be less treacherous and Miss Gleitze called for music and some refreshment, which was given at intervals.

We were now half way across the Dardanelles, having covered a distance of 3½ miles, Miss Gleitze still making splendid head-way, her courage never once deserting her. Steadily she scudded through the waves until within half a mile of the shore where she encountered a powerful current and abandoned the breaststroke for the trudgen, putting forth all her energy into the final struggle for the shore.

The sun was now beating down mercilessly upon us, the wind stirring up the sea in a very boisterous manner. We were tossed this way and that until eventually our boat made one terrific plunge, the sea by way of counter-attack slapping our faces, but this did not quell our enthusiasm.

Exactly at 12.05 p.m. Miss Gleitze set foot on the shores of Kum-Kale on the Asiatic side to the cheers of us all, looking wonderfully fresh and fit, certainly not as one who had expended all her energy on a 7 miles swim across the Hellespont at its widest part in 2 hours 55 minutes.

Once again in the motor launch we immediately headed for Chanak, congratulations being extended and refreshment freely indulged in. We were now a merry party indeed and, after a little sing-song, finished up with the English and Turkish National Anthems.

When we arrived back at Chanak at 2 p.m. I glanced at Miss Gleitze to see if she was showing any sign of fatigue, but not one trace could I find, only the happy smile of one who had achieved what she had set out to do – to swim the Hellespont.

Asia to Europe

On 23 August 1930, Mercedes successfully completed the return crossing of the Hellespont, this time from Halil Pash (Asia Minor) to Ak-Bash (Europe) in a time of 3 hours 5 minutes. During the course of the swim, four vessels passed by in the vicinity and the swim was witnessed by fifteen people, who subsequently signed the affidavit.

The following is a literal transcription of a report written by H. Ekrem, who acted as an official witness in the rowing boat:

Canakkale, 23rd August 1930

After a few days our luck changed for the better, with the sky slightly cloudy, the sea – which would soon embrace the swimmer – still and calm.

Miss Gleitze for the second time, without informing anyone of her inner thoughts, will – like in the lovers' tales of Leander – be swimming in the white froth of the sea.

The swim will start at 10.30 a.m. The official witnesses – Miss Gleitze's husband, Mrs Millington and myself – boarded a motor boat and after a sea journey of one and a half hours we reached the starting point of the swim at Halit Pasa farm, a place on the Anatolian coast.

The lady swimmer's husband and myself disembarked from the motor boat. The swimmer was covered in protective oil, and photographs and cine camera were used to record the moment as at 12.35 she entered the sea.

Everyone's eyes were affixed to her, observing every move she made. The tranquillity of the sea was broken, with waves attacking Miss Gleitze as she swam, but her eyes showed determination that nothing will frighten her off from her task. Myself and Mr Carey (Miss Gleitze's husband) in a guide boat and all other dignitaries in another motor boat, took the route, and the swimmer followed us, not showing any signs of fatigue, always smiling and going forward. The swimmer's husband was passing food and liquid refreshments to her and was singing her songs. Miss Gleitze's favourite song was 'Sonya' and after every two songs it was repeated to her.

Finally at exactly 3.38 p.m. the swimmer reached the opposite shore, Ah-Basa. Everyone was applauding and congratulating her, for she had swam a distance of eight miles in three hours and five minutes without showing any sign of fatigue or distress. Photographs and cine film was taken to record the moment.

I can confirm that Miss Gleitze successfully, for the second time, swam the Canakkale Strait.

Witnesses (for Municipal Police): H. Ekrem [signature]: Mehmet Behcet [signature]

Mercedes related later in an interview with *The Outspan*, while touring South Africa:

Swimming the Hellespont was easier than I had been led to expect. I crossed from Europe to Asia Minor and again the other way. The place where I landed on the first occasion was seething with malaria fever and almost everyone was down with it.

15

SEA OF MARMARA

This 10-mile swim was accomplished on 3 September 1930 in a time of 7 hours 20 minutes. The starting point was Doğan-Arslan, and the destination Alpata.

When Mercedes arrived in Gallipoli to tackle the Sea of Marmara, she discovered she had inadvertently mislaid her only swimming costume.

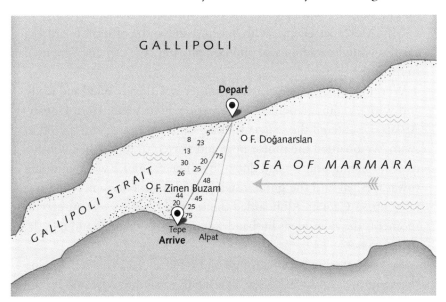

The Sea of Marmara – swum in an unconventional costume – a frock!

Unfortunately, she was unable to procure a replacement anywhere in the province. The women there were amazed when she described the garment, because they were never seen in such scanty clothing. She was, however, determined to do the swim, and the only thing left for her to do was to swim in her outer clothing. This she did, and during the 7 hours she was in the water she had no difficulty with her frock. All that she discarded for the swim were her shoes and stockings.

Mercedes recalled, 'At one spot in the Sea of Marmara the current was so strong that I swam strongly for an hour at one time without making any headway. Then I suddenly shot out of the current and crossed in just over seven hours.'

A report of the Marmara Sea swim translated (literally) from the Turkish language reads:

After the success at Canakkale Miss Mercedes Gleitze most famous and admired swimmer decided to swim the Marmara Sea.

This historical sea will again accommodate this courageous swimmer.

Yesterday we spent the day making preparations and today at 8 am, with all the officials and dignitaries, boarded a motor boat at Gelibolu.

The sea calm and blue with a soft breeze, we arrived at our destination at Dogan-Arslan, passing the rock and bell point at 10.15 am.

Miss Mercedes Gleitze with her husband and 2 officials boarded a small rowing boat, the usual photographs and cine camera were used to mark the event.

When we set foot ashore the swimmer was already oiled and ready, and with encouragement from everyone at 10.50 am from Dogan-Arslan she entered the sea via walking on a sandy area and started to swim. We boarded the motor boat and started to follow her, but due to gear malfunction we had difficulties. The swimmer was swimming towards Alpat and the guide rowing boat man, Huseyin, could not keep up, so Captain Ali boarded the rowing boat to assist. At certain moments the swimmer's husband was giving food and liquid refreshments to her.

At 14:00 the sea became rough and wind speed increased, forcing the swimmer towards Bogaz. The boats were duly affected by the adverse conditions.

The swimmer had been in the sea for 5.30 hours; her commitment and bravery increased my admiration of her.

After 7 hours 20 minutes in the sea, at 18:10, in the fishing port area of Alpatin, she came ashore. Photographs and cine film were taken to record the event. She momentarily fainted. Myself and 2 other officials massaged her and placed a fur coat on her to keep her warm.

We got her to a hotel in Gelibolu and got her hot tea to drink, and after 5–10 minutes she recovered, to be congratulated by the French Consulate official, M. Aleko, and duly by all of us.

After this great achievement from the swimmer I retired from her presence on 3rd of September 1930.
Gelibolu official: Bahactin [signature]

We confirm the feat on the 3rd of September 1930
The swimmer swam 10 miles from Doğanarslan to Alpata in the time of 7 hours 20 minutes across the Marmara Sea.

With our signatures we can confirm that Miss Mercedes Gleitze swam with her own physical capabilities and with only guide boats for assistance.

Witnesses in rowing boat:
Boatman: Captan Ali Osman ef [signature]
Boatman: Huseyin ef [signature]
Swimmer's husband: Patrick Carey [signature]

Witnesses in motor boat:
Port Official: Yakup Bey [signature]
Commisioner Assistant: Veysen Bey [signature]
Military Police: Hayder Bey [signature]
Military Police: Ibrahim Bey [signature]
Doctor: Fahri Bey [signature]
Muallim: Munire Hanin [signature]
Teacher: Arif Bey [signature]
Teacher: Ahmet Bey [signature]
Fabrikator: Hakki Bey [signature]

Logistic Manager: Ibrahim Bey [signature]
Polis: Ali Efadi [signature]
Mustentik: Mustafa Bey [signature]
Chemist: Marko Bey [signature]
Doctor: Behattin Bey [signature]
For the municipal stamp: K. Huseyin [signature]

16

NEW ZEALAND AND AUSTRALIAN TOURS

In September 1930, on their return to England from Gallipoli, Mercedes and her husband settled down temporarily in rented accommodation in the city of Leicester, where Mercedes had made friends on previous visits. During the months of September, October and November of that year she carried out five more endurance swims in Leicester, Dundee, Hull, Newcastle and Dublin, increasing her record to 42 hours.

It was a sign of the 'Britishness' in Mercedes that when she visited far-off lands she chose to tour the colonial countries of that era: New Zealand, Australia and the Union of South Africa – countries united by a common allegiance to the Crown. And at the end of November 1930, she and her husband set sail in SS *Corinthic* for the distant shores of Wellington, New Zealand. Mercedes had, in fact, made initial enquiries as far back as November 1928 about a visit to New Zealand, and the High Commissioner in London had then written her a letter of introduction to the General Manager of the Tourist and Health Resorts Department in Wellington. However, the trip didn't come to fruition for two years due to her busy schedule.

Although she had arranged this journey with the express purpose of tackling the Cook Strait, Mercedes had no illusions about her objective. She knew that the currents were almost as complicated as those in the Strait of Gibraltar, and the temperature of the water was almost as low as in the Irish Channel. She commented during a press interview, 'These long-distance sea swims are not altogether a pleasure. I feel the cold just as much as the average person, and sometimes more. There is no way of overcoming it, either – that's the worst of it. It's just a question of having the courage to stick to it.'[56]

The *Corinthic* docked at Wellington on 15 December 1930, and after bidding farewell to speedway stars 'Squib' Burton, Norman Evans and George Greenwood, whose company they had enjoyed on the long sea journey, Mercedes and Patrick sought and found suitable accommodation in the city. Mercedes then took initial steps to arrange a programme of swims to perform while in New Zealand.

During her spare time, she wrote a diary covering her time in Wellington. This is reproduced in Appendix 3 and gives a first-hand account of how someone with the unusual title of 'professional long-distance swimmer' went about furthering her career in new territory across the other side of the globe. She arranged to have the diary printed and put on sale to help finance her expedition. In it, she describes her hopes and fears, and tries to give an insight into the trials and tribulations of long-distance swimming. It highlights, in particular, the way the media are so responsive to sportsmen and women and go out of their way to help them organise events. Mercedes experienced this in whatever country she happened to be.

Wellington Harbour

The first swim in New Zealand took place on Christmas Day, 1930. It was across Wellington Harbour, which had never before been swum by a woman. The distance, as the crow flies, was 7 miles from Ferry Wharf to Days Bay, and Mercedes completed the crossing in 7 hours 3 minutes. The temperature of the water was a comfortable 61–62°F (16.1–16.7°C).

J. McNie (Wellington Centre of the New Zealand Swimming Association) and C. Thomas (Lyall Bay Surf Club) were official representatives of swimming interests on board the official launch, and John Tait accompanied her as her pilot. Mercedes recalled at a later interview with *The Outspan*:

A very happy swim. It took seven hours. I was accompanied by a boat-load of Italian fishermen who sang and played the guitar to me all the way over. The singing and the ukuleles of those on board made the hours fly by. It was a delightful way of swimming a long distance.[57]

Rangitoto Island to Cheltenham on the New Zealand Mainland

In between her two endurance swims in Auckland and Christchurch (see Appendix 2), Mercedes carried out an open-water swim on Wednesday, 21 January 1931 from Rangitoto Island to Cheltenham Beach – a distance of 4 miles – on a course never before attempted. During the crossing, which took 1 hour 30 minutes, Mercedes had to swim through a tropical thunderstorm. In a reception speech after the swim, she recalled:

> My swim from Rangitoto Island yesterday constituted a very easy task, in spite of the fact that I had no help from any current – having to swim across current all the time. I had plenty of water around me and above, and the crew of my rowing boat – thanks to the deluge from the sky – had a swimming pond of their own.

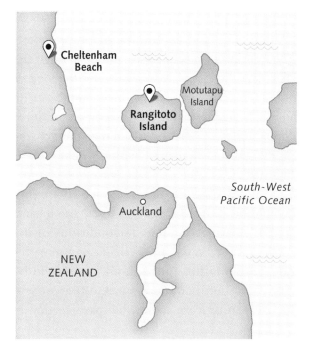

A comparatively short but 'very wet' swim through a tropical thunderstorm.

And in a later interview with *The Outspan*, she reminisced:

> When I swam from the island to the mainland, tropical showers fell all the time until the people in the boats were almost swimming also. When I got to the mainland I was amused to see that hundreds of people had waded into the water down the gently sloping beach to meet me. Although they were soaked to the knees, most of them held umbrellas over their heads to keep the rain off.[58]

Manly International Swimming Marathon, Sydney, Australia

During her stay in New Zealand, Mercedes received an invitation to enter the Manly Endurance Swim, which was to take place in the Manly Open-Air Baths in Sydney over the period of 24 January to 1 February 1931. She accepted the challenge and interrupted her schedule of swims in New Zealand to travel to Sydney, staying at the Wentworth Hotel in Lang Street. The timing was fortunate, because the New Zealand house in which she and her husband had been staying collapsed in an earthquake shortly after they left.

This was the first competition of its kind in Australia, and its promoters were offering a total of £500 in prize money, to be shared out amongst the six competitors (male or female) who stayed in the water for the longest time. Entries included contestants from New South Wales, South Africa, Italy, the USA and England, and Mercedes' name was used on promotional leaflets, along with Lily Copplestones, the New Zealand marathon champion. The arrangement was that the Gentlemen's Division would go first, followed by the Ladies' Division.

This event in Manly was not a true test of endurance swimming because the competitors would be allowed to stay afloat by any means: swimming, treading water or floating. Under the conditions of the competition, once they entered the water, they 'shall not thereafter during the entire endurance swim either touch, hold, or be held by anyone or anything whatsoever, and that any infraction thereof will immediately disqualify the competitor from any further participation in the swim'.

There were sixty contestants, so the event had to be staged over several days. A maximum of five swimmers would be allowed in the water at any one time, and as each competitor withdrew, he or she would be replaced by another competitor.

Mercedes wore a veil over her face as protection against sunburn in the open-air baths, and to help pass the time in the water she sometimes read newspapers and signed autographs. The endurance swim, especially in the concluding stages, attracted very large crowds. The spectators encouraged the swimmers with community singing, and during the final hours of the competition the police had to intervene twice in order to control the throng.

Mercedes won the marathon by staying unsupported in the water longer than any other competitor and was awarded the first prize of £300. Of note, the first three winners were all women, beating the times registered by the male competitors. The times in order of the six finalists were:

1st	Mercedes Gleitze	(England)	48 hrs 13½ mins
2nd	Katerina Nehua	(New Zealand)	47 hrs 56½ mins
3rd	Lily Copplestones	(New Zealand)	40 hrs 7½ mins
4th	Frank Roberts	(New South Wales)	38 hrs 35 mins
5th	Roy Henderson	(New South Wales)	38 hrs 10½ mins
6th	W. (Billy) Morris	(New South Wales)	35 hrs 36 mins

All six finalists appeared at the Empire Theatre on 5 February to receive their cheques from the Mayor of Manly.

The Advertiser, on 3 February 1931, pointed out the difference in temperament of the two sexes:

The men completed their ordeal first. As the hours dragged by and the water chilled their limbs, several became testy and liverish, thrusting biting remarks at their rivals. The women, however, were cheery and companionable. They gossiped, talked shopping and scandal, discussed the films, read the newspapers, and indulged in community singing.

When interviewed at the end of the swim, Mercedes told reporters that she stopped shortly after she knew she had completed the winning time, but that she felt so fit she could have stayed in for many more hours. She compared the competition with her recent 43-hour endurance swim at

Auckland, during which she had to swim all the time, 'which is much harder than swimming or floating as one pleases, which was the case at Manly'. At the latter competition, she had absolute control and for that reason was able to rest on the water without exerting a single muscle. She explained:

> It is a more complete rest than sitting in an armchair. One is in a complete state of relaxation. Also, during the Manly competition the danger from sleepiness was not great because it was held in an open air pool, whereas my endurance swims are always held in indoor pools where the air becomes close and hastens drowsiness.

The competitor who came second was a New Zealander, a lady of Maori origin called Katerina Nehua (Mrs Darley), and her share of the prize money was £100. Katerina was mother to four children, the youngest of whom was only 9 weeks old. The family had been residing in Collaroy, a suburb of Sydney, for some time, but they were in dire straits, as Katerina's husband, Joseph Darley (a motor mechanic), had been out of work for nine months due to the economic depression of that time. On hearing of the family's circumstances, the crowds were wonderfully supportive throughout Katerina's swim. She completed just under 48 hours in the water before giving up on Sunday evening due to exhaustion.

Mercedes, too, was so impressed by Katerina's courage that she declared that if she won the competition she would give Katerina £100 of her own prize money. She later fulfilled this promise and invited Katerina and her husband to afternoon tea at the Wentworth Café, where the cheque was handed over. This meant that she and Katerina ended up with £200 each. Katerina was very happy with the money she received.

The human interest story surrounding the dire living conditions of Katerina's family received wide publicity, and it was commented that:

> Sportsmen everywhere will applaud the generosity of Mercedes Gleitze in giving a third of her hard-won £300 prize for the Manly Endurance Swim to her Maori rival, Mrs Nehua. The grit of the two women lifts the contest from mere money-making to a real epic.

It was a successful start to her time in Australia, and Mercedes was asked to give a talk on Radio 2FC (the first radio station to be licensed in Sydney) about her future plans in that country.

There had been other offers for her to consider, one of which came from the organisers of the Manly Swimming Carnival. They asked if, apart from competing in the endurance competition, she would be interested in swimming across the harbour from Sydney to Manly in a specially constructed shark-proof net. They tried to tempt her by saying that the waters would be much warmer than any prevailing in New Zealand at that time of year and would prove a more lucrative event than the proposed Cook Strait attempt. However, she declined the offer, which to her appeared to be more of a risky stunt than a genuine open-water swimming challenge. It was clear that her focus was still on the Cook Strait, which was the main reason for her journey across the globe.

The Cook Strait Project

On 3 March 1931, Mercedes and her husband left Australia and returned to Wellington on the SS *Maunganni*, and from there they travelled by ferry steamer to Christchurch, primarily to ascertain the conditions for an attempt on the Cook Strait. This channel connects the North and South Islands, and the distance across in a straight line is 20 miles. However, it was estimated that in reality she could expect to swim 30–35 miles.

Mr John Tait of Island Bay, who helped organise the Wellington Harbour swim, had already been engaged as her pilot. Conditions on Mercedes' arrival in Christchurch were unfavourable and had been for the past month but, if they improved to her pilot's satisfaction, she hoped to carry out the swim between 14 and 21 March. On 10 March, John Tait wrote to Mercedes saying that he did not think the weather was going to favour her with the proposed swim. The summer season that year had been unsettled and cold. If he thought there was any chance at the weekend he would let her know, but so far as he could see, the prospects were very poor.

Lily Copplestones, the young New Zealand marathon champion, had made a failed attempt on the Cook Strait the previous year. Lily doubted whether it would be within the ability of any swimmer to conquer this strip of water, because the intense cold made it impossible for anyone to remain in the water for more than 3 or 4 hours. Mercedes, who had previously survived 8 hours in water temperatures averaging 48°F (8.9°C) in the North Channel, understood too well that cold was the worst enemy of an open-water swimmer, and told representatives from the press:

> I will not start unless the day is fine and sunny. My experience of pre-vious long-distance swims is that it is futile to attempt to stay in cold water, which Cook Strait undoubtedly is, unless there is compensating hot sunshine. It would be foolhardy to make the attempt on a dull day.

Mercedes knew it would be a formidable swim, but she said, 'Given satisfactory weather conditions I feel very confident. Cook Strait may be compared with the Irish Channel, which as yet has not been swum. When I attempted it I got to within a mile and a half of the shore.'

After a prolonged and frustrating wait for the conditions to become right, and following a final consultation with John Tait on 20 March, Mercedes reluctantly accepted his advice to abandon her attempt that season because of adverse conditions. The sea temperature was too low for a prolonged swim and it was unlikely to rise in the near future. Added to that, the prevailing heavy swells would make conditions too risky for the swimmer and the accompanying boats.

It must have been a huge disappointment to Mercedes, as she had made the journey to New Zealand with the express purpose of an attempt on the Cook Strait. She told Tait it was probable that she would return in 1933 as she was loathe to give up the project entirely. Sadly, this return visit did not happen because the circumstances of her life changed and she was unable to fulfil that particular dream.

End of the Tour

Mercedes revisited Australia on 27 March, at the end of her New Zealand tour. On this trip, she carried out two endurance swims, which she had arranged on her earlier visit – the first in the Unley Swimming Pool in

Adelaide on 11–12 April (44 hours), and the second in the Brunswick Baths in Melbourne on 17–18 April (44½ hours).

From Melbourne, Mercedes travelled to Perth and then set sail for Dublin on the SS *Esperance Bay* on 10 May 1931. There, she met up with her husband, who had returned to Ireland a month earlier, and she started training for her next major open-water swim across Galway Bay.

Apart from the disappointment she must have felt on the cancellation of the Cook Strait attempt, Mercedes' swimming achievements in New Zealand and Australia justified the long journey to the other side of the globe. All in all, it had been a sporting and financial success.

Mercedes' tour of New Zealand has been remembered in more recent times in a book celebrating the emancipation of women by Sandra Coney. Her status as a pioneer sportswoman was documented in Coney's 1993 book *Standing in the Sunshine: A History of New Zealand Women Since They Won the Vote*, in the chapter covering 'Forgotten Visitors: Acclaimed Women Who Visited New Zealand's Shores'.

17

GALWAY BAY

A potential swim across this beautiful bay on the west coast of Ireland had first been proposed by the *Irish Independent* newspaper in 1930, just before Mercedes set sail for a swimming tour of New Zealand and Australia, and she immediately accepted the challenge. While she was abroad, details of the Galway Bay swim were relayed by cablegram and arrangements

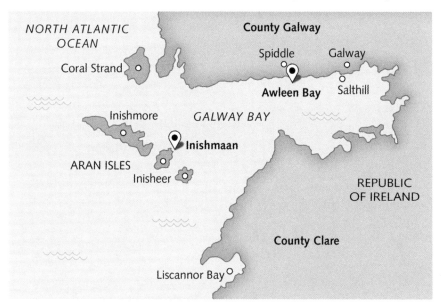

Galway Bay – another huge swim lasting 19 hours.

were placed locally in the hands of J.G. Browne, secretary of the Galway Chamber of Commerce.

On her return from Australia in June 1931, Mercedes re-joined her husband in Dublin, where she spent the next few weeks visiting Patrick's relatives and training for her proposed open-water swim across Galway Bay. That month, T.A. Grehan, the advertisement manager of the *Irish Independent*, liaised further with Browne at the Chamber of Commerce, and a new proposal was made (and agreed by Mercedes) that the course should be from the Aran Islands to Salthill – a distance, as the crow flies, of approximately 23 miles. Mercedes was informed by Browne:

Dear Miss Gleitze,

Arrangements are now nearing completion for your proposed swim. I have practically definitely fixed on a boatman for the rowing boat (he will have two helpers, of course, although he may manage with one). In addition we will have the parent boat. I am also arranging all other matters, log, those in attendance in boat, etc, and will write you finally within the next week.

The point on which I wish to obtain your views now is with regard to the time you will go over to Aran. As mentioned to you in Dublin, the usual sailing days are Wednesday and Saturday. In order, however, to bring in any Islanders who may be coming into the Galway Races (held on Wednesday and Thursday), the midweek sailing is being altered to Tuesday, leaving at 8 o'clock in the morning from Galway and arriving in Aran about 11 o'clock. The boat leaves Galway on the Saturday, 1st August at 11 a.m. and arrives in Aran about 1 o'clock that day. I shall be glad to know on which day you think it best for you to go over.

With regard to hotel accommodation, I thought it better to make inquiries on this point for you myself, although you may wish to make your own arrangements. The reason I did so is that hotel charges are enormously inflated here during Race Week, and charges frequently reach fancy figures. However, I have arranged with the proprietor of the Royal Hotel, Mr J. Costello, who is one of our members, that he will put up yourself and Mr Carey, or whoever you bring, at the ordinary rate. At Kilronan, Aran, the principal hotel is Ganly's. I enclose herewith list of charges at both places, and if you let me know your proposals I will arrange to make reservations at both places for you.

Although the pilot boat would be free of charge, Browne informed Mercedes that she would have to bear the expenses of the crew and firing, but that the charges for both boats should not exceed £12.

And so, on 2 August, with arrangements all in place, the first crossing of Galway Bay by a swimmer began at 12.34 a.m. from Inishmaan – the middle of the three Aran Isles – and finished at 7.17 p.m. at Awleen Bay on the mainland, where, just under the schoolhouse at Knock, and within 2 miles of Spiddal, Mercedes decided to go ashore, having been the best part of 19 hours in the water. The actual distance from Inishmaan to Awleen Bay 'as the crow flies' is 20 miles, but because of her zigzag course it was estimated that Mercedes had covered at least 40 miles. A *Connacht Sentinel* special correspondence was on board the accompanying boat (the *Nab*), and a *précis* of his first-hand account of the event can be accessed at www.mercedesgleitze.uk.

After the swim, she expressed her gratitude for everything that was done for her on both Inishmore and Inishmaan Islands and in Galway. She told the *Connacht Sentinel* on 3 August 1931, 'I am particularly grateful to Mr Ward and to all the observers for all they have done for me.' The observers included Paddy Mullins and William Gorham of Kilronan, who had accompanied and encouraged her throughout the swim, and a number of local fishermen from Loughannbeg, who had laid a course for her with two canoes along the coastline.

She added that, although the landing place was not the one originally intended:

… once I had swum to the mainland the attempt must be taken to have been a success. Long-distance open sea swimmers always strike for the mainland, not for any particular point of it, except for a beach considered favourable for landing, and so long as they land safely without having to be taken out of the water into the boat, they are regarded as having completed their task.

The *Connacht Sentinel* wrote that Mercedes had placed Galway Bay in a position in which it had never hitherto been regarded – as a magnificent sheet of water for long-distance swimming. The interest in the swim had been huge. The following extracts from local newspaper coverage show the extent to which Irish people were inspired by the image of a woman attempting to swim across such a large stretch of water:

Almost from noon onwards the crowds began to pour in. The number of private motor cars parked at Salthill – along the front, at the promenade and in the park – broke all records. A string of omnibuses plied between Salthill and Galway all day and each one was crowded on every trip during the afternoon and evening. The traffic at the Salthill terminus was particularly heavy. Along the promenade, in the park and on the strand the people swarmed in the almost overpowering heat. Excursion trains from Dublin, Limerick and Tuam brought large parties. Eight hundred passengers arrived in the Dublin train; 440 came by the Limerick train, 650 from Athlone and 440 from Tuam and Athenry.

Aeroplane flights over the bay were available from Oranmore and several availed themselves of the opportunity to get a glimpse of Miss Gleitze in the course of her long swim.

Disappointment was expressed when it was learned that she would not land at Salthill, and a large number of people motored out beyond Spiddal to watch her as she came in near the shore and to be present when she landed.[59]

Mercedes managed to make amends for the disappointment by agreeing to give a demonstration at Salthill on the following Tuesday, 4 August. The demonstration was described in the *Connacht Sentinel* as follows:

Several thousand people, many of whom had come from Athenry, Tuam, Gort, and other places outside Galway, thronged every available space along the promenade and beach at Salthill on Tuesday evening when Miss Gleitze gave a demonstration swim.

The demonstration had been arranged at very short notice; in fact it was not until the announcement appeared in the *Connacht Sentinel* earlier in the day that most people were aware of it. Crowds thronged the promenade and beach and many others witnessed the demonstration from boats.

The weather was very fine, and whilst the crowd were waiting for Miss Gleitze to arrive at the Blackrock springboard where her swim commenced, many local swimmers gave demonstrations of their skills.

A Presentation: Miss Gleitze upon her arrival at Blackrock in a motor car driven by Mr J.J. Ward, President of the Galway Chamber of Commerce, was loudly cheered. Mr Ward then presented Miss Gleitze with a Claddagh ring 'on behalf of the Galway Chamber of Commerce and the people of Galway as a fitting souvenir of your great and plucky adventure on Sunday last in attempting to swim Galway Bay.'

Mr Ward went on: 'If the thousands from all parts of Connacht and from far outside it who gathered here on Sunday to see you after your hazardous effort were disappointed, the fault certainly was not yours. Only those observers who had the unique privilege and experience of accompanying you through that long night and day can realise the full measure of your effort: your splendid heroism and unquenchable faith in your own powers coupled with an indomitable will to win through. To the debt that the people of Galway already owe you, you are tonight adding another by generously agreeing to give a demonstration swim so that all who come may witness your prowess.'

Accompanied by a small boat Miss Gleitze then took the water and, swimming with marvellous grace and ease, soon out-distanced those swimmers who tried to keep up with her. She gave demonstrations of many strokes including the crawl and trudgeon strokes, breast and side strokes, and treading, feeding, reading and writing in the water, and she also signed a number of autographs.

Miss Gleitze was mobbed by admirers when she finished her swim at the ladies bathing pool. For a while Miss Gleitze was kept busy shaking hands with those of the crowd who could get near her, and signing autographs, and in the rush to greet her some bicycles were smashed and some children were slightly crushed.[60]

Criticism from the Church

Not all was well, however. A report appeared in the *Irish Independent* on 3 August concerning a protest from a parish priest:

An unexpected development as far as the public is concerned has occurred in a vigorous denunciation by The Very Rev. Patrick Egan, P.P., Aran Islands, of the decision to hold the swim on Sunday:

'I protest against it because I regard it as a premeditated desecration of the Lord's Day, and deliberate contempt for the laws of God. There is no justification whatsoever for having selected Sunday, because the swim could have begun early on Monday, which is a Bank holiday, and more in keeping with the spirit of the event.

'The selection of Sunday was most unfortunate, and will mean the loss of Mass to all who take part in the swim, because they can have no possible opportunity of hearing Mass. As to the swim itself, I have no objection had it been arranged for any time except Sunday morning.'

Father Egan explained that when he heard of the arrangements he wired a protest to the Galway Chamber of Commerce, which was hosting the event. 'More will be heard about this,' added Father Egan.

The wording in the protest is very strong, but it should be noted that the swim was arranged by Irish people, native to Galway and the Aran Isles – local government officials, and men of the sea. These same people would surely not have agreed to take part in the event if they had felt they were countenancing a 'premeditated desecration of the Lord's Day'.

It is clear to me that Father Egan was deeply outraged by what he viewed as contempt for the Catholic way of life, but hopefully his feelings would have been soothed a little after reading the *Connacht Sentinel*'s report covering the swim:

The islanders, the crews informed us, had offered up their prayers that morning for the success of the swim. At 10 a.m. the crews and observers on board the row boat and the pilot boat joined together in reciting the Rosary, the devotional scene being particularly impressive on the still waters of the Bay. Miss Gleitze also joined in the devotions.

Donation of a Gleitze Cup

An editorial in the *Connacht Tribune* reporting on the gift of a swimming cup from Mercedes to the Galway Chamber of Commerce commented:

It would almost appear that swimming is a lost art in Galway, and, indeed, throughout most seabourne Irish towns. We are too prone to neglect the advantages and facilities that Nature so bounteously bestows, and if Miss Gleitze's plucky swim on Sunday had achieved nothing more than to stimulate swimming in Galway, it will have served the people well. As a fact, of course, that swim has done much more, for it has shown thousands of people the advantages that Galway possesses as a tourist resort, and it has given a resounding advertisement to Galway Bay.

The *Connacht Sentinel* of Tuesday suggested that a serious effort should be made to re-establish a swimming club in the City and to obtain the services of an instructor for at least a brief period next year. This is a matter in which the residents of Salthill should display an energetic interest. An enclosed swimming pool that could be available all the year round is a very obvious need. This would not cost a considerable sum, and it would more than repay the expenditure in a few years.[61]

Profile of Mercedes
Gleitze. (Gleitze archive)

George Henry Allan
(1899–1957), engineer
and swimming coach,
was Mercedes' trainer
during her successful
1927 season. (Allan
family collection,
reproduced courtesy
of Glenda Exley)

Mercedes' pilots: standing, Henry Gare Sharp (1874–1959), together with his son, Henry (Harry) James Sh
(1895–1961). Backdrop is the Dover–Folkestone coastline. (Reproduced courtesy of Alan F. Taylor)

Preparing for a further Channel attempt from Folkestone on 26 August 1926. On Mercedes' left, crouchi
USA Channel swimmer Mille Corson helping to apply grease. (PA Images)

raining session on 24 July 1926. In the boat, Henry Gare Sharp and Horace Carey; in the water, ping Mercedes into the boat, Dr Dorothy Logan. (Stanley Sharp collection)

rcedes, resting en route to Cap Gris-Nez for an English Channel attempt on 18 September 1926. With on board are her pilot, Harry Sharp (centre), and on left, with his elbow on the rim of the boat, news ptographer Stanley Devon, who joined them to cover the event. (Stanley Sharp collection)

Above: Mercedes with M. Leon Vincent, Mayor of Calais (centre), before the start of her English Channel attempt on 18 September 1926. On the right, with hands in pockets, another Channel aspirant, Egyptian Ishak Helmy, who eventually succeeded in 1928. (Photographer: Stanley Devon. Stanley Sharp collection)

Left: Mercedes at Cap Gris-Nez, with sister Doloranda Gleitze helping to prepare her for the 18 September 1926 attempt. (Photographer: Stanley Devon. Stanley Sharp collection)

...participants at the White Rock Baths, Hastings, on 2 October 1926. Back row: English Channel swimmer ...ian Derham (centre) with gala officials. Left to right: Verrall Newman, Eileen (Beatrice) Armstrong, ...edes Gleitze, Mrs Fitzroy and Isabelle (Belle) White. The three Olympic divers in this photograph are ...ng rectangular badges on their costumes. (Dr Ian Gordon collection)

"CRYING" A SPLENDID VICTORY

...HN "CHOPPER" ANDERSON. Folkestone's worthy Town Crier, ...nouncing to the townspeople the happy result of Miss Gleitze's Channel swim. Story on this page.

Folkestone's salute: a walkabout with John 'Chopper' Anderson, the town crier, the morning after Mercedes' successful Channel swim. (Photographer unknown. *Daily Herald*, 10 October 1927)

Illustrated article in the *News of the World*, 9 October 1927: 'TYPIST SWIMS CHANNEL. Miss Gleitze b received yesterday at Charing Cross Station by Lord Riddell (on her left). Her trainer, Mr Allan, is behind on her right.' (Topical Press Agency/Stringer/Getty Images)

The start of the vindication swim from Cap Gris-Nez on 21 October 1927. In the foreground, Mercedes the water and George Allan, her trainer, in the rowing boat. Illustrated London News article, 29 October (*Illustrated London News* Ltd/Mary Evans Picture Library)

Above: An aerial photograph of Mercedes on her vindication swim, taken by *The Times*, 21 October 1927. (News UK)

Left: Vindication swim. Illustrated London News article, 29 October 1927: 'Girt by a towel used to pull her out against her will, Miss Gleitze supported in the boat by George Allan, her trainer, when her second Channel swim was stopped.' (*Illustrated London News* Ltd/Mary Evans Picture Library)

A Folkestone welcome! Returning to base with her coach and pilot, George Allan and Harry Sharp, after being forced to abandon the vindication swim. (*The Times*, 21 October 1927/News UK)

Smiling through! Mercedes and her pilot, Harry Sharp, recovering after the disappointment of the failed vindication swim. (*The Times*, 21 October 1927/News UK)

Channel Swimming Association

Michael Read M.B.E.

President

This is to certify that

~ Mercedes Gleitze ~

swam the English Channel

France to England

on 7th October 1927   in 15 hours 15 minutes

The swim was duly entered in the
Record Book of the Association
on 1st November 1927

Michael P. Read   **President**

Alan Vooen   **Chairman**

Julie Bradshaw   **Secretary**

Channel Swimming Association
Certificate validating Mercedes'
successful swim across the English
Channel on 7 October 1927.
(Gleitze archives)

For her swim Miss Gleitze wore a veil instead of a helmet to protect
her head from the hot sun. In the picture this can be plainly seen.

...e of four pioneering wild swimmers. From
...ilda (Laddie) Sharp, the Zeitenfeld twins and
...des. (Bernice and Phyllis Zeitenfeld from
...SA were to act as bridesmaids at Mercedes'
...ng in August 1930.) (Photographers unknown.
... Chronicle, 1 May 1930)

Sunblock! Mercedes protecting herself from the sun's
rays and sea salt by wearing a veil over her face. The
image was taken on an English Channel attempt
in the reverse direction, England to France, on
3 August 1933. (Unknown photographer. Daily Mail,
3 August 1933)

Blackpool Tower Circus programme. Mercedes gave swimming demonstrations throughout the summer season of 1928, and her event drew in 2,000 spectators at each of the twice-daily sessions. (Gleitze archives)

Preparation for her first attempt, on 16 December 1927, to cross the Strait of Gibraltar. Illustrated London News article, 31 December 1927: 'Miss Gleitze's Gibraltar swim. A feminine touch. The greased swimmer consulting her hand-mirror.' (*Illustrated London News* Ltd/Mary Evans Picture Library)

Mercedes' first attempt on 16 December 1927 at the Gibraltar crossing. Illustrated London News article, 31 December 1927: 'A Channel swimmer's endeavour to swim from Tangier to Gibraltar: Miss Gleitze hauled out of the water at 10.40 after swimming since 2.30 in the morning.' (*Illustrated London News* Ltd/Mary Evans Picture Library)

Formal image of Mercedes, *c.* 1928. When not swimming, this is how she always dressed her long hair. (Unknown photographer. Gleitze archives)

Mercedes en route to Donaghadee on 21 June 1928 for her first North Channel attempt. (*Northern Whig & Belfast Post*/British Library/Gleitze archives)

A Donaghadee welcome, 21 June 1928. (*Northern Whig & Belfast Post*/British Library/Gleitze archives)

he start of Mercedes' first attempt at the North Channel from Robbie's Point, Donaghadee, on
June 1928. (*Northern Whig & Belfast Post*/British Library/Gleitze archives)

cond attempt across the North Channel, 26 July 1928: Mercedes, accompanied by her pilot boat.
orthern Whig & Belfast Post/British Library/Gleitze archives)

Constable Archie McVicker in the sea with Mercedes for a short while during her second attempt at the North Channel, after she said she would be glad of the company. (*Northern Whig & Belfast Post*/British Library/Gleitze archives)

Above: August 1928. At the request of her pilot, Andrew White, Mercedes christened his new boat *Mercedes*. (*Northern Whig & Belfast Post*/British Library/Gleitze archives)

Right: The *Mercedes* pilot boat at rest in the beautiful Strangford Lough, Co. Down. The boat (registration number B329) was located in 2012 by Brian Meharg MBE, North Channel pilot. Image shows Brian and Mercedes' daughter, Doloranda, surveying the boat at low tide. (Gleitze archives)

Above: The ever-constant Nettie Muir, who accompanied Mercedes on many of her swims. This image was taken on her third 1928 attempt to cross the North Channel. (*Northern Whig & Belfast Post*/British Library/Gleitze archives)

Left: Swimming due east at daybreak on Mercedes' third attempt to cross the North Channel from Donaghadee to Portpatrick, on 26 August 1928. (*Northern Whig & Belfast Post*/British Library/Gleitze archives)

Being rowed to the starting point of a swim, *c.* 1928/29. (Venue and photographer unknown. Gleitze archives)

The start of a swim, *c.* 1928/29. (Venue and photographer unknown. Gleitze archives)

Three images covering Mercedes' 1929 attempts to cross the North Channel from Kintyre to Cushendun. These were taken at the rocky starting points of Lice Point (*Rubha na Lice*) and Deas Point (*Sron Uamha*) on the rounded, south-western headland of the Mull of Kintyre. (Duncan Watson collection and Gleitze Archives)

Mercedes aboard the Lough Neagh Cruises boat *White Heather*. Included in the organising party are Mr N.M. Clarke and Mr F.J. Smith JP. (Courtesy of *Belfast Newsletter*, 9 July 1929)

Testing the waters in Antrim Bay – a warm-up swim from Maine Water Point to Six Mile Water in advance of Mercedes' planned breadthways swim across Lough Neagh. (Courtesy of *Belfast Newsletter*, 9 July 1929)

The Berne, Portstewart, Co. Derry – the start and finishing point of Mercedes' double swim across Lough Foyle in August 1929. (Sketched and gifted by Maurice McAleese, Portstewart)

Portstewart clifftop, August 1929. Frank Martin (Portstewart Town Clerk) pointing out to Mercedes the course across Lough Foyle to Donegal. Amongst others in the group are Bob Bacon (pilot), his son Jim Bacon, Harry Gibson and Thomas Murphy. (Gifted by Dr Michael Thompson, Portstewart/Belfast)

Lough Foyle swim on 17 August 1929. Midway, Greencastle (Moville) to Portstewart. (Gleitze archives)

Lough Foyle swim on 20 August 1929. Wading out at White Bay on the reverse crossing, Portstewart to Moville. (Gleitze archives)

Lough Foyle landing. On the beach at Moville at the finish of the Portstewart to Moville crossing, 20 August 1929. (Gleitze archives)

A plaque situated on the Causeway Path at the Berne, Portstewart, to commemorate the first crossing of Lough Foyle by Mercedes in August 1929 and the second crossing by Heather Clatworthy (née Holmes) in July 2016. (Courtesy of Causeway Coast and Glens Borough Council)

Firth of Forth swim: Mercedes, together with Mr A.N. Cameron, Mr Thomas Bunyan and Eastern Counties Swimming Association officials prior to her first attempt on 21 July 1929. (*Evening Dispatch*, 22 July 1929, courtesy of *The Scotsman* Publications Ltd)

vedding of Mercedes and Patrick Carey at St Paul's Roman Catholic Church, Maison Dieu Road, Dover, August 1930. Her adult bridesmaids were the 'Channel Twins', Bernice and Phyllis Zeitenfeld from New (Photograph by Whorwell, Dover. Topical Press Agency/Stringer/Getty Images)

Across the Hellespont. Mercedes
with husband Patrick at the finish
of her double crossing in August
1930. (Gleitze archives)

A publicity image taken at the start
of Mercedes' New Zealand tour
in December 1930. (Unknown
photographer. Gleitze archives)

ington Harbour, Christmas Day 1930. *Evening Post*, 26 December 1930: 'Miss Gleitze Swims The Harbour. centre, the crowd lining the beach at Day's Bay as Miss Gleitze approached the shore after being in water for seven hours. Below, some of the launches and boats which accompanied the swimmer, who is ming between the two rowing boats on the left. Left & right, Miss Mercedes Gleitze before and after her our swim.' (Alexander Turnbull Library/National Library of New Zealand)

Manly International Endurance Competition, Sydney, Australia, February 1931. The three finalists – from left: Mercedes Gleitze (48.13 hours), Lily Copplestones (40.7 hours) and Katerina Nehua (47.56 hours). (Alexander Turnbull Library/National Library of New Zealand)

'Reading to pass the time.' Image taken at the Manly International Swimming Marathon in Sydney, Australia, in 1931. Mercedes won the competition by staying afloat for 48 hours 13¼ minutes, swimming, floating and treading water. (Gleitze archives)

Illustrated article in the *Connacht Sentinel*, 8 August 1931: 'Charming camera studies of Miss Mercedes Gleitze taken during her tour through Connemara. On the right Miss Gleitze is seen with Mr P Carey, her husband.' (Courtesy of *Connacht Tribune* Newspaper Group, Galway)

Galway Bay crossing, 2 August 1931. An illustrated article in the *Connacht Tribune*, 8 August 1931: 'Images taken whilst the swim was in progress: (1) Breakfast on board the pilot boat, Nab; (2) Currachs from Aran following the swimmer; (3) and (4) Miss Gleitze doing the trudgeon. She dispenses with a bathing cap during her long swims, but is wearing a handkerchief on her head as a sunshade; (5) The attendant rowboat. In the boat are Mr P. Carey, Mr Jasper Kelly and Mr Sean O'Beirns. (6) A snack on board.' (Courtesy of *Connacht Tribune* Newspaper Group, Galway)

...urgh endurance swim (26 hours), 31 December 1929 to 1 January 1930. Mercedes being assisted from the ... at the Infirmary Street Baths in Edinburgh after setting a new British endurance swim record. (*Edinburgh* ... 2 January 1930/courtesy of *The Scotsman* Publications Ltd)

DERBY CORPORATION PUBLIC BATHS

32 HOURS
ENDURANCE SWIMMING

BY

MISS MERCEDES GLEITZE

AT

Reginald St. Baths, Derby,

COMMENCING

FRIDAY, MARCH 28, 1930

AT 2 P.M. & CONTINUING TO 10 P.M.

SATURDAY, MARCH 29th

Miss GLEITZE swam The English Channel. Straits of Gibralter,
The Wash. Lough Neagh. Lough Ryan, Firth of Forth, &c.

ADMISSION—

FRIDAY (Day & Night) to 12 Noon SATURDAY. **6d.**
SATURDAY 12 Noon to Close, **1/-**, including Tax.

The Baths will be Open all Night on Friday, March 28th.
If necessary, the Swimming Bath will be cleared at intervals.

MUSIC provided by H.M.V. RADIO GRAMOPHONE. supplied by
Mr. H. KEELING, Pear Tree Road, Derby.

WALKER & SONS, PRINTERS, LIVERSAGE STREET WORKS, DERBY

Left: Derby endurance swim poster, 28–29 March 1930 (32 hours). (Gleitze archives)

Below: Belfast endurance swim (34 hours), 21–22 April 1930, at Ormeau Street Baths. Included in the group are Cllr George Gray JP, Cllr J.D. McClure and Cllr J. Kilpatrick; members of the Baths Committee; Mr J.S. McNamara (General Superintendent); Messrs J. Caughey, H. Lemon and S. Auld (UDIASA) observers and timekeepers; Dr J.S. Jowett Lee, Nurse Mason and Miss Edyth Burnett (the swimmer's attendant – and future mother of ILDSA President William Wallace). (*Northern Whig & Belfast Post/* British Library/Gleitze archives)

Miss Mercedes Gleitze.

It will be remembered that in May last Miss Mercedes Gleitze carried out n endurance swim at Cossington Street Baths, in which she broke her own ecord of 34 hours set up in Belfast during April.

Owing to the interest shown by the public on that occasson and the disppointment of so many people in not being able to see that remarkable xhibition of skill, patience and perseverance, the Committee have arranged or another endurance swim on the 12th and 13th September, in which Miss leitze will endeavour to again beat her record of 39 hours set up at Wolverampton in July. She will enter the water at 7-30 a.m. on the 12th and finish t 11-30 p.m. on the 13th.

The Baths will be open during the whole of the time, and there will be mple opportunity for those who take an interest in the healthy sport of wimming to see "how it is done", and for the more curious, how swimmers ho are in the water for such a lengthy period are fed and encouraged to roceed.

Leicester endurance swim (40 hours), 12–13 September 1930. A page from a booklet produced by Leicester Corporation in connection with the reopening of the refurbished Belgrave Baths in Cossington Street, Leicester, in September 1930. (Gleitze archives)

lashlight photograph taken after 11 p.m. of a section of the crowd of severa! thousands which failed to secure admission to Dundee Central Baths to see the concluding stage of Miss Gleitze'S swim.

lee endurance swim (40½ hours), 24–25 September 1930. An illustrated article in the *Dundee Courier*, ovember 1930: 'A flashlight photograph taken after 11 p.m. of a section of the crowd of several thousands n failed to secure admission to Dundee Central Baths to see the concluding stage of Mercedes' swim.' nown photographer. Courtesy of D.C. Thomson & Co. Ltd)

Dublin endurance swim (42 hours), 2–4 November 1930. A group photograph with Dublin officials, taken at Tara Street Baths prior to start of the swim. (Photographer: J. Merriman, Amiens Street, Dublin. Gleitze archives)

Wellington endurance swim (42½ hours), 30 December 1930 to 1 January 1931. Mercedes was entertained during the swim by a quartet of Maori singers with refrains and *hakas* (traditional posture dances). (Sketched by Kara Campbell)

No. 8   MERCEDES GLEITZE   PHOTO BY NAVANA LTD.

Gleitze charity – one of a series of fundraising postcards Mercedes had printed to raise awareness of the plight of unemployed, destitute people during the years leading up to the Great Depression. (Photograph by Navana Limited. Gleitze archives)

Gleitze charity – *Leicester Mercury* illustrated article, 22 July 1935: 'Mrs. Pollock with her two children, Raymond (in arms) and Henry, who have entered the Mercedes Gleitze Home in Sparkenhoe Street, Leicester, with the husband, Mr Henry Pollock.' (Courtesy of *Leicester Mercury*)

Social welfare awareness – during the wild-swimming 'closed season' (November 1928 to April 1929), Me lodged at the home of Mr and Mrs J. Froggert, 14 Eagle Street, off Chester Street, Hulme. She used her ti in Manchester to gain personal experience of the conditions under which various classes of working girls and earned their living, working alongside them, barefooted, in local weaving mills. (Gleitze archives)

The guest of honour at the opening ceremony of the Blue Lagoon Sea Swimming Pool in Hunstanton (built under an unemployment scheme). It was officially opened on 26 May 1928 by Mercedes, supported by Edmund Maurice Burke Roche MP, 4th Baron Fermoy (Gleitze charity trustee), Alfred Ransford JP, and members of the Urban District Council. (Sheila W.B., Ancestral Voices)

A bed for the night! In the autumn of 1928 Mercedes gave up her flat in London for financial reasons and lived a nomadic life, travelling from sea to sea and place to place, staying in local B&Bs and inns. (Gleitze archives)

A working-class sportswoman alongside society women: an illustration of how people gradually became more equal by removing distinctions based on status or privilege. Illustrated London News article, 23 July 1927. (Photograph by Stanley Devon. *Illustrated London News* Ltd/Mary Evans Picture Library)

Cartoon by David Lowe, *Evening Standard*, 10 April 1928: a satirical political point being made using Mercedes' Strait of Gibraltar swim. (Solo Syndication/The British Cartoon Museum)

A cartoon by Gordon Brewster on the them[e] taxation in the *Sunday Independent*, Novemb[er] 1930. (Courtesy of *Irish Independent*/Irish Newspaper Archives)

Cartoon – 'Encore'! (Unknown source/ Gleitze archive)

Cartoon by D.G. John in the *South Wales Echo & Express*, 12 July 1930. (Courtesy of Media Wales Limited)

18

SOUTH AFRICAN TOUR

After her successful Galway Bay swim, Mercedes travelled to New York on the liner RMS *Homeric* at the end of August 1931 and stayed for one month. She had, in the past, received invitations to perform swims in the United States and Canada, and she made the journey to explore the possibility of future swims in waters warmer than those in the British Isles. However, family commitments eventually put paid to any plans that might have been envisaged to revisit America.

Nevertheless, after returning from the United States, Mercedes completed two more endurance swims – the first in Rotherham from 31 December 1931 to 1 January 1932 (45 hours), and the second in Chesterfield on 15–16 January 1932 (45 hours 30 minutes).

The next set event in her calendar was a swimming tour in South Africa – the main item on her programme being the double crossing between Cape Town and Robben Island. This small island (known in Afrikaans as *Robbeneiland* – Dutch for 'seal island') lies in Table Bay, approximately 9 miles off the coast of Cape Town. Historically, it has been the site of an early penal settlement, a hospital for what were then considered socially unacceptable groups (namely lepers, lunatics and paupers), a military base during the Second World War, and in more recent times a maximum security prison for political prisoners during the apartheid years, before its final closure as a detention centre in 1996.

In February 1932, Mercedes and her husband sailed on the SS *Guildford Castle* to establish new swimming records along South Africa's Eastern Cape. On arrival, her entry into the country was held up for a day and a half because she hadn't brought sufficient funds with her to satisfy the immigration authorities. She spent the time reading and writing letters until guarantees were lodged with the authorities. Help eventually came in the form of a representative from *The Cape Argos*, who boarded the ship to interview her, and after she explained the circumstances, sporting bodies were notified, and a guarantee was signed by a leading citizen. Mercedes and her husband were then permitted to enter the country. E.C. Baker, prominent in swimming circles, accompanied the couple to the immigration offices and attended to the details. He invited them to stay with him at Haddon Hall while Mercedes studied the conditions in relation to open-water swims. Afterwards, she told a local newspaper:

> Please understand I have no complaint to make. With the exchange as it is I did not bring as much money with me, and the result was that we were held up. We have received the greatest kindness from everyone. The Beach Manager, the Harbour Guard Agency and the Chief Immigration Officer have all vied with each other to show us courtesy, and I certainly would not like it to get back to England that we are at all annoyed. There are immigration laws in every country, and those in South Africa are no more stringent than any other.[62]

A Warm-Up

Prior to embarking on the Robben Island swim, Mercedes' first event in South Africa took place in the Long Street Baths in Cape Town, commencing on 17 March 1932. This was another of the endurance swims that she had been carrying out in indoor swimming pools, mainly in Britain, in her endeavour to break the world record. The Long Street Baths swim was successful, and she reached her target of 46 hours of non-stop swimming.

Apart from the endurance swim, all her principal swims in South Africa were carried out in open waters. One of those on her list was a crossing from the Cape of Good Hope to Cape Town Pier (50 miles), but she was strongly advised by experts not to attempt it because of the danger she might face if she encountered a shoal of snoek (large, edible fish with an extremely painful bite). The local fishermen warned her that if she did, there would be little hope for her.

Cape Town to Robben Island ... and Back

In 1926, South Africa's own Peggy Duncan had already successfully swum from Robben Island to Roggebaai on the foreshore of Cape Town, and seventeen years earlier Henry Charteris Hooper had crossed from the island to Cape Town Docks. However, no one had ever swum in the reverse direction from Cape Town to Robben Island, or envisaged swimming there and back. It aroused much interest, and the *Cape Times* on 24 March 1932 commented, 'Cape Town is to have the chance of watching a Channel swimmer in serious action.'

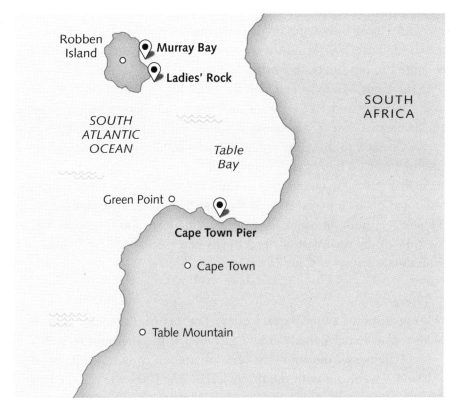

Cape Town to Robben Island and back – the biographer's favourite swim.

Mercedes was taken by surprise at the coldness of the waters around the Cape. When she waded in from the Pierhead at 11.18 on the morning of 25 March 1932, the water temperature was 50°F (10°C), and a bitingly cold wind together with a blanket of fog was the order of the day. It was reported that the siren at the breakwater and the foghorn at Robben Island sounded continually.

The outward swim was full of high drama. Apart from the cold winds and the dense fog enshrouding them, at a later stage in the swim the pilot boat (*The Flora*) had to leave Mercedes with just a small rowing boat for company, in order to refuel at Robben Island. In the absence of the pilot boat, and with darkness approaching, Mercedes swam off her course. It was only through the use of rockets fired from another vessel carrying spectators (*The Chance*) and answering rifle shots from the rowing boat, which thankfully had managed to stay with her, that the small party was located after a search lasting well over an hour.

As well as having to endure atrocious weather conditions, Mercedes was also badly stung by blue bottle jellyfish. Because she had become feverish, she had to postpone the return crossing for 24 hours until her body temperature had returned to normal.

In the event, Mercedes completed the first leg on Friday, 25 March 1932, in a time of 9 hours 12 minutes, and the homeward swim on Sunday, 27 March, in a time of 7 hours 36 minutes, and claimed two new records: the first person to make the crossing from Cape Town to Robben Island and the first to achieve the double swim.

Apart from the main charting of both crossings, a *Cape Times* journalist published his own perspective of the first 2 hours of the outgoing swim ('There …') from on board an accompanying boat, *The Chance*, as well as his view of the final part of the return swim ('And back …'), witnessed from the shorelines of Cape Town:

There …
Long-distance swims have a queer fascination for many people. Yesterday a considerable crowd gathered at the Pierhead to watch Miss Gleitze set out on her successful attempt to swim to Robben Island. I went out with the motor yacht *The Chance* to see the first stage of the swim. Along the Random Mole the water was calm, but at the turn a little north-west wind ruffled the surface.

The fog swept past us in great tongues that sometimes hid even the Mole from view, and sometimes cleared so much that we could see half-way up the sheer of the mountain. A vessel lying in the Bay now took on the ethereal outline of a ghost ship, and now the solid body of a humdrum cargo steamer. There were noises over the water. The bell of the ship at anchor as she was enveloped in the thicker wreaths of fog, the wail of the foghorn on the breakwater, the clashing of the bell-buoy in the little swell, and the croaking of the great diaphones on Green Point and the Island. At one time I could hear all three foghorns at once. At another – only a few minutes later – I could hear the breakwater horn alone. Sound travels mysteriously in fog, and the ear is not always to be depended upon as a guide to direction or to distance.

I like the system on which *The Chance* is working in connection with this swim. The two-hourly trips which she is running give one just sufficient of the performance. During those first two hours Miss Gleitze had rounded the Random Mole, cleared the breakwater, and set out past Mouille Point for the fog and the open sea. Then we came back to lunch in peace ashore. Cape Town had gained a little in mystery seen through a veil of mist. Familiar buildings had taken on other forms. Even the solid Pier Tower had become a minaret in an Eastern fantasy. I think I shall go out on *The Chance* again to watch Miss Gleitze come back.

And back …
Miss Gleitze's weather yesterday was in striking contrast to that which so nearly brought her Friday swim to an untimely close. After the early morning fog had cleared away the day was bright and warm, with a following wind and excellent visibility. The results were reflected – literally – in the faces of a very large number of Cape Town people. Mine was by no means the only one that reflected the brightness of the sunset. With a little effort one could have picked out of the crowd streaming away from the pier after the finish, all those who had been out to watch the progress of the swim in *The Chance*. But those faces paled besides the features of the party which had spent the whole day on the awning-less official launch and in the rowing boat. They had my fullest sympathy.

I watched the swim first with a pair of powerful glasses from the upper path on Signal Hill. We could see the little flotilla that accompanied Miss

Gleitze creeping slowly past the Whale Rock far out across the Bay. The movement at that distance was barely perceptible, and even when we had finished our morning stroll the gap between the boats and the Island was not very great. In the early afternoon I went out on *The Chance*. Miss Gleitze's armada had increased by then. A couple of yachts had been added to the strength and two redwing dinghies played about nearby. Later in the afternoon I had to go down to the docks and, being near the East Pier, strolled out along the breakwater to watch her pass. There was a considerable crowd there before me. People who had been watching from Mouille Point and along the Green Point front came hurrying along to give her a cheer as she passed outside the bell buoy – still clashing, but without the menace that it had held in the fog on Friday.

The interest in the swim was amazing. Well over 3,000 people watched the finish at the Pier. Every place of vantage along the docks and the Random Mole was occupied, and the esplanade was black with people. Miss Gleitze's effort is a remarkable one. She deserves every congratulation. The Friday swim was an example of dogged determination and fine courage. To have carried on after the launch had broken down and disappeared in the mist was a piece of real grit. For myself I should hate to be left with only a row boat for company in the middle of Table Bay in a thick fog.

In the 24 and 27 March editions of the *Cape Times*, both crossings were covered in detail, and a précis of these reports can be accessed at www.mercedesgleitze.uk.

Controversy

The rescheduling of the return swim from Robben Island to the mainland caused a reaction from the Church for the second time in Mercedes' swimming career, because it took place on a Sunday.

The Reverend Peter Williams, speaking on behalf of the Cape Peninsula Church Council, said that had there been time for the council to have made a protest, it certainly would have done so. He appealed for the maintenance of the sanctity of the Sabbath, and greatly deplored the completion of the recent Robben Island swim on a Sunday. He said it might be argued that it was the original intention of Miss Gleitze to complete her swim on the Saturday, but the fact remained that her act caused the desecration of the Sabbath.

This attack on Mercedes, however, was balanced by *The Cape Argus* also giving space to responses from other prominent churchmen in Cape Town. Father John Morris, a Roman Catholic priest, questioned the wisdom of Williams' view and told *The Cape Argus*, 'God is not a god of gloom, and Sunday should be a joyous day. Rome rather encourages recreation on Sundays. Provided a man or woman attends church service, we have not the slightest objection to the rest of the day being spent in healthy recreation.'

The Reverend Ramsden Balmforth of the Free Protestant Church also considered that a more liberal view should be taken of Sunday, and declared:

I do not think that this event was a desecration of the Sabbath. I think that the more modern religious leaders of the town take a liberal view of the Sabbath question. I myself see no harm in healthy recreation on Sundays, and I do not mind playing a game of tennis myself.

A more strongly worded response to Williams' criticism came from the local swimming authority:

One had thought that by this time the valueless shibboleths of another time would have vanished. Can it be seriously suggested that we should behave as in the days when to darn a sock on Sunday was a sin?

The truth about Miss Gleitze's swim is this: She put up an extraordinary performance on the Friday in crossing the stretch of water to Robben Island. She had intended to return next day, but she was so feverish on account of the bluebottle stings she had suffered that she had to postpone the attempt for a day. So she made the swim on Sunday. Because the swim took place over the weekend, many more people were able to see her than could otherwise have done. I think they gained considerably by being able to see just what can be done in the way of pluck and endurance, and for folk who do not always have many things of interest to see, undoubtedly the swim was a feature that must have provided food for thought and discussion.

Churches are intellectual institutions, and I consider that they should play a part in all phases of mental life. It is all very well to be interested in physical matters such as swimming alone, but the mind matters even more. I do actually consider that the swim made by

Mercedes Gleitze had value even in such an obscure way as making people think. What Mr Williams and other churchmen should have done was to have seized the feat that was occupying people's minds, and attached to it some moral. In that way they could have made valuable use of the swim. As it was, the condemnation appeared to the average man as slightly absurd and certainly not evidence of the Church's close connection with modern life and feeling.[63]

Two Female Pioneers

After the Robben Island swim, Mercedes indulged in what she called a Channel swimmer's best luxury – a Turkish bath. She had a normal night's sleep and awoke 'ready for any bit of water you can find me'.

She and Patrick spent the next three days exploring Cape Town and meeting people – including aviators Amy Johnson and Jim Mollison, who were also touring South Africa, and who called on Mercedes at her hotel to congratulate her on her Robben Island swim.

When Mercedes left Cape Town she took with her three mussel shells from Robben Island to add to her collection of treasured souvenirs from her various swims around the world. She also left a lock of her hair on the island to mark her visit there.

Eastern Cape Inland Waterways

After leaving Cape Town, Mercedes carried out pioneering swims over set distances in six of South Africa's rivers, lakes and dams. On arrival in each province, she first approached its local authority (as she had always done throughout her career) to ask if they could facilitate a swim in their local waterways.

Her reputation had preceded her, not least because of her successful Robben Island swim, and collaboration was always forthcoming. Once identified, each event was advertised and drew crowds of spectators. The first of these tour swims was in Port Elizabeth.

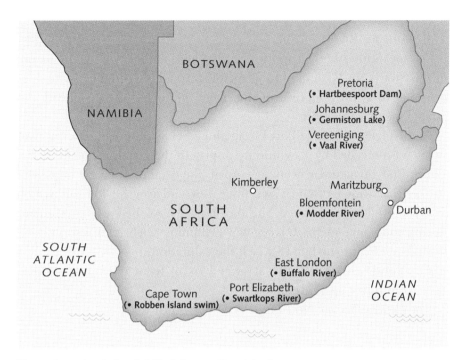

Pioneering swims in South Africa's Eastern Cape inland waterways.

From Cape Town, Mercedes and Patrick travelled by train along the Eastern Cape to Port Elizabeth, and on their arrival *The Eastern Province Herald* reported on 5 April 1932:

Within the space of a week Port Elizabeth has had the privilege of visits from two British celebrities – first Miss Amy Johnson, the famous aviatrix, and now Miss Mercedes Gleitze, Britain's greatest long-distance swimmer.

The *Herald* went on to report that Mercedes still bore the marks of her Robben swims, where her lips were blistered by the battering of the waves and exposure to cold and sun. She ruefully explained that her intended swim to St Croix Island had to be abandoned. She had been forced to take the advice of experts who informed her that the danger from sharks presented too great a risk.

The Swartkops River

In the meantime, she had approached the local authority as to the nature of the Swartkops River and its adaptability to a long-distance swim. Her proposal to swim a section of that river was given the go-ahead and arrangements set in motion.

At the invitation of the Port Elizabeth Ladies Swimming Club, the river swim was preceded by a swimming display in the Trafalgar Square Baths, North End, on Saturday evening, 9 April. She demonstrated the numerous strokes that a long-distance swimmer uses, and also the 'log roll' which she employed when fatigued. She also showed how she took refreshments during endurance swims. Interest in a swimming celebrity was strong, and several hundred turned up to watch the exhibition.

On Sunday, 10 April, the arranged swim from the mouth of the Swartkops River up to Redhouse took place.

The Eastern Province Herald reported on 11 April 1932:

> Probably for the first time in history the Zwartkops River has been conquered by a swimmer. This honour has fallen to Miss Mercedes Gleitze, the distinguished English lady swimmer, who entered the river at the mouth at 2.20 yesterday afternoon, and covered the 6½ miles to Redhouse in 3 hours 31 minutes.
>
> A large crowd witnessed the achievement. Miss Gleitze was led all the way by a party of Sea Scouts in their boat. When she stepped from the water at Redhouse she was accorded a hearty reception by the large gathering, and was handed a beautiful bouquet on the completion of her great performance.[64]

The Buffalo River

The next stop along the Eastern Cape was at East London. On 18 April 1932 *The East London Daily Dispatch* covered her stay, informing its readers that: 'The name of Miss Mercedes Gleitze is as familiar to followers of aquatic prowess as the name of Jack Dempsey is to boxing enthusiasts.'

An announcement of her intention to swim from the mouth of the River Buffalo to Green Point and back, a total distance of 7 miles, was published both in that paper and in the *Sunday Times*. The merit of this swim lay not so much in the distance as in the adverse conditions she would have to contend with in a river notorious for its exceptionally strong and swift currents and whirlpools. Although the notices only appeared a few days before the event, thousands of East Londoners turned up to witness Mercedes forge her way steadily against wind and tide along the river.

The East London Daily Dispatch reported that there was a great crowd to see her off as she waded in from the little sandy beach of the eastern bight between the pier and the harbour. She swam an easy and powerful breaststroke ninety per cent of the time. Sightseers were massed all along the mile and a quarter of the harbour up to the bridge, every vantage point being made use of to get a better view. It was apparently the most animated scene of its kind that had been witnessed in the harbour for many years. The crowds invaded the harbour crafts moored alongside the various wharves and quays, crowding the decks, bridges and rigging. Similar scenes, though less thronged, took place on the opposite west bank, and from eleven o'clock onwards there were signs of the same thing happening still higher up the river.

Mercedes proceeded 'unhurriedly and relentlessly' towards her goal accompanied by a number of small boats, a couple of launches, and a Royal Naval Reserve cutter with the officials on board. During the swim she wore a net veil over her face to protect herself from the sun. Wherever the crowd was thickest, as she drew abreast she acknowledged the friendly applause by lifting the veil and waving cheerfully. She was, in fact, cheerful and smiling all through the swim, talking brightly with those in the cutter, and enjoying the music being played on a gramophone in the stern of the boat. At various points she was fed with hot soup and with milk when the soup ran out.

Her choice of day was unfortunate with regard to the conditions in the river, which were extremely miserable. A buffeting wind was against her the whole of the way up and retarded her progress considerably, with the result that the tide was running out pretty fast against her long before she reached Green Point – which halfway point she achieved in a time of just over four hours. She lay on her back for 2 minutes gathering strength to set out on the return journey, which she completed in a remarkably good time.

Although she made up for lost time on the return swim, she again found the tide against her (incoming this time) before she reached the harbour mouth. As she passed Buffalo Bridge on her homeward journey the crowd seemed even greater. Enthusiasts on the western side of the river had followed her progress by making their way along the rough hillside and foreshore all the way up and back again. The harbour itself was again crowded, and when Mercedes finally waded ashore at the eastern bight after completing the entire swim in 6 hours 21 minutes, she received a wonderful welcome, which she acknowledged by waving happily, apparently not in the least distressed after her long battle with the elements. She was greeted by officials of the swimming clubs, and the crowd so thronged around her that she had considerable difficulty in making her way through it.

Later on in her life, Mercedes told me how on many occasions she had 'felt the strength of a crowd, and was always thankful that it was a friendly one'.

The Modder River

An exhibition swim in the Modder River in Bloemfontein was next on Mercedes' itinerary – the word *modder* being Afrikaans for 'mud'. The river forms part of the border between the Northern Cape and the Free State provinces.

The swim was organised by the staff and students of the School of Agriculture and Experiment Station at Glen. It took place on 23 April 1932 and covered a distance of 5 miles. Mercedes started at Glen weir at 2.50 p.m., swam 2½ miles upstream, turned and swam back to the weir in a time of 2 hours 25 minutes. It was noted that the water was 'dead' and 'no currents assisted the swimmer'.

While in Bloemfontein, Mercedes also gave a demonstration swim at the open-air swimming baths in Vanaand, on 25 April.

Germiston Lake

Mercedes journeyed on to Johannesburg early in May and made her first public appearance at Germiston Lake. She had been challenged to establish a new 6-mile record for South Africa. A ½-mile course in Germiston Lake had been measured off so that the mileage covered during an estimated 5 hours could be accurately calculated. Officials from the Transvaal Amateur Swimming Association authenticated the swim, and the Mayor of Germiston acted as official starter.

This was her first high-altitude swim, and she found the water heavy. The swim was nevertheless a pleasant one. At first the water was cold, but the midday sun gradually warmed it up. About 150 people witnessed the start. As the morning wore on the sightseers increased rapidly, gathering around the pier, and Mercedes was cheered each time she passed the buoy marking the completion of 1 mile. The spectators were able to watch her glide effortlessly through the water in rhythm with the distant music from the gramophone in the accompanying rowing boat. At intervals, she swam with one arm while she took hot chicken broth for nourishment.

She waded out of Germiston Lake after successfully establishing a South African 6-mile record of 5 hours, 38 minutes and 3 seconds. At the finish of the swim, the *Rand Daily Mail* (9 May 1932) reported that '3,000 voices lustily cheered Miss Gleitze on her performance'. The Mayor of Germiston (W.S. Grace) was the first to congratulate her, adding that the Town Council was particularly appreciative of her choice of Germiston Lake as the scene of her attempt. He said she had definitely placed the town on the map!

On the following Monday and Tuesday, Mercedes gave special demonstrations of distance-swimming strokes and methods to hundreds of schoolchildren in the Ellis Park Baths and the Doornfontein Baths, both located in Johannesburg.

The Hartbeespoort Dam
The Hartbeespoort Dam in the North West Province was designed for irrigation purposes. Its name derives from the Afrikaans for 'pass of the hartebeest'. On Sunday, 15 May, Mercedes performed a 4-hour and 45-minute endurance swim in this dam. The course was from the Agnes Hotel to Pelindaba and back. It was a feat that had not yet been attempted by any other swimmer.

Two members of the Northern Transvaal ASA (J. Gabron and J. Bosanquet) accompanied her. The weather was wretched, with a heavy headwind and choppy water on the 12-mile swim. There was a fair attendance, and, despite the conditions, Mercedes described the swim as a very enjoyable experience.

She found the dam the most pleasant of all the waters she had swum in South Africa, and suffered discomfort only from the winds. She commented that in spite of the strong wind that sent the spray into her face, she had no burning sensation in the eyes, which is usually the case when swimming in rivers and seas.

While she was in Pretoria, the Pretoria Women's Club called a special meeting on 13 May in her honour, and leading swimmers in the area were given the opportunity to meet and interview her. In reply to a question on what the most difficult task she had performed was, Mercedes described her experience when swimming the Irish Channel. She told her audience that she had made many attempts, and her nearest approach to success had been to reach within 1½ miles of the coast, in 11 hours 20 minutes. She said its great depth, its icy waters, and the rough weather in that channel, which created immense waves, made conditions terribly hard, and the actual distance of 40 miles was covered by reason of her being carried out of the direct course. She added that cold water sapped the strength and froze the blood.

This swim was followed the next day with an exhibition of long-distance swimming methods at the Pretoria Swimming Baths.

The Vaal River

The Vaal River is the largest tributary of the Orange River in South Africa. It is approximately 1,200km (750 miles) long, and forms the border between Mpumalanga, Gauteng and the North West Province on its north bank, and the Free State on its south. It is one of the world's oldest rivers, and during the winter months the faster-flowing water creates the muddy torrent for which the Vaal ('grey-brown') is named.

An invitation from the Vereeniging Estates was extended to Mercedes to establish a record for a 7-mile stretch of the River Vaal, which flows through Vereeniging. She was only too pleased to accept the challenge. The organisers held a dance at the Riviera Hotel to welcome her.

On Sunday, 22 May, Mercedes entered the starting point at 11.09 a.m. and was given a send-off by a large cheering crowd. The course was from opposite the Riviera Hotel to a buoy half a mile upstream. Her accompanying boat contained the mayor (Mr Haskins) and a representative from *The Star* newspaper. Transvaal Swimming Union officers (Alan Snyman and Hugh Paton) were the official timekeepers.

She felt the cold immediately she entered the water, and this troubled her throughout the swim. She remarked that the water temperature was lower than any she had been in since the Robben Island swim. Despite the chilly conditions, however, she remained in good spirits. The mayor operated the gramophone and also gave her soup at each ½-mile mark.

On 23 May, *The Star* went on to report that the sun had already set when she approached the finishing post, and the crowd of about 400 people gave her a rousing cheer upon 'the most remarkable performance ever accomplished in the Vaal River'. Mercedes had swum a steady pace throughout, averaging just under one hour for each mile – the established time for the 7-mile course being 6 hours, 44 minutes and 23 seconds.

Final South African Venues
The Vaal River was the last of the open-water swims carried out in South Africa, but to wind up the tour Mercedes visited three more towns – Pietermaritzburg, Kimberley and Durban – where she gave demonstrations in their local swimming baths.

Homeward Bound

Baby on Board
Mercedes sailed with her husband in the *Llangibby Castle* for England on 27 July 1932 – just three months before giving birth to her first child in October of that year. She had carried out all her South African swims while pregnant.

When she first realised she was pregnant on the outward journey to South Africa, Mercedes consulted the ship's doctor about the wisdom of carrying out her proposed swims. He was a very enlightened doctor for that era and reassured her that if it was the 'norm' for her to use her body in that way, then no harm should come to the baby. She had previously been strongly advised by a physician to curtail her swimming activities or she would never be able to have children, and after her endurance swim at the Brunswick Baths in Melbourne she received a letter from a medical officer congratulating her on her performance, but advising her not to do back-to-back swims or 'there will be the usual physiological sequence, viz. a greatly enlarged heart'. This was a further example of Mercedes breaking through existing prejudices and challenging the perception of women in general, and her as an individual, as fragile human beings.

Social Impressions
In an interview given to the *Rand Daily* a little while before her return to England, Mercedes commented on the marvellous advantage those South Africans who are keen on swimming have, living in a climate that is surely

ideal for the sport. She recommended that every beginner ought to get into the open as soon as he or she can, as it is so important when swimming to be on intimate terms with sea or river.

However, although Mercedes' tour of South Africa was a successful and pleasant one, and she was treated with courtesy and consideration everywhere she went, in a letter dated 6 July 1932 to Mr and Mrs Kelly (friends in England), she told them how astounded she and her husband were at the great differences between South Africa and New Zealand as colonies. She wrote:

> One misses when travelling in South Africa that spirit of unity and understanding existing between the New Zealanders and the Maori Race, and between New Zealand and the Home Country, but no doubt in time to come South Africa too will develop this social understanding.

And in a letter to the *Manchester Evening News in* June 1932, giving them her impressions of the countries she had visited, she observed:

> In South Africa the rules regarding native city life are, especially in the eyes of a traveller from England, very stringent.
>
> For instance, no native is allowed inside swimming baths, no Kaffir may use trains or buses, and at stations the black man may not use the white man's waiting rooms.
>
> The Zulus of Natal are the finest type of natives in the Union and in the cities they make very loyal workers. South Africa really owes its economic prosperity to the cheap native labour so easily obtainable.

During her voyage home to England she wrote to a friend, 'Throughout my travels in foreign lands I have been loyal to my swimming career.'

19

A STRONG AND FEMININE
SPORTSWOMAN

A central theme running throughout Mercedes' story is one of female emancipation. She was one of the 'new women' of the early twentieth century – young women who challenged the centuries-old tradition decreeing that a woman's place was in the home, and that it was only men who could realise their dreams and potential. She had to penetrate a glass ceiling in the male-dominated world of sport in order to achieve what was, in her day, a unique career as a female professional long-distance swimmer. Until she married in August 1930, she travelled alone, without an agent or manager, and, even after her marriage, she personally liaised with local authorities to arrange all her swims. This was a radical thing for a young female to do in those days. What made her even more extraordinary was she was from a working-class, immigrant background, without influence or financial support, just the sheer determination to succeed.

Mercedes strove for the absolute maximum the human body could achieve in her chosen element – water. By doing so, she pushed back the boundaries of physical endurance, especially for women. She told a South African publication, 'I have been nearly drowned several times during swims, caught in currents which dragged me down, whirled in a circle by torrents, and whisked off my course like a cork in a storm.'[65] But Mercedes possessed an inner calm, so the enormity of the task never overwhelmed her. She said, 'I know no sensation but that of calm pleasure at the prospect of another tussle with those "calling" waves. When one loves, one is not afraid.'[66]

It is notable that Mercedes achieved her open-water successes through perseverance, sometimes making as many as six or eight attempts at some of the sea crossings before finally succeeding. Although she did not complete all of her swims, by daring to be the first to try she opened the door for others to follow. In all fields of exploration and sporting achievement, once a benchmark has been set, others will attempt to go faster and higher and further, forever pushing boundaries.

Of all Mercedes' aquatic events, the twenty-seven endurance swims she performed in corporation pools offered the largest numbers of women and girls an opportunity to witness one of their own gender perform feats of strength. Not by a fictional character on a cinema screen or in a book, but by a real woman in real time – feats of strength that up until recent years had been thought to be the prerogative of men. It is significant that at many of her endurance swims, women made up the majority of spectators. However, it is also a sign of the times that, when arranging a swim, her advisors and event organisers were – without exception – male.

Mercedes was a pioneer in more ways than one. Credit was given to her for providing a big impetus to the art of swimming, which had never been properly developed in Britain during the early part of the twentieth century. Her endurance swims were witnessed by many thousands of people, and in some cities they motivated people to start new swimming clubs. Also, she must have been one of the first British female swimmers to advertise products for commercial companies, and one of the first sportswomen to institute a charity with the fees she earned from her activities. She was also one of the first female swimmers to be targeted by an exposé tabloid.

Although when performing a swim Mercedes seemed comfortable being photographed with loose, flowing hair and wearing just a swimming costume, she always dressed very formally at all other times, with her long hair coiled neatly around her ears. However, on one occasion she was caught breaking the rules. In 1927, a reporter saw her going for an early morning walk in Folkestone the day after her successful Channel swim 'without her hat on', and this fact was duly reported in the local paper.[67] The press also felt it was in the public's interest to report that the American Channel aspirants, the Zeitenfeld twins (Bernice and Phyllis), when attending as bridesmaids at Mercedes' wedding in 1930, 'were not wearing stockings'![68]

During those early years of female emancipation, the general perception of women who dared to show sporting prowess was that they were expected to be 'laddish' in appearance. It was as though the idea of women competing in athletic or swimming events was only acceptable or achievable if they displayed male characteristics. But Mercedes refused to comply and kept her natural feminine persona. She didn't crop her hair, and she wore pretty frocks. There were constant references in the press about Mercedes *not* conforming to type, and she was invariably described as graceful and 'surprisingly' feminine, with long, flowing hair. One journalist stated after an interview, 'One expected her to have the rather unattractive over-robustness of the average long-distance woman swimmer.' And the *Daily Sketch* (30 July 1923), in an article covering one of her Thames swims, felt obliged to point out to its readers that 'Miss Gleitze has no hint of "brawn" or masculinity'.

Female open-water swimmers often had to contend with barbed or derisory comments about their personal appearance. For example, Clarabelle Barrett, a highly respected and courageous contestant in the race to conquer the English Channel, had to endure repeated reminders in many of the media reports that she was not of average build. At 6ft tall, she was frequently described as the *large* lady from America, and varying estimates of her height and weight were often included in her press coverage. And across the globe at the 1931 International Manly Endurance Competition in Sydney, one journalist mockingly commented on 'the wider distribution of water' when the female contestants entered the pool.

The premise that female athletes can be beautiful and feminine and physically strong in equal measure is undisputed today, and attributes of strength, speed, grace and endurance are now foremost in the eyes of the genuine sports-minded public who turn up in their thousands to watch them compete. Regrettably, however, too many female (and male) contestants in all disciplines of sport are still subjected to shameful, unwarranted attacks about their personal appearance, notably via social media.

Mercedes' swimming ambition lay in juxtaposition to a feeling of wanting to do something to help the destitute people she witnessed on the streets of London during the years leading up to the Great Depression of the 1930s. She felt a strong empathy with these dispossessed groups and made up her mind to try to lessen their suffering. The records Mercedes stored in her attic illustrate how she remained true both to her swimming aspirations and her desire to help people living in poverty.

Role Model

Because Mercedes was a high-profile sportswoman, her name was used to promote female emancipation and to help change the behaviour of women who had been brought up to think in a narrow, limited way about their role in life. During her career she was approached by and supported various women's groups, including the National Political League, which Mary Adelaide Broadhurst MA founded in 1911 to further social and political reform on a non-party basis. Mary campaigned actively against the infamous force-feeding of suffragettes. In a letter to Margaret Milne Farquharson (secretary) dated 28 June 1928, Mercedes wrote that she greatly admired the principle of the organisation, which paid tribute to Mercedes herself at a ceremony held at the Mayfair Hotel in London to recognise the pioneer achievements of the modern woman.

Unsurprisingly in this period, national newspapers were giving more space to articles written in support of women's issues, and this meant that Mercedes was featured regularly in *The Guardian*, *The Scotsman* and the *Manchester Evening News*, amongst others. During the 1920s, apart from the usual announcements of the latest society engagements and weddings, women's pages were gradually featuring other female activities – including sporting achievement by women from outside of the Establishment. Mercedes' role in society as a successful and yet still feminine sportswoman made her a figure to be discussed and held up as a modern woman, for example:

It seems ridiculous to me that we should still be helpless females. Here we are with games fields and gymnasiums, with high schools and public schools, and physical-training courses and all other modern conveniences, but we still cannot look after ourselves. A few of us can. We have our Amy Johnsons, our Winifred Browns, our Rosita Forbeses and Mercedes Gleitzes and so forth. They have at least served to show us that our helplessness is a matter of choice and training. But the vast majority of us are still the sort of person for whom the cry *'Women and children first!'* had to be invented. It is a disgrace.[69]

Indeed, when the *Manchester Evening News* compiled a list of outstanding people from the worlds of international affairs, the arts and sport in 1927, Mercedes' name featured amongst such well-known figures as George Bernard Shaw, Ivor Novello and the Rt Hon. Ramsay MacDonald. Out of the fifty-five names listed, only eight were women: Tallulah Bankhead, Fay Compton, Anna Pavlova, Madge Titheradge, Mrs H. Dowdell, Mrs Victor Bruce, Mercedes Gleitze and Mrs Phyllis Satterthwaite.

Her prominence as a long-distance swimmer meant that Mercedes received invitations to join and support the growing number of campaign groups that were being formed to promote health and strength. She had a lifelong antipathy towards tobacco and alcohol, and spoke out publicly regarding these addictions, declaring: 'I am a total abstainer. I could not possibly carry out my profession as an endurance swimmer otherwise. I agree with Tilden [US tennis star] that alcohol must seriously affect the mind, and thus interfere with physical stamina.'

In 1934 in Scotland, the Temperance and Public Morals Committee stated that they, 'had the emphatic support of today's finest cricketers, Hobbs and Bradman, and of the famous swimmer, Miss Mercedes Gleitze, that alcohol was best left alone.'[70] Whilst on tour in Australia she told Melbourne's Young Australia Temperance League (which solicited statements from noted athletes to further their cause within the student community) that she supported the League's philosophy that 'Absolute physical efficiency is only possible when poisonous substances are rigidly excluded from the human system'. At their request, she provided them with the following testimonial:

It is my opinion that the world would be a far better, healthier, cleaner and more prosperous place if people refrained from undermining their moral and physical constitution by the habit of excessive drink. There is nothing in the world so wonderful as temperance and nothing so conducive to leading a healthy and useful life.[71]

Other Endeavours

Although the media had provided good coverage of Mercedes' many attempts to conquer the English Channel, her profile was raised considerably when she finally succeeded – not least because of the way she acquitted herself in the vindication swim, which was covered extensively at home and abroad. Because of her elevated profile, the invitations to attend galas, give demonstrations and lectures on sea swimming, open new or refurbished pools, model swimwear, appear on stage, and promote products, were numerous. Although focussing on future major swimming events, she willingly accepted and fitted as many of these invitations as possible into her schedule.

For example, after the vindication swim she appeared at the Plaza Theatre in London from 24 October for seven days, and gave a short speech before each showing of a film called *Swim Girl Swim* starring Bebe Daniels and featuring Gertrude Ederle. *The Daily Mirror* reported that she received a remarkable ovation.

Mercedes had given up her office work in July 1927 to pursue a swimming career, and the fees she earned in a celebrity role provided her with a much-needed income. She was paid between 5 and 10 guineas for some of the demonstrations, although most of the smaller swimming clubs could only cover her expenses. Reading through her personal letters, it is clear that she enjoyed attending these functions and at times travelled through the night straight from a major swim in order to fulfil an engagement.

Promotional Work

Mercedes was one of the first British female swimmers to be used to promote commercial products, making her a forerunner to modern advertising methods. Mercedes, of course, welcomed these opportunities. Her income from long-distance swimming was at times sporadic, and she needed to keep her finances in good order.

Modelling was not a career choice, but Mercedes was offered, and gladly accepted, short-term contracts to model and promote swimwear. As an indication of the times, although she was comfortable being photographed wearing a swimsuit in or near water, she only agreed to model swimwear in the confines of a store if she could also wear a robe. The stores who employed her included Brown, Muff & Co., Bradford, George Halls (Wolsey Bathing Suits), Huddersfield, and D. Kellett's Store, Dublin.

During her visit to Ireland, the *Dublin Evening Mail* of 13 February 1930 commented:

> The new role of Miss Gleitze may well give the death blow to the boyish-figure craze. This lead of Miss Gleitze, who has a very graceful

figure herself, may well turn the mode in the other direction. It is certain to be welcomed by women, who are weary of the rigours of slimming.

There was no shortage of swim-related companies who wished for Mercedes to model or advertise products of their line, but her influence was not merely limited to swim caps and bathing costumes; Lipton's Tea (sourced from then Ceylon) was promoted by Mercedes, while her testimonial was supplied for Horlicks malted milk tablets, Ovaltine chocolate malt drink, Nestlé products, and, of course, Bovril Limited, who had sponsored her attempts to swim across the North Channel.

By far the headlining promotional work that Mercedes carried out, however, was for Rolex. Indeed, she played a major role in launching the newly designed Rolex Oyster waterproof watch. In October 1927, there was extensive coverage in the national newspapers of Dr Dorothy Logan's hoax and of Mercedes' intention to swim the English Channel again. Rolex moved quickly and, through Messrs S.T. Garland Advertising Service of Brook Street, London, they asked her to wear a prototype watch on her planned vindication swim. She agreed to carry it on a ribbon around her neck. When she left the water, the watch was still working perfectly after being submerged for 10 hours. The following month, Rolex placed a whole front-page advertisement featuring Mercedes in the *Daily Mail* of 24 November 1927 to introduce their new product, the Rolex Oyster.

Through her agreement to test the innovative watch in such trying conditions, Mercedes helped establish Rolex as the global household name and leading brand it is today – a fact acknowledged by the company in its annals.

Dirt Track Riding

During the 1920s to 1930s (and beyond) dirt track riding was a popular international sport. En route to New Zealand, Mercedes had as travelling companions three British speedway stars – 'Squib' Burton, Norman Evans and George Greenwood – and in her 'Diary of New Zealand Tour' she writes, 'Dirt track riding is certainly a game that calls for grit, accuracy and pluck. A fine sport, interesting and thrilling, although I would enjoy watching it much more if the riders had a greater guarantee of safety.'

Mercedes was invited to three of these speedway events as a guest of honour. In 1929 she presented the *Manchester Evening Chronicle* Cup and Golden Helmet to the winner, the Australian track star A.W. Jervis, at the

White City Dirt Track in Manchester, and in September 1930 she was guest
of honour at the Leicester meet, where she gave a speech to the crowds
after a drive round the course. Later that same year, on 20 December, she
was invited to the Kilbirnie Dirt Track in New Zealand, where she presented the trophies at the finish of the meet.

A Secondary Ambition

While in Australia, Mercedes' admiration for the exploits of air pioneers,
such as her contemporary, Amy Johnson, developed into a personal aspi-
ration. She had already experienced what it was like to take to the air
courtesy of another British aviator of that era, Sir Alan Cobham, who took
her flying during his own pioneering years.

Judging from a medical clearance form in the archives dated 1931,
Mercedes was first assessed to fly that month and she was given the instruction, 'This memo must be shown to your instructor or club prior to the
commencement of training.' The form was addressed to Mercedes at
Osbourne House in Melbourne.

Later on, during the summer of 1931, in between swims, she also received
some initial instruction at the newly opened Iona National Airways & Flying
School at Kildonan, Finglas, in Co. Dublin. This was the first privately owned
flying company to be registered in Eire and it had three Moth aircraft available for tuition purposes. In an interview with the *Irish Independent*, the
company's managing director, H. Cahill, stated that he already had thirty
pupils training for their pilot licences and that the pupils included Miss
Mercedes Gleitze, the famous swimmer, and Miss Long, a young Dublin lady
(presumably the only two women). In those early days of female emancipation, the news of her registration with this flying school also found its way
into at least one American paper, the *Harrisburg Telegraph* in Pennsylvania.

When she returned to Leicester in August that year, Mercedes told the
Leicester Mercury that she hoped to continue tuition with the Leicestershire
Aero Club and ultimately qualify for her 'A' certificate. However, her
swimming and welfare commitments inevitably took up most of her time,
and all of her money, so she was unable to pursue this latent ambition.

20

INSTITUTION OF THE GLEITZE CHARITY

In a 1927 interview with the *Sunday News* following her successful English Channel swim, Mercedes explained why she felt she had to try to do something to help people 'who have been battered by life'. During the course of the interview, the special representative suggested that her proposed scheme for a hostel was one that bristled with manifold difficulties. He referred to London's poor as the 'wastrals of London' and implied that the casuals of the streets whom she hoped to reclaim were, often as not, past reclamation. But Mercedes listened to him undaunted, and answered:

> I don't believe there are any really bad people in the world. Life is kind to some of us, and it is very cruel to others. The people who are down and out, the poor creatures who have nowhere to lay their heads at night, are not wicked. They are just unfortunate. It might have been you, it might have been me.[72]

In the event, although in 1927 she had originally envisaged a charity 'to help the London poor', after her return from the South African tour in the autumn of 1932, Mercedes and her husband settled temporarily in rented accommodation at 350 Humberstone Road in her adopted home, Leicester. This city had hosted her on many occasions, and it is where her first child was soon to be born. And so it was in this Midlands city that an idea was conceived and a decision made to put the monies in her trust fund to good use – her aim being to help unemployed people to become self-supporting and regain their self-respect.

The constitution of the charity – formally named 'The Mercedes Gleitze Homes for Destitute Men and Women' – had been put in place according to Charity Commission Rules and Regulations, the first of which stated:

> 1. The Charity shall be administered and managed by the Executive Committee hereinafter mentioned in accordance with the provisions of a Declaration of Trust dated the 20th day of June, 1928, and made between Mercedes Gleitze of the one part and Mercedes Gleitze and Edmund Maurice Roche Baron Fermoy M.P. of the other part and the regulations hereinafter contained.

Mercedes concentrated her efforts on identifying and securing the help of a small, local group of professional men with similar ideologies to herself. The original committee comprised Amos Mann JP (Chairman), G.W.R. Searle (Hon. Secretary), F. Craston-White (Hon. Solicitor), Reverend A.E. Kimpton, C.T. Barton, F.C. Barber, Philip Ashwell, J.E. Quain and W.H. Topley, with Mercedes and Lord Fermoy as *ex-officio* members.

At this time in Britain's history, any of its citizens who, through no fault of their own, had fallen into a state of poverty due to widespread unemployment had only the demeaning 1834 Poor Law (based on a harsh philosophy that regarded pauperism amongst able-bodied workers as a moral failing[73]), or the 1934 reinvented means-tested but still inadequate Unemployment Assistance Board, from which to seek help. The comprehensive Welfare State as we know it now did not exist. Soup kitchens were commonplace, but without an adequate safety net to provide basic needs, people suffered from hunger and cold and many inevitably succumbed to ill health and depression.

The notion of setting up a charity specifically to help families in that situation had always been Mercedes' objective. However, in those bleak times, general interest in charities was lukewarm and innovative ideas by her and the committee members were put to the test. For example, she secured interviews with some of the Leicester cinema managers to ask if they would be prepared to run a Sunday cinema performance on behalf of the charity, and she was told that, providing the London chiefs agreed, they would be willing to do so.

Although the piloting and development of the proposed scheme in Leicester had to be carried out piecemeal, in March 1933 the newly formed committee made a practical start and a large property in Sparkenhoe Street, Leicester, was purchased with part of the trust funds. The purchase price was £794 19s, and the executive committee noted in its minutes that the house was a fair bargain and could not have been built for that sum. (This reflected the drop in the value of housing during those years.)

The freehold property comprised an entrance hall, two reception rooms, a kitchen, a scullery, an outside toilet and a coal house on the ground floor, and eight bedrooms, a bathroom and a separate WC on the three upper floors, plus a cellared basement, a back yard and a small garden. The premises were in good repair, but although sufficient funds were left in the charity's account for future maintenance, extra money would need to be raised to convert them into self-contained flats.

It was agreed by the committee that a local appeal for additional funds should be made to cover the conversion. Leicester-based business magnates were contacted, and a comprehensive list was drawn up of manufacturing and retail companies in the city, such as Woolworths and the Co-operative Society, as well as other organisations like Toc-H, from whom they could solicit financial support. Additionally, the *Leicester Mercury* and *Leicester Evening News* covered the story and appealed to the general public on the charity's behalf for donations.

During the summer of 1933 Mercedes was committed to performing three more swimming events. She carried out her final two endurance swims in Huddersfield and Worthing respectively, and in July she travelled to Dover to await the right conditions for one last (unsuccessful) attempt to swim the Channel in the reverse direction, from England to France. After this, she she was preoccupied in a search for somewhere permanent to live that, of necessity, had to be near her husband's new place of work in London.

In October of that year, however, she wrote to the trust's honorary secretary, Mr Searle, to let him know that she would be able to spend some time in Leicester 'to fulfil my promise to supervise things'. The letter is very long, and it underlines Mercedes' determination to get the charity up and running, as well as her willingness to scrub floors to make the Sparkenhoe Street accommodation habitable, despite her sporting celebrity status:

Dear Mr Searle,

I am writing to let you know that I am now ready to commence duties at 67 Sparkenhoe Street.

In the first place the question of a female companion for myself arises, as we must not give anyone the slightest opportunity of questioning the good name of the house. In this respect I am quite willing to share my room with a poor girl. This means that to start off with, instead of taking in two poor men, we will give shelter to one man and one woman. The woman will only be there so long as I am on the premises. When the time comes for me to leave, the remaining man, who in the meantime I shall have trained as regards the duties involved, can take over the supervision of the house.

Before taking in any one at all, it will be necessary for me to live in the house for about a fortnight, as there is a tremendous lot of preparatory work to be done – rooms and stairs to be cleaned, furniture to be selected and arranged, etc., and I am ready to get started. In order not to waste any time, I shall move straight into the house on arrival at Leicester, and to enable me to do so, I would be grateful if you would have the following preparations made for me:

1) Have electric light installed.

2) Have gas laid on.

3) Have a bag of coal, a packet of matches and firewood put in.

4) Have one bed (fitted with blankets, sheets and pillow) and one chair put into the small front room on the second floor.

5) Have a cleaning outfit delivered and placed in the kitchen ready for use, as follows: Two floor cloths, one scrubbing brush, one long brush for cleaning the walls, steps, one window leather, large and small broom, a few tins of black to stain the staircase edges and the edge of the reception room floor, a tin of Gumption to polish up the marble mantle pieces, a tin of Brasso, a tin of furniture polish for the staircase railings, some liquid stove polish for blacking the fireplaces (together with necessary brushes and cloths), polishing and dusting cloths, a large kettle, a rough broom for use in the yard, carbolic or Life Buoy soap for scrubbing floors, etc., three or four packets of Hudson Powder for cleaning cupboard doors and ordinary doors, five pounds of soda, two tins of pan shine, and two pails.

6) Have the lock on the front door repaired, as I cannot open the door unless this is done.

Perhaps it would be just as well to get the above cleaning articles from the Leicester Co-operative Society providing they are as reasonable as any other stores. With regard to the bed for my room, I can temporarily use one of those intended for the men's dormitories as selected and approved by the Executive Members (Mr Quain and Mr Topley) who were kind enough to visit Morgan Squires. Mr Warriner, the Manager, will remember which type of bed it was, and please tell him that the blankets (pure wool) should not cost more than 5/- each. (Some time ago he quoted 8/- per blanket; they are being sold at 5/- in London so we ought to get them at the same price in Leicester.) In view of Mr Warriner's promise to buy some rugs from us,[74] it would perhaps be just as well to let Morgan Squires supply the dormitory beds, but please do not commit yourself as regards purchase of any other furniture from them as we want to consult our Chairman and Committee members on the matter and buy according to their wishes.

I do not want anything else put in the room. I shall only have to turn everything out again as I want to clean the floor and walls before the lino is laid. I have a pair of curtains at Lower Hastings Street and I can fetch those and put them up temporarily.

It will probably take you about a week to get the above things fixed up, so I think the best plan would be if I leave for Leicester on Sunday afternoon, October 29th, so as to be able to start work early Monday morning. Our immediate plans now are as follows:

October 20th–29th: Mr Searle to see to light, gas, coal, cleaning materials, etc.
Sunday, October 29th: Miss Gleitze to move into Sparkenhoe Street.
Monday, October 30th – Morning: Rooms to be cleaned – 1) reception room, 2) kitchen, 3) scullery, 4) one dormitory, 5) supervisor's room, 6) work room, 7) bathroom. Afternoon – Allotment of rooms to be decided upon and approved by, say, two Executive Committee members. Arrange this appointment for me please Mr Searle, and get our Chairman's sanction for two Exeutive members to decide this point. Unless we know what we are going to use the rooms for, we

will not know what furniture to put into them. I can then use the members' decision as regards room allotment as a basis for preparing the list of furnishing articles required for submittal to the Committee. Tuesday, October 31st – Morning: Clean staircases, corridors, etc. Afternoon: Hold meeting of the Executive at Sparkenhoe Street. I would be glad and very grateful if the members in question could manage this.

Agenda

1) Submit list of furniture required for entire building.

2) Submit list of initial furniture needed and obtain Committee's approval.

3) Decide as to firm and/or firms from whom equipment is to be purchased.

4) Decide on best source of food supply for men.

5) Decide on date of Finance Committee meeting so that the Midland Bank form may be completed and a Maintenance Account opened.

6) Decided on date of first Subscribers' meeting.

7) Decide on date on which the first two people are to be taken in.

8) Formal acceptance of (a) Mr Philip Ashwell as Executive member; (b) Mr Payne as Treasurer, (c) the Midland Bank as our bank. This is just a matter of form so that the names in question may be duly entered in the Minute Book.

9) Any other business.

Wednesday, November 1st – Morning: Get manager of firm and/or firms selected by Committee to take measurements for the curtains, etc. at Sparkenhoe Street.

– Afternoon: Inspect – with the assistance of, say, two Executive Members – articles to be furnished at the warehouse and/or warehouses in question.

Thursday, November 2nd: Furniture to be delivered at Sparkenhoe Street and rooms as selected to be made ready for use.

Until we are able to put more men into the house I shall do most of the domestic work myself as I am anxious for the two initial people to spend 8 hours a day at rug-making because their output of work means a source of income.

I should be very glad if you would kindly let each of the five Executive members have a copy of my letter and then let me know whether you will be able to have things ready for me by Sunday, October 29th. In the meantime I remain,

Yours sincerely,

Mercedes Gleitze

During the following year (1934), Mercedes' ability to travel and act independently was curtailed further by a second pregnancy. However, during that year, plans for the house were expanded so that the charity would be able to offer accommodation to whole families, not just single occupants. The house was eventually converted into two family-sized flats, each having a bath, sink, gas stove and hot-water system. There was also a small garden that provided a communal area where children could play.

Leicester Rotary Club

Although Mercedes had put the bricks and mortar of the charity in place, and her trust fund would maintain the fabric of the building, it was the Leicester Rotary Club that eventually facilitated the project. There was high unemployment in Britain at that time, but the effects of the Depression were unevenly dispersed. Some parts of the country fared better than others, and extracts from reports in the archives relating to the charity's collaboration with the Leicester Rotary Club describe prevailing conditions:

The Rotary Club had been working on a scheme for the transfer of juveniles from distressed areas into Leicester where there was almost certain employment for children from the time they left school, and a good chance of employment for adults too. Rotarians P. Ashwell, F.L. Attenborough, G.I.H. Parkes, S.H. Russell and M.H. Taylor, with their wives, spent a weekend in County Durham where unemployment had risen by 23 per cent – way above the national average. They found that the workers there were losing vitality, becoming unemployable, and were sapped by depression. Approximately 29,000 juveniles had never had a job, whereas there was a definite shortage of juvenile labour in Leicester. There was a preference for younger workers who were more able to adapt to the new skills demanded of them in the expanding industries of the Midlands.

Through the initial scheme some 300 boys were brought to Leicester by the Rotary Club, although 50 per cent of them returned because of homesickness and other causes, and the Committee soon realised that it was advisable to transfer complete families if possible. However, the principal difficulty in carrying out such a scheme was the provision of accommodation for whole families. An arrangement was put in place under which the Gleitze Charity's Homes in Sparkenhoe Street were to be used to accommodate such families until they 'found their feet' in Leicester. A General Council to oversee the arrangements was elected from Rotary Club members and other people of good repute in Leicester, which in turn elected Executive and Finance Committees.

During the years of the collaboration between the Gleitze Charity and the Leicester Rotary Club, an unrecorded number of families were removed from areas where their prospects of employment were almost nil, and eventually integrated into Leicester after rehabilitation in the Gleitze Homes. The families given shelter in the homes came mainly from Shildon in County Durham, with a few from Aberkenfig in South Wales. Both of these areas were severely affected by the gradually shrinking coal-mining industry – unemployment in Shildon having reached almost 100 per cent, and the Welsh mining valleys being 'numb with distress'.[75]

Unfortunately the records of everyone who occupied the homes from inception are incomplete, but details were found of the following twelve families:

Chapman	17 weeks	Husband, wife and 7 children
Pollock	(unrecorded)	Husband, wife and 2 children
MacDonald	7 weeks	Husband, wife and 3 children
Beadle	27 weeks	Husband, wife and 2 children
Dalkin	25 weeks	Husband, wife and 2 children
Jacques	8 weeks	Husband, wife and 7 children
Connolly	25 weeks	Husband, wife and 5 children

Jobson	10 weeks	Husband, wife and 3 children
Thompson	26 weeks	Husband, wife and 8 children
Ellis	39 weeks	Husband, wife and 3 children
O'Connell	10 weeks	Husband, wife, 2 children and wife's brother
Jones	50 weeks	Husband, wife and 4 children

The Rotary Club's aim was, of course, to move families in and out of the flats speedily in order that as many destitute families as possible could be transferred to Leicester. This transition was only possible after employment was secured and the incumbent families were in a position to rent houses of their own. The underlying practice was to allow the families to occupy the charity's house rent-free for two or three weeks, and then to charge a rent not exceeding one-fifth of the family's income. It was estimated that the rent charged should cover the rates.

Throughout the mid to late 1930s, the economic crisis held Britain in a tight grip, and there are some notes in reports compiled by the executive committee highlighting the problems experienced by these people. On their arrival in Leicester, many were undernourished, had very little clothing, and were 'out of benefit' when illness struck – some examples quoted being a perforated eardrum in a boy resulting in deafness, a mother suffering multiple abscesses caused by a bacterial infection, and general depression brought on by prolonged unemployment and the ensuing poverty. (It was noted in the correspondence that assistance with the rehabilitation of these dispossessed families was also given by the local branch of the Suroptimists organisation.)

Extracts from the report read:

During the whole of 1937 the house has been occupied by one and two families at a time, none of whom has been in a position to pay rent, either owing to the size of the family or through illness.

One family who took possession in 1937 were the Thompsons (husband, wife and 8 children). They arrived in January and stayed for 26 weeks, the mother being seriously ill for the greater part of that time.

Then the family named Ellis came, husband, wife and 3 children (2 adult). Both daughters were ill to start with, and consequently were not at work. Then the mother was taken ill, with the result that a month before Christmas she was removed to hospital for three or four months' treatment. This woman, prior to her illness, did a lot of decorating work throughout her part of the house. The Ellis's are still in the house and the woman is still away in hospital. They were first approached for rent last November, but owing to their troubles this point has not been pressed.

In August another family, the O'Connells (husband, wife, 2 babies, and wife's brother), came and stayed for 10 weeks. The husband only was in work, and no rent was paid during the time they were in the house.

1938: The family named Jones is still in the house. The woman is trying very hard to find suitable alternative accommodation but all the houses she has so far come across have rents of 17/6d upwards, which she says is impossible for her to pay. She is visiting all the estate agents and going through the streets herself on the look-out. With the exception of one week at Christmas, they have regularly paid rent. For one week in July they paid 10/- rent. Then the husband fell out of work. Commencing August they paid 15 weeks rent at 5/-, then 10 at 7/- and one more at 5/-. For the last two weeks they have paid the full 10/-. As the house is badly needed for another family, can something be done to find a suitable house for them to move into?

Some of the special allowances made by the Rotarians in 1937 were to cover medical expenses for those out of benefit, assisting an occupant to visit her young son in Leicester Infirmary, providing clothing, helping with the cost of the removal of furniture, and paying for the transport of the body of a young man who had died in the infirmary.

It is to their credit that the charity's executive committee decided to take rent only from those families where it had been considered desirable to charge them, and the difference between income and total expenditure on council rates and minor incidental expenses was borne by the charity.

The Approaching War

In March 1939, recruitment into the armed forces and into vital industries connected with the defence of the country had taken care of unemployment in Britain, and the charitable homes were subsequently used for another purpose. In April 1939, the trustees received a request from the Leicester Committee for Refugees from Czechoslovakia to allow their refugees to be accommodated in the Sparkenhoe Street house.

The Charity Commissioners raised no objection to it being used for that purpose, and so in June 1939 the Czechoslovakian refugees moved in. The trust paid for certain alterations and repairs in preparation for the new tenants – who in turn redecorated the rooms and kept them in good condition during their stay. No rent was charged as the refugees were not allowed to work while awaiting visas, but the Leicester Committee for Refugees took responsibility for all rates and gas accounts. The refugees were given a 10s allowance plus 2s 6d pocket money, and a *News Chronicle* fund provided them with cash for any other necessities. Once a refugee had been granted a visa, the Rotarians endeavoured to find him work in the city. The Czech refugees occupied the house from June 1939 until November 1940.

Enemy Action

On the night of 19–20 November 1940, a high-explosive bomb made a close descent on the property, demolishing all but the ground floor, and rendering it useless for future habitation. When the house collapsed, the occupants were all together on the ground floor at the back and thankfully no one was killed. A demolition order was subsequently served by the city surveyor, and once the site was levelled the trustees gave permission for the Air Raid Precautions (ARP) organisation to erect a temporary water tank to help deal with firefighting emergencies in the locality. A peppercorn rent of 5s per annum was paid to the trust for this use.

In August 1941 the activities of the charity were formally suspended for the duration of the war. The following month the general council, on behalf of the trustees, registered a claim for £800 (the 1939 market value of the house) with the War Damages Commission. The value of the property after it was destroyed by enemy action was estimated at £25. This amount was deducted from the £800, leaving a net claim of £775. The claim, however, could not be processed until hostilities had come to an end.

By July 1948 the War Damage Commission and the Income Tax Authorities had settled outstanding claims, and all monies had been handed over to the Charity Commissioners for investment in 4 per cent Consolidated Stock until it was decided in what way the funds should be used. At that date, the amount standing to the credit of the Gleitze Trust Fund was £1,426 4s 3d. In addition, the charity was still the owner of the freehold site, which was derelict, and was to be sold as soon as a suitable offer was obtained.

Shortly afterwards, under the Acquisition of Land Act 1946, the Minister for Education authorised the compulsory purchase of the site comprising 67 Sparkenhoe Street, together with neighbouring bomb-damaged sites, for the purpose of building the Leicester Sparkenhoe Street Temporary County Infants School. The footprint of the charity's site measured 320 square yards, and the purchase price offered was 14s per square yard, which amounted in total to a sale price of £224. This was a favourable increase over the pre-war site value of £170. Mercedes and Lord Fermoy signed their acceptances of this offer.

The committee had earlier put forward a suggestion to Mercedes, Lord Fermoy and the Charity Commissioner, that the entire proceeds of the sale of the charity's real estate and all the charity's cash and investments should be handed over to the City of Leicester's Old People's Welfare Association. However, this did not happen.

When approached about the matter, Mercedes responded:

With regard to the subject of your letter and the possible transfer of the remaining monies to some other charity, although I agree with you that the organisation in question is extremely deserving, I prefer for the time being to leave the money of my Fund with the Charity Commission to earn interest a little longer. Although tied down by family reasons and forced into inactivity during the past years, I feel that the near future may give me a chance to resume active interest in matters dear to my heart … so please convey my regret that at the moment I cannot sanction any transfer of money from the Charity Commission.

As it turned out, the secretary of the Charity Commission was like-minded about not transferring the funds to the Old People's Welfare Association, and said, in a letter dated 15 December 1948 to Mr Taylor (honorary secretary of the trust's general council):

With reference to the question of an appropriate destination for the assets of the Charity, I am to point out that it must be borne in mind that the object is to provide and maintain a home or homes for destitute persons of any age or sex.

The object of the Leicester Old People's Welfare Association is to promote and assist the general good of all old people in the City of Leicester. Its annual report for 1947/8 suggests that what is proposed is to provide a residential hostel for lonely old people who apparently are not required to be poor.

It is true that no one need now be destitute as it is the duty of the National Assistance Board to assist persons who are without resources to meet their requirements, but nonetheless these Trust assets cannot properly be applicable other than in some way for the benefit of those who are very poor.

In the event, the invested funds remained with the Charity Commissioners, accruing interest for four decades. And then, on 1 May 1990, as both trustees of the charity – Lord Fermoy (1885–1955) and Mercedes Gleitze (1900–81) – had long since passed away, the Charity Commissioners wrote to the Family Welfare Association (FWA) with the following proposal:

Given the charity's objects – the maintenance of a home(s) for the destitute – I wonder whether the trustees of the Family Welfare Association would be willing to consider taking on the trusteeship? This would have to be effected by a Scheme of the Commissioners, and it may also be necessary to provide for modern relief-in-need trusts, but we can consider this further if the trustees of the FWA agree to the proposal in principle.

The FWA was an appropriate choice to take over the trusteeship. Not only were its aims comparable, but the association was experienced in managing over seventy other small trusts, many of them the result of an individual's bequest. The FWA's responsibility was:

… to ensure that funds are disbursed in accordance with the governing instruments of each Trust which, even when changed, are structured so as to remain as close to the spirit of the founder's intention as is practicable, having regard to changing social circumstances.

From 1991, the Mercedes Gleitze Homes for Destitute Men and Women (since renamed the Mercedes Gleitze Relief in Need Charity) has been under the trusteeship of the Family Welfare Association (since renamed Family Action). At that time, the funds handed over to the FWA amounted to £52,435.16 in 4 per cent consolidated loan stock. They are currently being used 'to relieve either generally or individually persons who are in conditions of need, hardship, or distress by making grants of money or providing for items, services, or facilities calculated to reduce the need, hardship or distress of such persons'.

This chapter cannot be completed without giving due credit to the Leicester Rotarians and others who served on the charity's general council from 1933 through to 1950, after which date the affairs of the charity's homes in Leicester were wound up. Their services were entirely voluntary and had to be carried out in their own time. These volunteers were businessmen, accountants, solicitors, builders, local councillors, etc., and the general council included amongst its members people from the Midland Bank, the Employment Exchange of the Ministry of Labour and National Service, the British Legion, HM Prison Services, the *Leicester Mercury* and the *Leicester Evening Mail*:

Members of the General Council of the Mercedes Gleitze Homes for Destitute Men and Women throughout part or all of the period 1933–50

Officers:
Mr Amos Mann JP (Chairman), Grasmere, 107 Keyham Lane, Humberstone.
Mr N.W. Payne (Hon. Treasurer), 11 Granby Street, Leicester.
Mr G.W.R. Searle (Hon. Secretary 1933–35), 45 Gaul Street, Leicester.
Mr Mark H. Taylor (Hon. Secretary 1935–50), 104 Stoughton Street, Leicester.
Mr C.A. Duncan (Hon. Auditor), 18 Millstone Lane, Leicester.
Mr F. Craston-White (Hon. Solicitor), 27 Belvoir Street, Leicester.

Edmund Maurice Burke Roche MP, 4th Baron Fermoy (*ex officio*),
Park House, Sandringham, Norfolk.

Mercedes Gleitze (*ex officio*), Leicester/London.

Committee members:

Mr P.E. Ashwell, P.A.S.I., c/o Andrew & Ashwell, Waterloo Corner,
45 London Road, Leics.

Mr F.C. Barber, c/o the *Leicester Evening Mail*, 37 London Road,
Leicester.

Mr C.T. Barton, c/o *Leicester Mercury*, Albion Street, Leicester.

Mr G.W. Brake OBE, 33 Alexandra Road, Leicester.

Mr T. Crewe (no address available).

Mr H. Davis-Herbert (Round Table No. 39), Oadby House, Oadby.

Mr Gadd (no address available).

Mr J.B. Graham (no address available).

Capt. H.D. Hempton, c/o H.M. Prison, Leicester.

Ex-Inspector A.E. Kendall, The Limes, 10 Baden Road, Leicester.

Rev. A.E. Kimpton, St Leonard's Vicarage, Woodgate, Leicester.

Mr W.F. Maw, 11 Chepstow Road, Leicester.

Councillor J. Minto, c/o Council Offices, Leicester.

Mr F.H. Parker, 350 Humberstone Road, Leicester.

Mr G.I.H. Parkes MBE, c/o Employment Exchange, Charles Street,
Leicester.

Mr E.H. Pickering (no address available).

Mr A.B. Plummer, 17 New Street, Leicester.

Mr J.E. Quain, c/o British Legion, 29 New Bond Street. Leicester.

Mr S.H. Russell, c/o Russell & Sons, Bath Lane, Leicester.

Mr W.F. Shaw, 11 Chepstow Road, Leicester.

Mr L. Swanwick, Temple Chambers, Belvoir Road, Coalville.

Mr W.H. Topley, 196 Scraptoft Lane, Thurnby.

Alderman J.M. Walker, 333 Humberstone Road, Leicester.

EPILOGUE

The End of the Affair

In 1934, with the practical organisation of her charity being managed by the trust's executive council, Mercedes settled permanently in London with her own family. She made a few trips by train to Leicester to attend executive meetings in her *ex-officio* capacity, but in the latter part of the 1930s, with war looming and her own children to care for, most of the contact between her and the committee was carried out by letter.

She had performed her last public swimming event in August 1933. All her savings, apart from £20 which she retained, had been donated to her trust fund. As she was no longer the breadwinner, it was necessary for her husband to provide for the family. He had the essential skills needed in the now vital aircraft industries, and he found employment first with the De Havilland Aircraft Company, and later with Handley Page Limited – both companies having sites in north-west London.

When Mercedes, Patrick and infant daughter Elizabeth first moved to London, they stayed temporarily at the home of Mercedes' elder sister, Stella Seaton, and it was in Hampstead in 1934 that I was born. Shortly afterwards, they rented a modest three-bedroomed terraced house in a private estate owned by the Liverpool Victoria Insurance Company in the London suburb of Kingsbury, where in 1940 Mercedes gave birth to my brother, Fergus. This is where she spent the rest of her life.

Mercedes' transition from a high-profile sporting celebrity into a mother and housewife was absolute. She deliberately closed the door on her ten-year love affair with the sea. She never swam again – except, perhaps, during quiet moments in her musings.

A Threefold Legacy

Mercedes' legacy in regard to open-water swimming has been acknowledged by the International Swimming Hall of Fame (ISHOF) and the International Marathon Swimming Hall of Fame (IMSHOF), into which two organisations she has been enshrined as an Honour Pioneer Marathon Swimmer. An assessment of her pioneering achievements posted in April 2014 by Steven Munatones, Editor of the WOWSA-sponsored online *Daily News of Open Water Swimming* magazine, states:

> Given the era, circumstances, and global expanse of her swims, there has been arguably no greater aquatic adventurer than Mercedes Gleitze. From Ireland and Spain to South Africa and Australia, she often went swimming where no man (or woman) went before her. Without jet transportation, GPS, or others to pave the way before her in many of her swims, Gleitze set forth to do many unprecedented swims that had to be mind-boggling at the time, both physically and logistically.

Secondly, Mercedes' contribution to the rehabilitation of a number of poverty-stricken families from the mining communities during the bleak 1930s, as well as to the subsequent housing of Czech refugees at the beginning of the Second World War, could be assessed as modest in the general scheme of things, but her trust fund, although small, is still being used today to help families in need. The results of a 2013 PSE research project 'Poverty and Social Exclusion in the UK'[76] reveal that 'the number of households which fall below the minimum standard of living has increased sharply in the past 30 years. One in three people cannot afford to heat their homes properly, and 4 million Britons are not sufficiently fed.'

Her third legacy is in relation to the role model she became to women and girls during that era, encouraging them to realise their potential. While the Pankhurst womenfolk and their sister suffragettes battled unwaveringly with politicians to secure for women an equal place in society, Mercedes led by example. She contributed as an individual by publicly demonstrating to many thousands of women and girls in Britain and overseas that it was within them to be physically strong, and that sporting activity, in whatever discipline, was not just the prerogative of men.

Sea swimming is a beautiful thing, in fact an art
whose mistress should be not the few, but the
many, for does not the sea and its dangers cross
the paths of thousands? Nay, millions! What could
possibly speak more for man's prowess as an
athlete than the ability to master Earth's most
abundant, most powerful element – water, no
matter what its mood.

Mercedes Gleitze,

Diary of New Zealand Tour, 1931

APPENDIX 1

OPEN-WATER SWIMS

1923

British Ladies' Record for Thames Swimming over the 27-mile stretch between Putney and Silvertown, in 10 hrs 45 mins.

1927

18–29 July   From Westminster Bridge down the Thames to Folkestone (120 miles in ten stages).

7 October   English Channel (France to England) – 15 hrs 15 mins.

1928

6 April   Strait of Gibraltar – 12 hrs 50 mins.

1929

21 June   The Wash – 13 hrs 25 mins.

12 July   Lough Neagh (breadthways) – 13 hrs 48 mins.

13 July   Loch Ryan – 3 hrs 38 mins.
28 July   Firth of Forth – 11 hrs 22 mins.
17 August Lough Foyle (Moville to Portstewart) – 8 hrs.
20 August Lough Foyle (Portstewart to Moville) – 7 hrs.
8 September Lough Neagh (lengthways) – 20 hrs 1 min.

1930

13–18 June Around the Isle of Man (100 miles in nine stages) 56 hrs
      45 mins total swimming time.
6 August   Hellespont (Dardanelles) – Europe to Asia Minor – 2 hrs
      55 mins.
22 August Hellespont (Dardanelles) – Asia Minor to Europe – 3 hrs
      5 mins.
3 September Sea of Marmara – 7 hrs 20 mins.
25 December Wellington Harbour, New Zealand – 7 hrs 3 mins.

1931

21 January Rangitoto Island to Cheltenham, New Zealand – 1 hr
      30 mins.
24 January Won Manly Swimming/Floating Endurance Competition,
      Sydney, Australia – 48 hrs 15 mins.
5 August   Galway Bay, Eire – 19 hrs.

1932

25 March   Cape Town to Robben Island – 9 hrs 12 mins.
27 March   Robben Island to Cape Town – 7 hrs 36 mins.

Set distances in the following rivers:
10 April   Swartkops River, Cape of Good Hope – 6½ miles in 3 hrs
      31 mins.
17 April   Buffalo River, East London – 7 miles in 6 hrs 21 mins.

23 April   Modder River, Glen, Bloemfontein – 2 hrs 25 mins.
8 May   Germiston Lake, Johannesburg – 6 miles in 5 hrs 38 mins.
15 May   Hartbeespoort Dam, Pretoria – 4 hrs 45 mins.
22 May   Vaal River, Vereeniging – 6 hrs 44 mins.

Swims Attempted but Abandoned due to Low Water Temperature or Contrary Tides

1927
22 October   Vindication English Channel swim.

1928
Jun to Nov   Four North Channel attempts (Irish Sea).
17 September   14-hour endurance sea swim at Blackpool (target: 25 hours).

1929
Aug–Sept   Four more attempts on North Channel (Irish Sea).

1930
2 June   Moray Firth.
30 June   Bristol Channel.
30 September   English Channel (England to France) – Dover Town Gold Cup.

1933
2 August   English Channel (England to France) – Dover Town Gold Cup.
29 August   English Channel (England to France) – Dover Town Gold Cup.
21 September   English Channel (England to France) – Dover Town Gold Cup.

ENDURANCE SWIMS

(All carried out in UK pools, except where indicated.)

Hrs	City	Date	Venue
26	Edinburgh	31 Dec 1929–1 Jan 1930	Infirmary Street Baths
28	Dublin, Eire	9–10 February 1930	Tara Street Baths
30	Cork, Eire	25–26 February 1930	Eglinton Street Baths
31	Liverpool	7–8 March 1930	Westminster Road Baths
32	Derby	28–29 March 1930	Reginald Street Baths
33	Huddersfield	4–5 April 1930	Ramsden Street Baths
34	Belfast	21–22 April 1930	Ormeau Baths
35	Leicester	19–20 May 1930	Belgrave Baths, Cossington Street
36	Sheffield	23–24 May 1930	Glossop Road Baths
37	Douglas	9–10 June 1930	Henry Bloom Noble Baths
38	Stafford	3–4 July 1930	Royal Brine Baths
39	Wolverhampton	18–19 July 1930	Municipal Baths
40	Leicester	12–13 September 1930	Belgrave Baths, Cossington Street
40½	Dundee	24–25 September 1930	Central Baths
41	Hull	9–10 October 1930	Madeley Street Baths

41½	Newcastle	24–25 October 1930	Northumberland Baths
42	Dublin, Eire	3–4 November 1930	Tara Street Baths
42½	Wellington, NZ	31 Dec 1930–1 Jan 1931	Boys Institute Baths, Tasman Street
43	Auckland, NZ	16–17 January 1931	Auckland Tepid Baths
43½	Christchurch, NZ	12–13 March 1931	Manchester Street Tepid Baths
44	Adelaide, Aus	10–11 April 1931	Crystal Swimming Pool, Unley
44½	Melbourne, Aus	17–18 April 1931	Brunswick Baths
45	Rotherham	31 Dec 1931–1 Jan 1932	Main Street Baths
45½	Chesterfield	15–16 January 1932	Central School Baths
46	Cape Town, SA	18–19 March 1932	Long Street Baths
46½	Huddersfield	31 Dec 1932–1 Jan 1933	Cambridge Road Baths
47	Worthing	18–20 May 1933	Corporation Baths

APPENDIX 3

DIARY OF NEW ZEALAND TOUR

Note: In the diary Mercedes refers to the 'Book of Life' (B.o.L.). This was her term for the world's press. She was an avid reader of newspapers throughout her life.[77]

December 15th, 1930

For five weeks good ship Corinthic has been ploughing the fields of the Atlantic and Pacific waters and now it has reached its goal, New Zealand – Wellington, to be precise.

It is midsummer, but a gale is blowing and it is bitterly cold. Husband takes me on deck for my first view of the wonderful new land. My main impression is 'hills' – mighty, fascinating, awe inspiring; – and 'sea'. As far as the latter is concerned I confine my gaze to the section that lies between the North Island and the ship. I do not seek the coastline of the South Island.

The Cook Straits are not in a happy mood – an expanse of white horses and howling wind, spelling an atmosphere of gloom and disheartedness which I refuse to accept. That spirit of hope and confidence which has prompted me to travel 11,000 miles is too precious to lose, so I ignore the tempest of the waves and (optically) hug the coast. How beautiful the gorse looks on Wellington's hills. How enchanting the layout of the City of Wellington – like a dot of jewels nestling on the curve of a silver horseshoe.

Wellington Harbour traversed, the time for disembarkation draws near – likewise the necessity to face a new world alone; but no, not alone. Wellington men have come aboard asking for me; representatives of 'The Book of Life', in other words, press reporters and press photographers – six men in all.

Husband and I bid our shipmates farewell, then disembark. A member of the B.o.L. offers to drive us to our hotel, but we are waiting our turn in the queue for Customs' examination, so, in fairness, ask him not to wait.

A last chat with the stars who had travelled out with us – 'Squib' Burton, Norman Evans and George Greenwood. George Greenwood seems full of fun and happy anticipation of thrills to come. Good luck to them and may their speedway thrills be free from spills.

Our luggage cleared, we instruct a taxi-driver to take us to the Occidental Hotel. Everything – rooms, beds, armchairs – seems strange to us after five weeks dwelling in the limited space of a ship's cabin. We decide 'no business till tomorrow', and go for a walk past the Government Building. What strikes us as peculiar is the fact that practically every house we pass is built of wood. Another peculiarity that impresses us is the quaint calls of the newspaper boys, which seem more musical than those of newsvendors of other countries.

After dinner at the hotel we retired to our room. My object in coming to New Zealand is to make an attempt to swim across the Cook Strait. The distance I shall have to traverse is about 16 miles. The currents I shall have to contend with run at an average speed of 3½ knots on a neap tide, and 5 knots on a spring tide, especially if the spring tide coincides with a gale. Personally, I feel inclined to make my attempt during a neap tide as there is less likelihood of being overtaken by a storm when the currents are not running at top speed. In most of my sea swims I favour the neaps, although my rate of travelling is only one mile per hour as against three miles an hour on a spring. The difference between neap- and spring-tide swimming is that, with a spring tide the swimmer reaches his or her objective on a very pronounced zig-zag course, making a distance of, say, 10 miles as the crow flies into anything between 27 and 40 miles according to strength of spring – and with a neap tide the goal can be reached on a fairly direct course, though this means swimming across tide and swimming hard every inch of the way without the benefit of a 4–5 knot drift. The position of the wind has a very great influence on the success or failure of a swim. To swim against a head wind, receiving frothing waves full force in your face once for every yard you swim, is real punishment – punishment which I have suffered for five continuous hours at a time, on numerous occasions, in numerous seas. Apart from the physical discomfort caused, a 'header' has the disheartening effect of taking you back about one yard for every yard of forward propulsion. With an accompanying wind on the other hand, that is, a wind true to your course, matters are vastly facilitated and the effect of a favourable wind as far as progress is concerned is almost as beneficial as the favourable drift of a current.

As far as my Cook Strait task is concerned, I consider the cold temperature of the water a greater enemy than either the distance or the currents. Difficulty with regard to currents can be overcome by careful study and by the necessary changes in the calculated course. The distance obstacle in my case can be considered as negligible on account of the greater distances I have already successfully traversed (Lough Neagh, Ireland, 19 miles), but when it comes to fighting the cold, when the temperature is estimated at being below 55 degrees, the chances are 100 to one that the battle will be a hard one. Here, we come to an obstacle which no study or effort can eliminate: the human body is simply not meant to cope with the icy temperatures of watery depths – we are not cold-blooded like fish and, consequently, not capable of acclimatising ourselves to the conditions prevalent in the regions of fish, which means that if we encroach upon the latter's elements, we must pay the penalty.

Most people seem to be under the impression that the grease long-distance swimmers are in the habit of applying prior to entering the water has the effect of keeping out the cold. This is not so. During the course of my career as a swimmer I have used many kinds of substances for greasing purposes – ordinary lard, olive oil, porpoise oil, sheep oil, and thick engine oil, but I have never found them of any use as a means of protection from the cold. My sole purpose in using grease prior to long immersions in water is to protect the skin from becoming waterlogged. The substance I shall apply prior to taking the water for my Cook Strait attempt will probably be whale oil.

The coldest sea I have swum in so far is the Irish Channel, the temperature in these waters varying between 44 and 58 degrees, and the mere memory of my attempts to conquer this Channel makes me shiver. If the waters in the Cook Strait are anything near as cold as those of the Irish Channel I doubt whether the swim can be success-fully accomplished. If, on the other hand, on the day of my attempt I shall have a steady average of 60 degrees, I consider I stand a good chance of successfully accomplishing the task. I wonder how long it will be before I make my attempt? I cannot conceive it possible that I shall do so just yet; it seems so cold, so windy – wintry in fact – and yet it is midsummer. However, a talk with one or two experts tomor-row should clear this point. I can then make my plans accordingly.

December 16th, 1930
Breakfast – press interviews – a complimentary studio-sitting in a Wellington studio (modern, beautiful and well on a par with English studios) – replies to telephonic enquiries. Lunch – and another morn-ing gone. And now for the business of the day.

One of this morning's callers – a member of B.o.L. – offered to take me to a Captain O'Neil (a man who had had many years' piloting experience in local waters) for the purpose of consultation. Gladly I availed myself of the invitation. The Captain proved to be a very interesting man who hails from Dublin. His father was a prominent Irishman who compiled some wonderful books containing beautiful reproductions of the ancient Celtic Crosses scattered all over Ireland. An original copy of these books is still in the captain's possession. The artistic, skilled and refined work on Celtic Crosses as shown by the reproductions prove that the Irish as a race were scholars already many hundreds of years ago.

Laying aside the Captain's wonderful book, our conversation drifted from a subject of ancient culture to one still more ancient – the time-old sea, eg the Cook Strait. (1) Is the present time an opportune one for making the proposed attempt? (2) Is the water at its warmest now? (3) Are there any dangerous fish to contend with? (4) Are there any suitable boats available for the job?

Very soon Captain O'Neil was able to put my mind at ease with regard to all these points: (1&2) The present month is not the best for the attempt, the water being as yet much too cold – wait until February, he advised – the sun will have had a better chance of penetrating the water and the temperature will have improved by at least one or two degrees. (3) From his experience no creatures frequent the Strait which might be regarded as a source of danger. (4) He knows a fisherman who has a good class fishing boat and spends his days fishing in local waters, who might be able to render me the required services – his name being Mr John Tait. The Captain promised to get in touch with Mr Tait and ask him to call on me tomorrow so as to go into the matter of a suitable course, requisite boating arrangements, etc. This completed the business part of our interview and, after a welcome cup of tea served by the Captain's wife, the B.o.L. representative took us on an inspection tour of Wellington's swimming pools.

At the Te Aro Open-Air Baths I had the pleasure of meeting the Wellington champion, Miss Kathleen Miller, a fine girl who seems to have the right physique as well as the real sporting and winning spirit necessary for aquatic feats. After Te Aro, we drove to the Boys' Institute Tepid Baths. The B.o.L. representative introduced me to Mr Jordan, the Director, who showed me the interior of Wellington's Tepid Baths. Asked the latter if he would allow me the use of his baths for an endurance swim. Forty-two hours is my present record, as established in Dublin a few days before sailing to New Zealand. To my great delight Mr Jordan seemed favourably disposed towards granting my wish and asked me to call tomorrow at 2 o'clock for his definite consent. The date suggested for my endurance swim is December 31st. A swim on New Year's Eve will mean that I will be ending the year 1930 the same way as I started it: 12 months ago, at Edinburgh, when I swam out the old and in the new at the Infirmary Street Baths. By swimming continuously for 26 hours I beat the existing record by one hour. I have devoted the months that followed this Hogmanay event to increasing my time.

After dinner at the hotel Hubby took me to the pictures. He is a rather heavy smoker and during the performance, as is his habit during shows in England, he puffed away at his cigarettes. Presently a tap on his shoulders and a remonstration: 'smoking not allowed'. Poor Hubby nearly collapsed – it wasn't so much the remonstration as the idea of 'no smoking' during a show! He had never heard the like of it before and I am afraid it will take him weeks to recover from the shock. As far as I was concerned, the 'shock' was merely in the nature of a pleasant surprise. What a wonderful regulation – if only it were in force at home. Think what it means: no layers of cigarette and pipe fumes to spoil the clarity of the screen – no streams of cough-creating fumes disturbing one's breathing – no continuous striking of matches to light obstinate pipes – a purer atmosphere – less distur-bances – general peace and, as a consequent, greater enjoyment and more beneficial entertainment. Only a trifling regulation, yet a boon to humanity, for think of the thousands of men who frequently spend two hours of their time at shows – and of these men's lungs and the benefit they derive by the enforced two hours' abstinence.

December 17th, 1930

Breakfast – telephone calls – more interviews – inspection of a ware-house – then another photographic sitting. This time in a commercial studio. After the sitting was introduced to the President of the Evans Bay Swimming Club, who invited me to the Club meeting to be held on January 10th.

Met Captain O'Neil by appointment at the Queen's Wharf and was conducted by him to the man in charge of the Harbour Board Signal Station. This man corroborated the gist of the information and advice given me by the Captain yesterday.

One thing is clear to me, therefore, and that is that I must post-pone activities as far as my Cook Strait swim is concerned until February next.

Lunch at 1 o'clock. At 2 o'clock a tramcar ride to the Baths to obtain Mr Jordan's definite approval of my swim. The answer was the one I longed for – an affirmative one. Now I can forget about the Cook Strait and the cold for a matter of six weeks and concentrate on my proposed 42½ hours' swim, and the organisatory arrangements. Thank you, Wellington, for giving me the chance to better my record.

Received an invitation to use the Lyceum Club any time I wish during my stay in Wellington. Just before dinner we received a caller – Mr John Tait – with a friend, half an hour's talk with whom convinced me that I could have no better man. He expressed his willingness to hire me his boat and give me the necessary piloting services. Mr Tait, too, agreed with the advice given by Captain O'Neil, namely, that activities should be postponed until February next. His opinion was that if I chose to swim on a neap tide I should start from the Wellington side, whereas, if I selected a spring tide I should enter the water on the South Island side. Told Mr Tait I should prefer a neap tide and a North Island start. The first neap in February is due on the 8th.

The outcome of our interview was that I accepted Mr Tait's offer of his piloting services for my proposed Cook Strait attempt and that we should meet shortly before the February neaps to go into the matter of a detailed course.

After dinner another visitor – a B.o.L. representative – one of the six who had met us on the boat. He offered to help us search the town for some nice private lodgings. Hotel life for a day or two, or even a week, is very nice, but when it comes to a stay of several weeks the matter of high cost makes the sojourn prohibitive. We were glad, therefore, to avail ourselves of our press friend's invitation.

Darkness had descended by the time we reached Wellington Terrace, where several houses displayed notice boards of 'Rooms to Let', and we could scarcely discern the house numbering plates. Quite by chance the car was stopped at No. 138, where a large, comfortable, front ground-floor room was vacant, although no notice boards were displayed. We decided to take the room for two or three weeks, and our press friend offered us his car for the luggage removal tomorrow morning.

December 18th, 1930

Packed our trunks after breakfast in readiness for removal to 138 Wellington Terrace. Friend pressman arrived at the appointed hour. Before proceeding to our new home he took me to a local elementary school where he had some business to perform. The occasion was the breaking-up ceremony prior to the Christmas holidays. Strange that I should witness this, for just a year ago, about the very same time, I witnessed a similar event – the Christmas break-up at one of Edinburgh's elementary schools.

The picture I witnessed today – boys and girls in many dozens assembled in the open school playground, a group of teachers near an improvised platform, a speech by the Head, then distribution of certificates to the accompaniment of enthusiastic clapping of all assembled little hands – brought back into my mind the Scottish picture of a year ago: boys and girls assembled in many hundreds in a large interior school hall, a group of teachers, Board of Education inspectors, a school choir seated in a row on the hall platform, an opening song by the choir, the soul-awakening Christmas hymn 'Still Night, Holy Night', a speech by the Head, a speech by the Board of Education man, distribution of class certificates, distribution of swimming certificates by myself, then an evacuation of the platform by grown-ups in favour of little amateur actors of the school who presented dances and short plays in happy termination of the day's function.

The Edinburgh scene of 12 months ago, over 12,000 miles north of New Zealand, is the Edinburgh scene of today, and the self-same scene is being enacted here today in Wellington. As coast-lapping ocean rollers engird New Zealand soil, so ocean waves kiss the shores of Bonnie Scotland. As the spirit of Christianity engirds the soul-land of Young Scotland, so the voice of Christmas calls to festivity the childhood of New Zealand.

By noon we had moved in and settled down. We are having breakfast in and all other meals out. Meals in Wellington restaurants are just as cheap – if not cheaper – than those in home restaurants. In England, for instance, the usual price for a good square midday meal is half-a-crown, while here in most restaurants 1/6d or 2/- will cover the cost of an equally good meal.

One or two points which have struck me as being of outstanding nature are the following: the meat seems to be more tender, the green-stuff, lettuce and the like, seems to be more plentifully served and of nicer quality, and fresh cream seems to be more frequently apportioned.

After lunch at the Wattle, husband and I spent a quiet afternoon at home. A B.o.L. representative had recently suggested that a swim across Wellington Harbour would constitute an aquatic performance of interest. Only one man had so far successfully accomplished the swim, whilst three others had tried and failed. The distance is about seven miles across. Decided to follow out the suggestion and swim Christmas Day, so the question of the moment is: 'Would Mr Tait be free to give me his piloting services and loan of a boat for that particular day.?' B.o.L. again to the rescue – a car drive to Island Bay to the pilot's house.

By reason of Mr Tait's acquiescence to my requirements the proposed harbour swim was definitely fixed to take place December 25th, weather permitting of course. This means I have now three New Zealand swims on hand – the Cook Strait, February next; the Wellington Harbour swim on Christmas Day; and the 42½ hours' endurance swim on New Year's Eve. Shall I successfully achieve them all – or shall I fail?

With a sea swim one can never really guarantee success. So much depends on it – position of wind, condition of sea, state of temperature, run of tides, physical fitness, etc – so much so that any definite prediction of success merely serves as an emphasis of boastfulness and lack of real experience on the part of the predictor.

December 19th, 1930

Decided to spend the day fixing arrangements for my endurance swim. A record swim of this description entails a great deal of organisatory work. Devoted the morning to business calls. Placed order with the Tramway Department for posters, placed order with B.o.L. Jobbing Department for printing of posters, etc. In the afternoon we tackled the question of timekeepers to supervise the swim and vouch for its authenticity. Here again things were made easy for us by B.o.L.

A press friend drove us to the Post Office in Kilbirnie, a suburb of Wellington, where he introduced us to Mr Pete Coira, Secretary of the Wellington Amateur Swimming Club. After placing my requirements before this gentleman, he expressed his willingness to do his best, though, most people being out of town for the New Year holidays, it might be difficult to enlist the service of sufficient men to tackle the job. Mr Coira rang up Mr McNie, another prominent member of the Association, and the result of his enquiry was most gratifying, for Mr McNie agreed to cooperate with Mr Coira to assure of my having the sportsmen necessary for the event.

December 20th, 1930

Breakfast at 8.30 a.m., then a continuation of yesterday's business calls, the Office of the Entertainment Tax officials being our first port of call. Here I found the laid-down regulations and mode of dealing with cases such as mine (where it is impossible to foretell the number of tickets likely to be sold) extremely efficient and satisfactory. Instead of having to lay down a large sum of money on a roll of advance entertainment stamps (as is the case at home) which, if the audience is small, will never be used, it is only necessary to fill in a form registering the entertainment and a guarantee form witnessed by a responsible friend.

After lunch Hubby and I were taken for a car ride. Witnessed the Christmas party given to Wellington railway workers and relatives in one of the sheds at the Railway Depot. It was a wonderful gathering of men, women and children, and the event speaks well for Wellington's industrial social relationship and commercial good fellowship.

While I was standing amidst the throng I caught my first glimpse of New Zealand's wonderful native race. The musicians who supplied the melodies for this great Christmas gathering were Maori men.

The M.C., learning of my presence in the hall, asked me to step onto the platform. I conceded to his request and bowed to the assembled crowd while the M.C. introduced me through his megaphone. Husband stood beside me, and thus I faced my first New Zealand audience.

Later in the afternoon I witnessed another Christmas festivity – this time one given to the staff and relatives of a city commercial house. Here I found everyone in festive humour.

About 7 o'clock Hubby and I were driven to the Kilbirnie Dirt Track to witness the night's speedway races, the car we were fetched in being a pale blue Vauxhall Super sports car (the property of the speedway officials).

Towards the end of the night's performance we were summoned to the track, where I presented the winner of the silver gauntlet – a local rider – with his well-earned trophy.

After the presentation Hubby and I were driven round the dirt track in the Vauxhall. We stood on the running board of the car facing the audience, and as it encircled the track I waved my arm to the crowd in response to their clapping, cheers and smiles.

Frank Bond and Jim Kempster were the two English riders competing in tonight's event, forming a team of six with the noted

Australians H. Buchanan and L. Hale plus two others. Wally Kilmister, one of New Zealand's current stars, joined with Tim Wilkinson, Clarrie Tonks, Bill Harvie and two others to make up the local side. The event constituted my third public appearance during a speedway show, my first having taken place at Manchester in 1929, when I presented a silver cup and golden helmet to Rider Jervis, and the second in September of this year at the Leicester speedway, when I was driven round the course and spoke to the audience through the loud speaker. Dirt track riding is certainly a game that calls for grit, accuracy and pluck. A fine sport, interesting and thrilling, although I would enjoy watching it much more if the riders had a greater guarantee of safety.

December 21st, 1930
Accompanied husband to Sunday Mass. Had lunch in town. Found most restaurants closed. Spend the afternoon at home. Did some clerical work, bringing my letter book, telegram book, photo book, contract book, etc, up to date. Retired early.

December 22nd, 1930
Spent the morning completing endurance and harbour swim arrangements. Afternoon at the Lyceum Club, where I was introduced to some of the members and entertained to tea. The Club rooms are beautiful, and I felt much honoured by the kind invitation extended to me to use them at any time I wished.

Later had an interview in the D.I.C. Building with Mr Luckie, the Deputy Mayor, who consented to act as official starter of my endurance swim.

December 23rd, 1930
A Wellington business man very sportingly devoted the morning to us, taking us for a drive along the shore road to Lyall Bay and across to the harbour peninsula. We broke the journey at the golf pavilion, where the matron in charge entertained us to a welcome meal of tea, sandwiches and cake. After signing the visitors' book we proceeded on our way. I think for a car drive there is nothing more fascinating than a pretty coastal road, and New Zealand certainly seems to be well endowed with these. Had lunch at the Wattle. Another car drive in the

afternoon, this time in the direction of Petone, where a miniature fair was in full swing.

In the evening we were shown round the Broadcasting Station 2YA. Watched the announcer broadcast some gramophone records. A very fine station. Received an invitation to give a 10 minutes' talk. Agreed to do so tomorrow evening at 9 o'clock.

December 24th, 1930

Arranged about witnesses for tomorrow's swim. Bought the necessary requisites – food, drink, grease, etc., to take with us on the boat. Met Doris, a fellow passenger on the Corinthic, who took us into her shop to introduce us to her mother. Both Doris and her mother, also one of her brothers, will be members of my boat party tomorrow.

Lunch at one – then home. Had a visit from Mr Tait to discuss tomorrow's plans. The harbour waters have been very boisterous the past few days and the wind seems too strong to die down overnight. In Mr Tait's opinion there is little chance for a swim tomorrow. Though disheartened and disappointed, I accept the possibility of a cancellation of tomorrow's programme, but appealed to Mr Tait to let me have my swim if the morning should bring a slight improvement, even if conditions are not exactly what you might term 'ideal'. It was arranged that he should ring me up at 8 o'clock tomorrow morning to definitely advise me whether or not the swim would take place.

A little before nine husband accompanied me to the Broadcasting Station and, at 9 o'clock sharp, I gave the promised 10 minutes' broadcast covering the three swims I had planned whilst in New Zealand.

Wellington Harbour – Christmas Day, December 25, 1930

Wonderful Christmas news: The wind had dropped – the squall had died down – conditions seemed favourable for the intended harbour swim. Soon Mr Tait's telephonic confirmation of the suitability of weather conditions came through, and husband and I felt glad at heart.

Breakfasted – packed our gear ready for transport to the harbour, then went to Church to attend Christmas Mass. About 11 o'clock two parties of friends arrived simultaneously with a car to drive us to our taking-off point – the Eastbourne Ferry Wharf – so Husband went in one of the cars, I in the other. On arrival, Husband helped me grease

(with lard) in one of the private offices on the wharf, then, all prepared for the plunge and an old coat around me, I was conducted by
Mr J. McNie (who is to officiate my swim) to the extreme end of the
wharf; a halt on the way for some photographs by B.o.L. and a formal
introduction to the thousands who had collected to witness my start.

With every swim it is my custom to grease my legs and arms on the
very spot from which I am taking off, just prior to entering the water.
If I applied the grease some distance away from the starting place
there is the possibility that by the time I get to the water's edge most
of it will have rubbed off or melted if it happens to be a sunny day.

At 11.30 exactly I plunged into the harbour waters, my surrounding audience wishing me 'good luck'. Until acclimatised to the
harbour temperature – which, by the way, fluctuated between 61 and
62 degrees, I used the trudgen stroke, then I settled down to using
breaststroke all the way across, with the exception of three or four
spells of trudgen in the fourth and fifth hour of the swim.

As is the custom on all my swims I kept to a swimming position
about a yard or two behind my attendant rowing boat. For the space
of about one hour we were followed by a small fleet of skiffs, some of
the manipulators of which sang to me. The sea remained smooth till
1 o'clock, when a change of wind caused some choppiness. We were
now passing Jerningham Point, our point of steering being slightly to
the north.

At twenty minutes past one I had my first feed – just a cup of hot
milk in one of Mr Tait's enamel fisherman's mugs. By 2 o'clock we
had reached a position opposite Point Halswell, although the drift of
tide, which was rather strong, was still taking us out of our course. By
2.45 we were well in sight of Soames Island, and by 3.45 abreast of it.

To our delight we were joined by two gaily flag-bedecked launches
containing a crowd of Italian fishermen who had steamed out from
Island Bay with the express purpose of cheering me up with songs.
What wonderful voices they had and what a fine repertoire of Italian
songs. At my request they sang 'Santa Lucia', a favourite melody
of mine, to the accompaniment of the string instruments they had
brought with them.

It was lovely, but I must not forget mention of the Scottish part of
the afternoon's musical programme – the songs rendered by merry

Scotsmen on board, which too I enjoyed. My favourite Scottish song is 'Rolling Home to Bonnie Scotland', and the pilot's wife, Mrs Tait, gave me a very fine rendering of this lovely melody. I love the song, not merely because of its beauty, but because it brings back to me a wonderful memory – the last fighting hour of my successful swim across the Firth of Forth when, in the depth of darkness, about 50 rowing boats brought out to me from my prospective landing shore, full of well-wishing, singing and cheering Scotsmen, accompanied me in the last laps of my swim. It was like a page from a fairy-tale book which nothing can ever efface from my mind. Pitch darkness – the mast lights of my pilot boat – a yard in front of me the guiding lantern of my attendant rowing boat – to the left and to the right of me, in fact all around me, the flickering, star-like lights of the 50 rowing boats – just darkness and twinkling hurricane lamps – and voices, voices producing melody – the tune of 'Rolling Home to Bonnie Scotland'.

At 4.35 pm Hubby rowed to the pilot ship for my third feed of hot milk. The only solid food I had during the swim comprised two egg sandwiches and some iced cake made by my landlady. An event of interest during the swim was the passing by of the ferry boat, the passengers of which waved to me in appreciation of my endeavour.

At 5.30 pm, the sea – which for the past two hours had been fairly calm – again changed its mood, choppiness gradually changing to roughness. About this time, too, we were taken out of our course, adverse wind and contrary set of tide hampering progress. Nearing the prospective landing shore a calm sea once more favoured us, the landing being successfully effected at 6.45 pm in the presence of a large crowd of spectators, whose warm and enthusiastic welcome was most inspiring. What surprised me on reaching the line of waiting humanity after wading through about 25 yards of shallow water, was the fact that the crowd level was not the land line. So keen was the spectators' interest that the people comprising the front rank were actually standing in the sea. As my landing goal I took that part of the crowd where Hubby had been made a fixture. B.o.L. was there three-strong, with cameras. The photographs taken, I walked to Hubby's side, who wanted to take me by the arm to drag me through the crowd. 'Don't touch me yet,' I said to him, 'this is still sea, let my feet touch dry land.'

Dry land reached, I allowed Husband to take me to the pavilion, the proprietor of which had very kindly offered me hospitality. With an old coat of Mr Tait's on top of my greasy costume, I paced the pursuing crowd – my steps being almost faster than those of the crowd, so fit and fresh did I feel after my seven hours' swim.

The pavilion duly reached, I had a hot bath, after which I joined my official boat party (about 20 strong) at table for a welcome hot dinner of soup, roast lamb, potatoes and peas, pudding and tea. Dinner over, we retreated to the pilot ship and steamed full speed ahead to Island Bay, where we arrived about half past eleven. A refreshing drink at the pilot's house in Island Bay, then home by taxi to Wellington Terrace, well satisfied with the outcome of the day's adventure.

Today's swim constitutes one of the easiest of my career. There was nothing difficult, complicated or gruelling about the venture. The swim was 'play' from start to finish, so much so that I feel sure it will be swum many times after me. Also, if the start is timed to fit the set of tides and if an overarm stroke is used all the way across, it can easily be done in quicker time. Here is a swim which can be classed as falling into the range of Wellington swimmers who possess the greatest staying power, the best stamina, the least energy-exerting stroke, the longest power of endurance, the strongest will power, the ability to cope with any condition of sea, and the physique most suitable for the work involved.

I am sure that amongst New Zealand's athletes a sufficiently large number of swimmers could be found to warrant the inauguration of an annual season for swims across the harbour, a trophy for victory to be given to the competitor whose achievement is ranked as the best swim. The prize should be given not necessarily to the one who had effected the quickest landing, but to the one whose successful crossing constituted the finest exhibition of a conquest of adversities – capable manipulation of rough seas, winning fight against cold temperature, etc. A conquest of a certain stretch of sea under adverse conditions in, say, six hours, is a greater achievement than a successful crossing of the same waters under ideal conditions in, say, three hours.

As far as my own Harbour swim achieved today is concerned, I am proud to be the first woman to have accomplished the feat, and I thank all those who have today so willingly and sportingly sacrificed their time in order to help me on to success. To them in the first place credit of the event is due.

Sea swimming is a beautiful thing, in fact an art whose mistress should be not the few, but the many, for does not the sea and its dangers cross the paths of thousands? Nay, millions! What could possibly speak more for man's prowess as an athlete than the ability to master earth's most abundant, most powerful element – water, no matter what its mood.

SWIMS ABANDONED DUE TO LOW WATER TEMPERATURE OR CONTRARY TIDES

(Note: The eight North Channel attempts that Mercedes made in 1928 and 1929 are documented in full in the main body of this memoir.)

Vindication Swim (English Channel)

A special correspondent from the *Kent Evening Echo* was amongst the group of journalists accompanying Mercedes on the vindication swim, and he sent on-the-spot messages of the swim's progress at intervals to his editor via pigeon post – the only means of communication available to the little group of vessels out in the English Channel. These 'winged' messages were published in the *Kent Evening Echo* on 21 October 1927. They were also reprised in the *Folkestone Herald* on 22 October 1927, with the addition of the final three dispatches which reached the mainland after the *Kent Evening Echo* had gone to press.

THE MESSAGES
(By our Special Representative accompanying Miss Gleitze)
(The whole of these messages were received by pigeon)

I left Folkestone last night at about 6.20 in the *F.E.11*. After an uneventful crossing in a calm sea, we arrived off Gris Nez about 10 p.m.

At midnight I sat in the forecastle of the *F.E. 11* riding off anchor at Cape Gris Nez when Mr Allen, Miss Gleitze's trainer, came aboard to discuss fine details with Mr Sharpe, the pilot.

To me he said: 'She is as fit as can be. She has done a long walk to-day as exercise. She feels very confident.'

I asked, what do you think of her chances?

He replied: 'I believe she will do it.'

I had travelled over in the *F.E. 11* when the temperature was suggestive of frost. To me it seemed impossible that I was going to see a woman on October 21st start a swim.

Moon's Welcome

Yet into the water she waded and was as cheery as if going to picnic. The moon peeped out over calm sea as if to welcome her.

The party of London journalists who have been staying at Cape Gris Nez awaiting the start looked a piteous band aboard the tug.

They had to wade thigh deep to a small boat and spent the early morning in pyjamas and overcoats awaiting clothes being dried.

Mr Pollock who removed his shoes to wade into the water ran a large codfish hook through his foot and the doctor had to come aboard the tug from the *F.E. 11* to remove it. All the newspaper men are on board the tug '*Alsace*'.

7 a.m.

ABOARD BOULOGNE TUG 'ALSACE'

Miss Mercedes Gleitze started at 4.15 Cape Grisnez.

Dark, but favourable, light breeze, S.S.E. Icy cold aboard.

Water temperature 56.

The start of the swim was witnessed by Mr A. Hirst representing the National Swimming Association, two medical officers, and a large party of journalists.

Swimming steady breaststroke. Miss Gleitze left on the finish of the ebb tide and was taken westwards past the Grisnez lighthouse.

At the end of 2 hours she was 2½ miles N.W. of the lighthouse and received her first refreshments.

When Mr Allen, her trainer, suggested food, she insisted that she would only be fed every two hours.

Told that time had expired she remarked: 'I thought it was only half-an-hour.'

NOT UNDER LEE OF BOAT

She refused to swim under the lee of the boat, and when Mr J.H. Sharpe, acting as pilot, manoeuvred the *F.E.11* to shelter her she refused the cover of the boat and swam away.

At intervals she carried on an interesting conversation with the crew. Now about three miles N.N.W. of Cape Grisnez lighthouse, and Miss Gleitze is swimming very wide of the boat.

Two small boats are in attendance.

Miss Nora Baker is aboard the *F.E.11* as swimmer's companion.

9 a.m.

Grey skies obscure the sun and a wind freshening from S.E. has whipped the sea up until it has become moderately choppy. Still it has the effect of causing the water's movement to come from behind. Musicians were hired to provide some music and for that purpose were placed on board the official boat. Their condition was soon pitiable.

MAL DE MER

Seasick beyond hope of recovery they were transferred to the more commodious tug where they were soon lost in the safety of the crew's quarters.

Journalists sought to deputise but their efforts as instrumentalists were as inefficient as their apparel was scant.

MORE 'TIPPERARY.'

Still they sang and Miss Gleitze showed her appreciation as she asked for more. 'Tipperary,' 'Smile, smile, smile,' and 'Britannia Rules the Waves' they tendered, and in turn – at least those to whom the action of the drifting tug did not turn seasick – did.

Her observers shivered, but on went Miss Gleitze without showing the slightest effect of the cold.

Just in front of her sat her trainer in the stern of a small boat watching all the time, occasionally talking to her, and now and again passing out the feeding cup.

CHRISTMAS CAROLS

Spirited airs, the latest jazz and eventually carols which felt seasonable were sung by the Pressmen, and in this way at 8.30 the French coast was lost sight of by those in the small boats and was barely discernible to those on the tug.

At that hour we were favoured with a sight of the sun. It made things happier, but the cold air was intense.

Meanwhile Miss Gleitze was forging ahead with a spirit that was absolutely indomitable. Maintaining the breaststroke with very few reversions to the side stroke she plodded on with a smile that would have done credit to a modern Hercules.

Tramp steamers and steam trawlers passed by and hooted a syren of encouragement.

Trainer, pilot, and all concerned in the swim wondered at the rate of progress. Would she stand the cold?

From shivering lips aboard words of encouragement were handed out, to all of which Miss Gleitze had a cheery answer.

I have never seen anything more game in my life. Her face is a trifle blue, she has no complaint.

11 a.m.

By 10.30 the French coast disappeared and an hour later the South Foreland cliffs were visible through haze.

There is a slight sun and the sea is a trifle smoother.

The wonderful pluck, cheerfulness and indomitable perseverance of the swimmer are amazing.

She swims on cheerily using the breaststroke the greater part of the time and occasionally varying with short stretches of side stroke.

NO COMPLAINT

She made no complaint of cold and smiles cheerily as though she was perfectly happy, whilst onlookers are far from happy.

'Let's have more community singing' she asked when the small band of Pressmen – reduced from 20 on the French coast to 11 on the boats, ceased from the chorus singing. Everything from Tipperary, Christmas hymns, carols, and school songs were lustily bawled out by way of cheer.

At half past ten one of the musicians 'came back to life.'

He played 'Tea for Two,' the 'Froth-blowers' Anthem,' and 'God Save the King,' and then he was joined by another, but either the music or the singing sent them back to their hiding places.

AIR GREETING

At 11.10 a.m. the Paris Air Mail circled round the swimmer and continued its flight.

Changes in the attendant boat were made from time to time, Mr Hayward occupying the stern while Mr Allen prepared food.

We are opposite the South Foreland, and the tug master computes that we are at least within 10 miles of the land.

The cliffs are getting whiter and the pilot has caused the red ensign to be hoisted on the F.E. 11 in order that people on the Kentish coat may see the approach to the English coast.

SECOND TIDE

The second tide has served Miss Gleitze wonderfully well and hopes are becoming far more confident as to the issue.

Last night there were many pessimists, but now they look far more hopeful.

The band has come back to life. The tug too has just run up a strong of flags denoting her business.

Journalists with dried clothes are becoming more cheerful. Enforced inactivity prompts them to sing and as Miss Gleitze appreciates the 'music', they carry on. Wind still E.S.E., trifle fresher, sea lumpy, but clouds appear to be approaching from behind with some rapidity.

12 NOON

Swimming strong and still as cheery as ever. Miss Gleitze joined in the jokes of accompanying Pressmen.

The complete failure of the 'band' has led to a spirit of revival, and amongst other songs going 'Another little drink won't do us any harm,' as she gets her bottle of nourishment.

The tide is helping the swimmer along the Channel towards Folkestone.

She shows no sign of cold or fatigue.

SIGHTED BY CALAIS BOAT

The Captain of the *Isle of Thanet* outward bound for Calais, reports at 1.26 having seen Miss Gleitze swimming nine miles off the pier head, Dover.

The official in-shore sea temperature at Dover this morning was 56.3 degrees.

1.45 p.m.

The mail boat Calais to Dover passed us a quarter of an hour ago.

We were abreast of St. Margaret's Bay with the tide sending us up towards Folkestone.

The tug *Alsace* acted as a buffer for the wash from the mail boat, but it was not sufficiently near to be harmful to Miss Gleitze.

Mr Allen has been in the boat for over two hours with her. He is watching and encouraging and she still smiles on especially when she shows her wilfulness in the matter of getting away from the lee of the *F.E.11.*

'Amazingly wonderful,' is how she is described by those aboard.

I have admired my colleagues. Unable to work from loss of means of communication, they are giving themselves fully to cheering the swimmer on.

All songs are lively.

MISS GLEITZE CHOOSES HYMN

Miss Gleitze chooses the hymns which are occasionally sung, but real variation is the order of the day.

I have just watched her as she smilingly chatted to Harry Sharpe. She has got great faith in her pilot and so has the trainer. Both have eyes like hawks and have used them watching her since 4 a.m.

Their conversation guides them as to the condition of Miss Gleitze.

GETTING SLEEPY

She is getting sleepy now, and as soon as she appears as though she will relapse into anything approaching that condition the whole crowd roar at her and she wakes up, as it were, smiling and struggling on.

As the pigeon is about to leave the ship she is being sung to hymns she has asked for, and 'Abide with me,' is being sung.

To me it suggests sleep. We are about seven miles off Dover and all is being well. There is every hope of success.

Kent Evening Echo, 21 October 1927.

At this point in time the *Kent Evening Echo* went to press, but the final three messages were published the next day in the *Folkestone Herald*:

2.15 p.m.

Miss Gleitze flagging considerably, and now appears to be suffering from cold.

She is struggling on manfully, but I see no hope.

She is getting much slower, and to us men it seems cruel that she should endure. Temperature water 53. Those on boat could not keep warm.

2.38 p.m.
Expecting every minute to see her come out now. The land has disappeared and no headway is being made whatever.

Continually Mr Allen has to shout to arouse her and Arthur Saunders who has rowed all the time has to come back or wait.

She is making the bravest struggle woman ever made.

The ladder is over the back of the boat facing her.

Mr Allen has removed his sweater and the forecabin of the *F.E.11* is being cleared to put her in warm.

The pilot is forced to tell her as she refuses to come out that she is swimming back instead of forward, but she carries on and the ladder is hauled on board.

A private aeroplane above circles around. Sharpe gets in small boat with Allen. Towels are ready to get her out.

2.50 OUT OF WATER

Folkestone Herald, 22 October 1927

Blackpool – Open-Water Endurance Record Attempt

In between her circus performances and three attempts at crossing the North Channel, Mercedes fitted in an attempt to break the endurance record of 25 hours' continuous swimming currently claimed by Dr Dorothy Logan in a failed English Channel attempt.

The swim took place on 17 September 1928. The sea at Blackpool was calm at 8 o'clock that morning, and many people went out in motorboats to watch her. However, at 10.35 p.m., after 14 hours in the water, Mercedes was forced to abandon the attempt by her advisors. An hour before, she had been swimming strongly, but a considerable drop in temperature occurred within the space of half an hour. Despite this, she refused to stop and finally had to be roped and pulled into the boat as it was obvious that she was succumbing to the cold.

Mr Harry Bradburn, a friend who helped organise the swim, said that she was suffering with a bad cold when she entered the water, which must have had an effect on her stamina. He predicted that she would probably make another attempt at this particular record in a fortnight's time.

However, this did not happen, as she refocussed on one more attempt to cross the North Channel before the winter set in.

Moray Firth Attempt

The year 1930 was a busy one for Mercedes. In between an organised programme of endurance swims carried out in corporation pools in the UK, six major open-water swims were planned. The first of these was the Moray Firth crossing. She had in mind to use this swim to 'harden' her body in advance of her Isle of Man project and another attempt on the North Channel.

During the month of May, in order to help cover her living expenses, Mercedes gave costume demonstrations at Brown Muff department store in Bradford. A representative of *The Observer* interviewed her at the store on Saturday, 31 May (the last day of her contract) and she told him she was planning to travel to the north of Scotland for an attempt on the Moray Firth. Local journalists were always eager to help her, and the man from *The Observer* was no exception. He went with her to arrange her travel and later wrote:

We found there was a convenient train, and within two minutes we were off to book the ticket for Inverness. If the conditions are good on Monday or Tuesday she will attempt the difficult swim; if not she will study conditions for a future attempt.

As we hurried on Market Street to get the ticket – I carrying Miss Gleitze's case and umbrella – she remembered that she had made some arrangements at Cook's for a visit to Turkey in August when she will attempt to swim the Hellespont. So we called on the way to settle the Turkey arrangements, and everything was fixed up before we left. Nearly three months ahead she has the passage booked, the passport, the visas, and all the incidental affairs arranged!

'I might as well get it all done now,' she remarked casually, as we examined a map of the Hellespont. This girl, who swims more miles than most of us care to walk, thinks nothing of long journeys abroad. When I asked Miss Gleitze the reason for her decision to attempt the Moray Firth she said she thought the swim would acclimatise her to the cold water for her subsequent long distance efforts.

When Mercedes arrived in Inverness on Saturday, 31 May, she initially took up her quarters at the old Highland hostelry, the Caledonian Hotel. Help with the organisation of the swim was soon forthcoming from local seafaring folk, in particular Bailie Anderson, and after consideration it was decided that she should proceed to Burghead that same day and start the swim from there early on Monday morning, 2 June. The chosen course was from the Morayshire side to Balintore on the Ross and Cromarty coast – a distance of 14 miles.

One of the party accompanying Mercedes wrote the following (abridged) account of the swim, which was published in *The Elgin Courant & Courier*, 6 June 1930:

From the practical obscurity of its every-day hum-drum existence, the little Moray seaport of Burghead found itself this week thrust suddenly into the lime-light of publicity through the announcement made that from there Miss Gleitze, the famous Channel swimmer, was to set off on the first attempt that had ever been made to swim across the Moray Firth to the Ross-shire coast.

Miss Gleitze arrived at Burghead from Inverness on Saturday evening and put up at the Station Hotel. She retired early on Sunday evening so that she would be rested for the ordeal ahead.

It was my happy privilege, at the invitation of Miss Gleitze, to accompany her, and the experience I shall not readily forget – for more reasons than one! Falling in with Miss Gleitze's wishes, early on Monday I accordingly found myself one of the party that sailed out from the Burghead harbour in the dim, grey light of a somewhat uninviting June morning – the heavy clouds carried with them more than a suspicion of rain.

Despite the comparatively early hour of the morning a large crowd assembled on the pierhead and gave Miss Gleitze an encouraging send-off.

The little craft in which we set out was the local motorboat *The Swan* belonging to Mr Alexander Mackay, whose crew consisted of his son, Mr Alex Mackay and Mr Daniel Mackenzie, Harbourmaster. Along with Miss Gleitze, Dr Sutherland of Burghead, three journalists and a press photographer made up the boat's complement, while in tow of the motor boat was a small fishing yawl belonging to Bailie Jas.

Anderson of Burghead, who was responsible for the making of the
local arrangements for the swim. With him in the yawl were Mr Alex
Anderson, his brother, and Mr Louis McArthur.

Our troubles began early – the press photographer not finding his
sea legs so readily as the others, falling an early victim to the lurching
of the vessel in the somewhat heavy swell that was running. To him
at least the broad expanse of desert sand on the Culbins to the west
of Findhorn was a welcome sight, and after being fortified in some
measure with the best wishes and 'spirits' of his companions on board,
it was with very apparent relief that he made ashore along with the
famous swimmer to return, not again to the motor boat, but to hike
his way as best he could across the Culbins and for home.

To reach the shore at the point selected for the start of Miss Gleitze's
swim, known locally as the Buckie Loch, the small craft had a somewhat hazardous passage. Heaved and tossed by the breakers on the
old bar of the Findhorn, the yawl shipped a heavy sea, the occupants
being badly drenched.

The while Miss Gleitze undressed in preparation for her great venture, it was more than a fair test for the skill of the navigators on board
the yawl to keep it near the landing point, and it was driven swiftly
westwards before the tide, being taken in tow by the motor boat only
after considerable delay and difficulty.

The surf had again to be crossed for Dr Sutherland and Bailie
Anderson, who had gone ashore with Miss Gleitze, and further seas
were shipped as the yawl re-crossed the current. Those on board were
badly soaked, and a bucket had to be requisitioned in order to bale the
water out of the boat.

After being greased with seal oil Miss Gleitze entered the sea at
11.13 in her daring attempt to conquer, for the first time in history,
the stormy waters of the Moray Firth.

Her stamina was early taxed when she had to battle her way through
extremely strong breaking inshore surf for almost half a mile. Once
through this she made considerably better progress, although she was
severely handicapped by having to cut across at almost right angles a
particularly heavy stream tide that was running westwards.

From the moment she entered the water, however, she realised that
the swim was doomed to failure by reason of the icy cold nature of

the water, but she battled on bravely in the wake of the motor boat and yawl.

A gramophone brought by a member of the party, as well as vocal efforts by Bailie Anderson, assisted in keeping up the swimmer's spirits and to cheer her on her way.

While Miss Gleitze was fighting gamely on in the water, the journalists on board by this time were feeling less happy, first one and then the other having recourse to prostrate themselves on the deck in an earnest study of the rocking billows. One, indeed, held a precarious grasp of the hold in blissful indifference as to the grave risk which he ran of being pitched overboard!

While all in the boat were wholehearted in their desire to witness Miss Gleitze succeed in her valiant effort, one may be forgiven for wondering whether the journalists, at least, heaved an inward sigh of relief when the swimmer, after being fortified by a helping of brandy, had at last to give in.

This was after having swam for close on six miles and being in the water for exactly an hour and three quarters. By that time she was so exhausted and benumbed by the icy cold nature of the water that she was able only to sign to those on the yawl to lift her aboard. The motor boat immediately headed for Burghead, the while Miss Gleitze required careful medical attention. It took her close on three quarters of an hour to come round. She was however able to walk ashore when the boat reached Burghead Harbour again. The hundreds of children and fisherwomen who had given Mercedes a rousing send-off were waiting to give her an equally rousing welcome back.

Frozen Jaw: Afterwards she told me that she knew she was a beaten woman from the moment she stepped into the sea at Findhorn. She said:

'Never in the whole of my career have I experienced conditions so excruciatingly cold. I was thoroughly benumbed after half an hour, but decided to carry on, always hoping for the best. However, when I found myself unable to shout to the boatmen I knew the game was up, as my jaw was virtually frozen.'

Although she failed, Miss Gleitze deserves the congratulations of the whole community for her bravery in attempting to conquer the Moray Firth so early in the season, and from the progress recorded

I am justified in the belief that her proposed second attempt later in the year will meet with success.

By her quiet, unassuming and likeable demeanour the renowned swimmer commanded the admiration and esteem of those who were associated with her in her record-breaking endeavour, and if she did not succeed, her abilities, stamina, and brilliant career are by no means impugned – no-one could ever resist such cold waters. Rather should we rejoice that the country can produce such a woman who can undergo Monday's trying ordeal. And it was an ordeal – for more than Miss Gleitze![78]

The second try planned for September unfortunately did not come about because of her prolonged involvement that year in further attempts to conquer the North Channel.

Bristol Channel

Mercedes had earmarked the Bristol Channel as a possibility as far back as 1928. Following the English Channel and the Gibraltar Strait swims, and just before commencing her contract of work with the Blackpool Tower authorities, she paid a visit to Penarth in Wales and made contact with the Welsh Amateur Swimming Association. The incumbent general secretary, Mr Linton, looked after her during her visit and they discussed an attempt on the Bristol Channel during the latter part of August.

Mercedes also secured the enthusiastic support of a journalist associated with the Welsh press, H.H. Mayford, who wrote to her:

Your willingness to attempt the Bristol Channel swim – providing the necessary financial aid was forthcoming – has aroused much interest in the district, and I should deem it a great favour if you would kindly inform me of the dates and your training arrangements in the event of your decision to add the Bristol Channel swim to your attainments.

However, no doubt due to the extension of her Blackpool Tower contract, and her four attempts on the North Channel that year, the 1928 plans were put on hold, and it wasn't until the summer of 1930 that they were reactivated. During the first six months of that year, Mercedes had carried out ten endurance swims and had achieved her ambition to swim around the Isle of Man in stages. During her stay in Douglas, she wrote to the Welsh Amateur Swimming Association suggesting an exhibition swim, and on 11 June R.P. Green, the honorary organising secretary, replied:

> I find it impossible to arrange anything earlier than August at Barry, so that the pleasure of a visit from you must be delayed. Have you thought anything more about the Barry–Minehead suggestion and want any further details, kindly let me know and I shall be only too pleased to be of any assistance possible?

Mercedes wrote back to Green on 15 June:

> Many thanks for your very kind letter. I should very much like to carry out my Bristol Channel swim during the last few days of June, say between June 25th and 30th. On the 1st July I am due in Stafford to prepare for my endurance swim there on the 3rd July. At the moment I am swimming around the Isle of Man. Douglas Swimming Club officials are members of my crew. They are responsible for the log and general organisation of the swim. A Manx man has loaned me his yacht for a week for the job.
>
> In accordance with your offer, I would like to – if it is not inconveniencing you too much – enlist your very valuable help for my Bristol Channel venture. What I should like you to do in this respect is the following:
>
> 1) Enquire of Barry whether there is anyone who possesses a yacht or motor boat who would be sporting enough to lend it to me for my swim.
> 2) Whether there is any hotel proprietor willing to put me up for the few days necessary to accomplish my task.
> 3) Could you form a small committee of volunteers (men of good repute like yourself) who would act as official witnesses of my proposed swim?

As I shall not be deriving any financial gain from my Bristol Channel swim I am very anxious not to incur any loss, and I feel sure that local authorities approached will be just as willing to render me the necessary help – as has been the case with my Isle of Man swim. I should appreciate it very much if you would kindly send me a letter to the following address – c/o Douglas Corporation Baths, Douglas, Isle of Man – as soon as you have any news regarding a boat, so that I can arrange my plans accordingly. In the meantime please accept my very best thanks for any kind help you may be able to render me.

Green responded positively to her requests, and so, with arrangements in place, Mercedes travelled to Barry. Unfortunately, her tendency to arrange swims in close proximity to each other turned out to be one of the reasons she almost, but not quite, made it across the Bristol Channel.

The swim was planned for Monday, 30 June. Those, however, who were well qualified to know this dangerous stretch of water and its peculiarities as to tides and currents, were not at all optimistic about her chances. One pilot went so far as to foreshadow the result by predicting that the tide would be too strong for her to reach the Somerset coast, and that the strength of the tide that day would undoubtedly set her back towards Wales.

Mercedes was, of course, advised of the difficulties she was likely to encounter but, unfortunately, she was so pressed for time because of the need to fulfil an endurance swim contract at Stafford on 3 July she could not afford to wait until the weekend when, without doubt, falling tides would have enabled her to reach the other side with comparative ease. An abridged version of a media report by journalist Edith Parnell, covering the attempt, reads:

A little after nine a.m. on Monday [30th June] Miss Mercedes Gleitze entered the sea from the pebbles at Porthkerry Bay, Cold Knap. Bob and Dick Jones piloted her across and they, together with Dudley C. Luen, the 'doctor', were in the rowing boat. Mr Chris Jones, the Olympic swimmer and Captain of Barry Swimming Club, Miss Nancy Owen of Cold Knap, a Cardiff press representative and myself accompanied the swim in a small motor launch driven by Mr Teddy Lewis of Barry Dock.

Throughout the whole of the swim the tides, the winds and the general weather conditions were in favour of the swimmer. Apart from slight trouble with her eyes which were affected by the salt water Miss Gleitze was in fine spirits. After 12½ hours in the water, the sun had set and the skies were dull. The occupants of the rowing boat were silhouetted by flashes of lightning which periodically lit up the sky and which caused her some distress.

Dozens of motors boats packed with passengers came out from Minehead and the neighbouring coast to greet the party and circled around the swimmer during the last stages. At 10.15 p.m., when almost a mile from Minehead Pier, it seemed certain that she would effect a good landing. By eleven o'clock however, she had not only made no progress but had drifted out into the channel again owing to eddying currents off the pier. The impossibility of landing against such odds was soon realised by the launch party and Miss Gleitze asked if all were of the opinion that she could not fight the tide and that it was advisable to abandon the swim. All on board agreed with the advisability of giving up and Miss Gleitze was then pulled into the rowing boat and taken to the Barry Pilot Cutter *Barrian*.

Several Bristol Channel pilots expressed the opinion that if she had left the Welsh coast an hour or two sooner she would have been favoured with a flood tide on the other side and would have stood a good chance of reaching her objective. Mercedes had planned to return to Barry on 11 July to try again, but other major events in her life intervened, and this reprise never happened. Nonetheless – as with the North Channel attempts – she demonstrated that she was more than capable of crossing the Bristol Channel.

Reverse Direction English Channel (England–France, 1930, 1933)

After her successful swim from France to England in October 1927, Mercedes reached out for new horizons in Britain and across the world, but later in her career she was drawn back to the English Channel for four attempts in the reverse direction – from England to France. On all four attempts she was competing for the Dover Town Gold Challenge Cup.

1930

30 September: *The Guardian* (1 October 1930) reported that Mercedes entered the water just west of Admiralty Pier, Dover, at 5.47 p.m., and athough conditions were good at the start, she was forced to abandon the swim some distance in because of the intense cold. (Unfortunately, there are few details available in the archives covering this attempt.)

1933

On 2 August 1933, at the age of 32, and just nine months after giving birth to her first child, Mercedes entered the water at 10.15 a.m. at Dover to again attempt the reverse crossing from England to France. However, after 6 hours of swimming, and an estimated 9 or 10 miles out from Dover, the weather changed and rough seas developed. The waves were washing right over the small rowing boat accompanying her. Very reluctantly, she gave in to the advice of the weather experts and her medical advisor, and after a total of 8 hours in the sea, she was reluctantly lifted into the accompanying boat at 6 p.m. Despite her failure, thousands of holidaymakers cheered her when she returned to Dover in the *Ocean King* (piloted by Mr Brockman). She said afterwards that she was feeling quite fit for the further long swim, and the end was a great disappointment.

On 29 August Mercedes tried again. She started from the South Foreland at 7.30 a.m. in perfect sea conditons. But a dense fog suddenly developed in the Channel just before midnight, and this, together with adverse winds and tides, caused Mercedes to abandon the swim after 15 hours in the water and 7 miles from the French coast.

In September that year (exact day unknown, but around the middle of the month), Mercedes made her very last attempt to cross the English Channel from England to France (and her very last open-water swim). An article dated 21 September 1933, covering this attempt (reproduced in the *Evening Post*, 24 October 1933), reports that she entered the water at the South Foreland just after 11 a.m. and at 3.30 p.m. was swimming strongly about 5½ miles from the English coast, on the other side of the Goodwins. Again, however, she was beaten by the strong wind in her face, and sadly was forced to abandon the swim after 14 hours when only a few miles off the French coast.

RECIPIENTS OF GLEITZE CUPS

Cups Donated by Mercedes

Republican Swimming Club, Dublin
In March 1930, one month after her Dublin endurance swim, Mercedes returned to the city as guest of honour at a function held at the Wicklow Hotel by the Dublin-based Irish Republican Swimming Club. She presented a silver cup, inscribed 'The Gleitze Cup (to be used in competition amongst female speed swimmers)' to Mrs H. McEvoy, captain of the Ladies Section of the club.

In acknowledging the gift, the president of the club commented that Irishmen in a bygone age were great swimmers, but the art had declined. He said that Mercedes' achievements and her presence in Ireland had without doubt given a great impetus to the sport. Miss A. Boyle, on behalf of the ladies present, said that the trophy would be a great incentive to swimming, not only amongst the ladies of the Republican Swimming Club, but amongst women's clubs in general in Ireland.

Galway Chamber of Commerce
To acknowledge the reception she received from the people of Galway after her 19-hour swim across the bay in August 1931, Mercedes gave the president of the Chamber of Commerce a swimming challenge cup, inscribed 'The Gleitze Swimming Cup'. This cup was to be presented each

year to the school in the county that turned out the greatest percentage of swimmers in relation to the number of its students.

Although at the time the conditions for awarding the cup were still to be drawn up, the intention was that all schoolchildren – boys and girls, primary and secondary – would be eligible to compete.

Cups Donated by Mercedes' Family

More recently, in 2011, 2012 and 2017, three commemorative trophies have been donated by Mercedes' family.

Galway Bay Cup
The cup is to be used in connection with the Frances Thornton Memorial Swim across Galway Bay in aid of Cancer Care West. Members of the Thornton family are the driving force behind this race, which takes place annually across a 13km stretch of Galway Bay, from Aughinish in County Clare to the Blackrock Diving Tower in Salthill, County Galway. The event is hugely popular and draws in competitors from far afield. Since its inception in 2005 it has raised many thousands of euros for Cancer Care West.

Brighton Shield
This shield records the names of Brighton-based swimmers who have successfully swum across the English Channel. It is being kept up to date by local marathon swimmer/coach, Fiona Southwell. Mercedes was born in Brighton and spent many happy years in this popular seaside town and she would have been delighted to know that her name is being perpetuated in this manner.

The Mercedes Gleitze Trophy for the Most Pioneering Female Swim of the Year Across the English Channel
In November 2017 the first recipient, nominated by the Channel Swimming Association at its Annual Awards ceremony, was Pat Gallant-Charette from Maine, USA.

OPEN-WATER SWIMMING TODAY

Open-water swimming as a sport has a long history, going as far back as ancient Roman times when races were held in the Tiber River.[79] Indeed, in the early part of the twentieth century, some organised swims in local waterways had already been established, such as the Manhattan Island Marathon Swim and the River Liffey Swim in Dublin.

However, after Captain Matthew Webb's landmark crossing in 1875, the English Channel became the benchmark for international aspirants, and Mercedes made her own mark with her Channel attempts in the 1920s and 1930s. She encouraged others to share her passion for swimming in open waters through her own achievements and even her failed attempts.

Although today more challenging swims exist globally, the English Channel is still as alluring as ever – so much so that would-be swimmers are advised to book at least two years in advance to secure a good swim slot. In response to the increasing popularity, the Channel Swimming Association was founded in 1927 to authenticate swims specifically across the English Channel, and over the decades many other national and international associations have been formed to help categorise and validate other global open-water swimming courses. The British Long-Distance Swimming Association, the Irish Long-Distance Swimming Association, the Hawaiian Channel Swim Association and the Catalina

Channel Swimming Federation are amongst the early organisations that set the standards.

Other global organisations such as the World Open Water Swimming Association (WOWSA), the International Swimming Hall of Fame (ISHOF) and its sister organisation, the International Marathon Swimming Hall of Fame (IMSHOF) – all of which hold annual conferences and awards ceremonies to honour outstanding swimmers, officials and administrators – have become a welcome and integral part of the open-water swimming scene.

Mercedes would have been delighted to know that, since her own pioneering days, open-water swimming has increased enormously in popularity and has become an international sporting discipline in its own right. The FINA (Fédération Internationale de Natation) World Aquatics Championships have included open-water swimmings events in their programme since 1992, and from 2007 the FINA 10km Marathon Swimming World Cup has been held, in various formats, around the world. Additionally, the IOC (International Olympic Committee) officially introduced the triathlon event in the Olympic Games in 2000 (the open-water leg covering 1,500m), and in 2008 the 10km open-water swimming race was included in the Olympics.

It is estimated that globally there are at least 6,000 marathon swimmers, a good number of them having turned professional.

Solo and relay swims have also increased in number and diversity, and the bar continues to be raised. There are well over 200 major global bodies of water in which marathon swimmers can test themselves, and with the increasing popularity of the sport, local clubs and individuals are now organising events. Innovative challenges such as the Oceans Seven swim, the Five Islands Challenge and 'ice swimming', amongst others, have been introduced as aquatic trials of human strength and endurance. For example, over a period of six days in August 2013, in sea temperatures ranging from 2.5°C to 10°C (36.5 to 50°F), an international relay team of sixty-six elite long-distance swimmers from sixteen countries successfully crossed the Bering Strait between Alaska and Russia.

Many of the present-day open-water marathons are organised around fundraising, and the swimmers taking part are motivated – as was Mercedes – to help disadvantaged people.

Information about this sport is now easy to access and two specialist publications covering global events are the online WOWSA-sponsored *Daily News of Open Water Swimming*, edited by Steven Munatones, and the *Outdoor Swimmer* magazine (online and in print), founded and published by Simon Griffiths.

As with most sporting activities, open-water swimming has only been able to progress because of the invaluable help and expertise given by the dedicated, often long-serving members of the various governing bodies, and the support provided by on-the-ground volunteers who organise and oversee the swims. During her own career, Mercedes repeatedly acknowledged that she could never have achieved her goals on her own.

It is to be hoped that both the swimmers and their support teams continue to enjoy the resurgence of interest the sport is enjoying in the twenty-first century.

APPENDIX 7

ORIGINAL MAPS

The original map of Mercedes' swim across the Marmara Sea with the official stamp and witnesses' signatures.

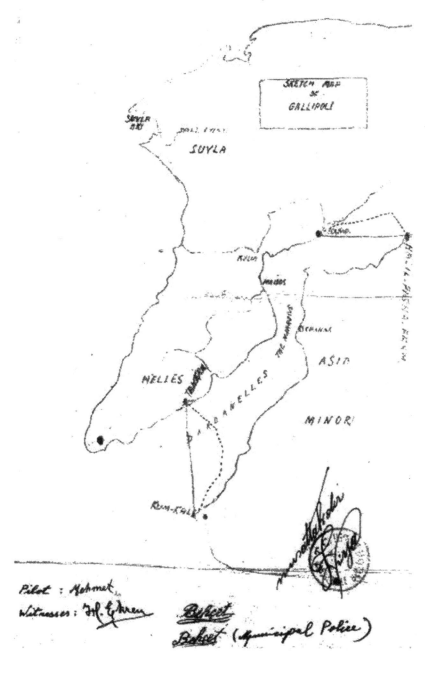

The original map of Mercedes' swim across the Hellespont with the official stamp and witnesses' signatures.

NOTES

1   Dr Jean Williams, Senior Research Fellow, International Centre for Sports History and Culture, De Montfort University.
2   The Voluntary Aid Detachment (VAD) was a voluntary organisation providing field nursing services. The organisation's most important periods of operation were during the First and Second World Wars.
3   Kate Adie, *Corsets to Camouflage* (Hodder & Stoughton, 2003).
4   Rosemary Rees, *Britain 1890–1929* (Heinemann Advanced History series, 2003).
5   Stephen Constantine, *Social Conditions in Britain 1918–1939* (Lancaster Pamphlets, London: Methuen, 1983).
6   Drages was one of the first furniture retailers to offer hire-purchase facilities to the newly housed working classes.
7   *Dundee Courier*, 16 September 1930.
8   *The Australasian*, 14 September 1931.
9   *Daily Sketch*, 30 August 1926.
10 *Rand Daily Mail*, 5 May 1932.
11 *The Guardian*, 19 July 1927.
12 *The Outspan*, 25 March 1932.
13 *The Gloucester Citizen*, 30 July 1927.
14 *New York Times*, 4 August 1922.
15 Stanley Devon, *Glorious: The Life Story of Stanley Devon* (George G. Harrap & Co. Ltd, 1957).
16 *Dover Standard*, 23 September 1926, p. 3.
17 She was later re-employed by Mesrs T.J. Eaton and remained with them until 1 July 1927.
18 *Kent Evening Echo*, 8 October 1927.
19 *News of the World*, 9 October 1927.
20 *Kent Evening Echo*, 18 October 1927.
21 *Daily Herald*, 19 October 1927.
22 *Daily Express*, 19 October 1927.

23 A special representative from the *Kent Evening Echo* on board the tug *Alsace* used pigeons to relay a series of messages to keep his editor informed of the progress of the swim as it was happening. (See Appendix 4.)

24 *The Guardian*, 22 October 1927.

25 *Daily Mirror*, 23 November 1927.

26 On 12 December 1927 the *Daily Express* printed an abridged form of this letter.

27 *The Scotsman*, 17 December 1927.

28 *Daily Express*, 25 January 1928.

29 Jesús Castro, www.eyeonspain.com.

30 *The Outspan*, 25 March 1932.

31 *The Guardian*, 12 April 1928.

32 *Daily Mail*, 7 April 1928.

33 *Daily Mirror*, 10 April 1928.

34 Reproduced from Mercedes' archives; any forthcoming information about the poet, C.C.S. of Donaghadee, will be included in future reprints.

35 *Belfast Telegraph*, 6 November 1928.

36 *Belfast Telegraph*, 6 November 1928.

37 *Belfast Newsletter*, 6 November 1928.

38 Taken from a letter from Mercedes to Mr Roe, dated 4 June 1928.

39 *The Guardian*, 19 December 1928.

40 The White Heather Fund was run under the patronage of the *Manchester Evening News*. On its committee were representatives from that paper and from the *Manchester Guardian*.

41 *Daily Mirror*, 20 December 1928.

42 This letter was written before Mercedes' August 1928 attempt on the North Channel when, for the first time, she did sustain injuries to her leg muscles because of the low temperature of the water, from which she took two weeks to recover.

43 A précis of a report published in the *Mid-Ulster Mail* on 13 July 1929 can be accessed at www.mercedesgleitze.uk.

44 These records can be accessed at www.mercedesgleitze.uk.

45 'Diary of New Zealand Tour' (1931).

46 Article reproduced courtesy of the *Northern Constitution*.

47 Detailed coverage of both crossings can be accessed at www.mercedesgleitze.uk.

48 The story of the swim by Bernard Hurrell, the official log keeper on board the accompanying boat, can be accessed at www.mercedesgleitze.uk.

49 Article written by G.B. Newe and published in an unidentified Northern Irish newspaper. Any forthcoming information about the author and publication will be reproduced in future reprints.

50 *Ballymena Observer*, 4 October 1929.

51 Martin, Angus, 'North Channel Swim', in *The Kintyre Antiquarian & Natural History Society Magazine*, No. 72, Autumn 2012.

52 Article in *The Glensman*, Vol. 1, No 11, August 1932; (Glens Publishing Company).

53 *Sheffield Independent*, 26 May 1930.

54 *Dundee Courier*, 25 September 1930.

55 A complementary detailed description of each stage of the swim can be accessed at www.mercedesgleitze.uk.

56 *The Christchurch Star*, 6 March 1931.

57 A log and witness statements relating to this swim can be accessed at www.mercedesgleitze.uk.

58 A log and witness statements relating to this swim can be accessed at www.mercedesgleitze.uk.

59 Article reproduced courtesy of the Connacht Tribune Newspaper Group, Galway.

60 Article reproduced courtesy of the Connacht Tribune Newspaper Group, Galway.

61 Article reproduced courtesy of the Connacht Tribune Newspaper Group, Galway.

62 *Cape Argus*, February 1932.

63 *Cape Argus*, April 1932.

64 *Eastern Province Herald*, 11 April 1932.

65 *The Outspan*, March 1932.

66 'Mercedes Gleitze: A Personal Interview', H. O'B, Dublin, 1929.

67 *Kent Evening Echo*, 8 October 1927.

68 *Dover Standard*, 14 August 1930.

69 *The Guardian*, 17 July 1930.

70 *Dundee Courier*, 9 June 1934.

71 *The Clarion Call*, 2 March 1931, see also Appendix 3: 16 December entry.

72 *The Sunday News*, 16 October 1927.

73 *Encyclopædia Britannica*.

74 In an interview with *The Sunday Times* (16 October 1927), Mercedes mentioned her plan to teach handicrafts to those entering her proposed hostel for the unemployed.

75 Charles Loch Mowat, *Britain Between the Wars, 1918–1940* (Methuen, 1955).

76 Gordon, Professor David (lead author), *The Impoverishment of the UK, PSE First Results: Living Standards* (Townsend Centre for International Poverty Research, Bristol University, 2013).

77 Gleitze archives.

78 *The Elgin Courant & Courier* ceased publication in 1960.

79 Steven Munatones (ed.), *The Daily News of Open Water Swimming*, 19 April 2013.

BIBLIOGRAPHY

Adie, Kate, *Corsets to Camouflage* (Hodder & Stoughton, 2003)

Boyd, Ruth, *A Focus on Fleet Street: Stanley Devon, News Photographer* (Derek Harrison, 1995)

Chambers, Dr Ciara, 'An Advertiser's Dream: The "Construction" of the "Consumptionist" Cinematic Persona of Mercedes Gleitze' in *Alphaville Journal of Film and Screen Media* (Issue 6, Winter 2013)

Coney, Sandra, *Standing in the Sunshine: A History of New Zealand Women Since They Won the Vote* (Viking Penguin Books NZ Ltd, 1993)

Constantine, Stephen, *Social Conditions in Britain 1918–1939* (Methuen, 1983)

Conway, Thomas (ed.), *The Oberon Anthology of Contemporary Irish Plays: This is just this. It isn't real. It's Money* (Oberon Books Ltd, 2012)

Davies, Caitlin, *Downstream: A History and Celebration of Swimming the River Thames* (Aurum Press Ltd, 2015)

Devon, Stanley, *Glorious: The Life Story of Stanley Devon, Twice British News Photographer of the Year* (George G. Harrap & Co. Ltd, 1957)

Dou, Montserrat Tresserras, *Nadando el Estrecho, Sus Origenes Y Su Historia* [*Swimming the Strait, its Origins and History*] (Consejería de Deportes: Dirección General de Promoción Deportiva, 2007)

Encyclopædia Britannica (Encyclopædia Britannica Inc.)

Gordon, Professor David (lead author), *The Impoverishment of the UK, PSE First Results: Living Standards* (Townsend Centre for International Poverty Research, Bristol University, 2013).

McAleese, Maurice, *Golden Days on the Summer Shores of Old Portstewart* (Impact Printing, 2011)

Mowat, Charles Loch, *Britain Between the Wars, 1918–1940* (Methuen, 1955)

Rees, Rosemary, *Britain 1890–1929* (Heinemann Advanced History, 2003)

INDEX